shifra stein's

day trips® from
kansas city

D1403571

help us keep this guide up to date

Every effort has been made by the authors and editors to make this guide as accurate and useful as possible. However, many changes can occur after a guide is published— establishments close, phone numbers change, hiking trails are rerouted, facilities come under new management, and so on.

We would love to hear from you concerning your experiences with this guide and how you feel it could be improved and be kept up to date. While we may not be able to respond to all comments and suggestions, we'll take them to heart, and we'll make certain to share them with the authors. Please send your comments and suggestions to the following address:

The Globe Pequot Press
Reader Response/Editorial Department
P.O. Box 480
Guilford, CT 06437

Or you may e-mail us at: editorial@GlobePequot.com

Thanks for your input, and happy travels!

day trips® series

shifra stein's

day trips® from kansas city

fifteenth edition

getaway ideas for the local traveler

shifra stein

with

diana lambdin meyer

gpp

travel

Guilford, Connecticut

The prices and rates listed in this guidebook
were confirmed at press time. We recommend,
however, that you call establishments before
traveling to obtain current information.

To buy books in quantity for corporate use
or incentives, call **(800) 962–0973**
or e-mail **premiums@GlobePequot.com**.

Text design by Linda R. Loiewski
Maps by XNR Productions Inc. © Morris Book Publishing, LLC
Spot photography throughout © Cliff Keeler/Alamy

ISSN 1538-4993
ISBN 978-0-7627-4774-0

Printed in the United States of America
10 9 8 7 6 5 4 3 2 1

contents

day trips from kansas city

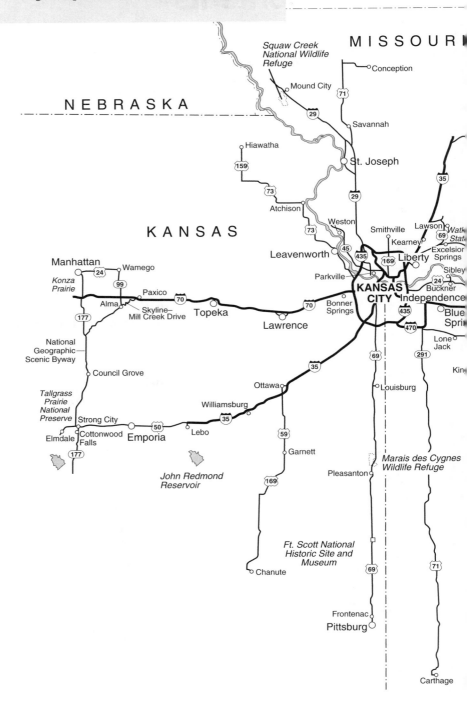

Jamesport

MISSOURI

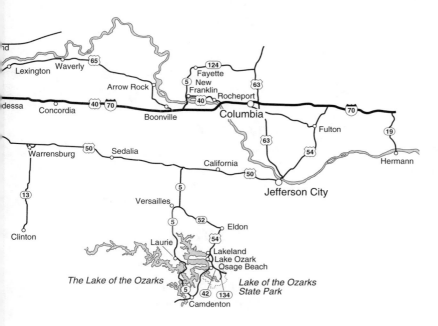

Lexington Waverly **65**

124
Fayette
5 New
Franklin **63**
Arrow Rock Rocheport

dessa Concordia **40** **70**
Boonville **40** Columbia **70**

Fulton **19**

50 Sedalia **63** **54**
Warrensburg California Hermann

13 **50**
5
Jefferson City

Versailles
Clinton **5** **52** Eldon
54
Laurie Lakeland
Lake Ozark
Osage Beach
The Lake of the Ozarks *Lake of the Ozarks*
5 **42** **134** *State Park*
Camdenton

0   10   20   30 miles

south

day trip 01

precious moments

southwest

day trip 01

apple cider, wildlife, and history

day trip 02

safaris and suppers

day trip 03

front porch to the flint hills

west

day trip 01

history, culture, and agriculture

day trip 02

state capital

day trip 03

scenic drive into the past

day trip 04

the "little apple"

day trip 05

national geographic scenic byway

day trip 06

presidential town

worth more time

northwest

day trip 01

military memorabilia, mansions, museums, and memorials

day trip 02

shop 'til you drop

day trip 03

the start of "snail mail"

day trip 04

bird heaven and haven

acknowledgments

Special thanks to Diana Lambdin Meyer whose invaluable help made this edition of *Day Trips*® *from Kansas City* a better one. I am grateful for all the assistance given to me by the chambers of commerce, state and regional tourism departments, and convention bureaus of the states of Kansas and Missouri. I am also indebted to photographer Bob Barrett, whose love of the prairie, back roads, and all things wild and beautiful made this book possible.

—Shifra Stein

using this book

Restaurant prices: Designated $$$ (expensive, most entrees $15 and over), $$ (moderate, most entrees $5 to $15), or $ (inexpensive, most entrees $5 and under).

Lodging rates: Designated $$$ (expensive, $100 and over per night), $$ (moderate, $50 to $100 per night), $ (inexpensive, $50 and under per night). Rates often change seasonally, so be sure to call first for current prices.

Credit cards: Establishments that do not accept credit cards are indicated with the notation "no cards."

Highways: Designated I– for interstate highways and U.S. for federal highways. State routes are designated K– in Kansas and "Highway" in Missouri. County and state roads are identified as such.

Hours: In most cases, hours are omitted in the listings because they are subject to frequent changes. Instead, phone numbers are provided for obtaining up-to-date information.

Wheelchair accessibility: The designation ♿ is provided only for those wildlife areas and historic sites that provide amenities for the physically challenged.

Lewis and Clark Trail: The designation 🎒 is provided to highlight sites associated with the Corps of Discovery Journey through this region in 1804–06.

>> preface

Day Trips® from Kansas City has had a long and happy life. It was first published in 1980 and has been updated and revised ever since. Over the years there have been letters and calls from people throughout the country wanting to know when the book was going to be expanded to include more places. Well, it's time to toss out your old editions. You are holding in your hands a brand-new, chock-full-of-stuff publication that features sections devoted to the Lake of the Ozarks region; the Flint Hills; Tallgrass Prairie Preserve; Manhattan, Kansas; Columbia, Missouri; and other areas.

Many of you have written to tell me how much you love cheap eats, old-fashioned soda fountains, and great ice cream, so I took it upon myself to devour my way through Kansas and Missouri to provide you with the latest information on establishments that know no bounds when it comes to butterfat. (It was hard work, but somebody had to do it.)

I also expanded my pants by two sizes—all in the interest of research, mind you. I was forced to eat mini mountains of filet mignon and whopping twenty-two-ounce porterhouses and to gorge myself on homemade biscuits and gravy, real hash browns, and real mashed potatoes. It was terribly difficult for me to cram my mouth full of roast pork with honey-bourbon sauce and bouillabaisse while at the same time sampling fine wines from around the world. And, oh, the decadence of those desserts: chocolate cake topped with "evil fudge icing," peach praline pie, and homemade bread pudding with New Orleans bourbon sauce. Well, I hope you can appreciate to what lengths I went to make you the beneficiary of my gastronomic investigations.

Then there were those close encounters with the very exceptional and the very strange—what comedian Robin Williams might call "richly bizarre." Consider, if you will, hosting your wedding beside an eleven-million-pound steam shovel, or initiating a carp-feeding frenzy while munching on barbecued ribs. Who knows what adventures await as you frolic your way through a two-state region?

Armed with this book and a good map, you will find that you no longer have to trek to New Mexico, Arizona, or California to be in bed-and-breakfast heaven. Kansas and Missouri have sprouted so many superior new establishments that it was difficult to find space to include them all. Many offer upscale amenities, acres of land on which to stroll, and full gourmet breakfasts prepared by trained chefs. Some of these places have been touted in national magazines and newspapers; others are just about to be discovered.

Day Trips® from Kansas City holds plenty of breathtaking vistas, prairies, wildlife refuges, and places steeped in history. You'll travel pathways where settlers drove their Conestogas through towns that marked the beginnings of the Santa Fe, California, and Oregon Trails. As you drive the back roads, you'll discover that the nineteenth century is still with us, in the elegant mansions, antebellum homes, and exquisite buildings that line the streets of small midwestern towns fewer than two hours from your doorstep.

The book's longevity attests to the fact that there is yearning in each of us for something that speaks to the heart. Kansas City borders a prairie that once grew soybeans and sunflowers. Today our burgeoning metropolis is crowding out the prairie and its fragile ecosystem. Wildlife is being decimated as we rip up fields to make way for business complexes, cinema multiplexes, strip malls, shopping centers, and gated residential communities. Chalk it up to "progress," but the fact is that we now must go farther and farther away from the city to find peace of mind and fresh air to breathe.

So prepare to detach yourself from the Internet, your fax machine, your monthly planner, and your cell phone and live life in the slow lane for a while. Join other readers who have already made *Day Trips*® *from Kansas City* part of their lives. As you read this book, you'll gain insight into what makes this part of America so special. There are maps to follow, but perhaps you'll seek your own roads to places you've never been before. Having seen them, you may grow to love them all the more because they are home.

—Shifra Stein

northeast

day trip 01

northeast

city by the lake:
smithville, mo

smithville, mo

Humphrey Smith came to Clay County in 1822 and built the first grain mill north of the Missouri River on the Little Platte River. The town that developed was known as Smith's Fork but later was incorporated as Smith's Mill. At some point, the town became Smithville, which it remains today.

Most people envision Smithville Lake when they think of this community about twenty minutes north of downtown Kansas City. The lake was created in the late 1970s and is managed by the U.S. Army Corps of Engineers. Many flights coming into Kansas City International Airport circle over the lake to get a perfect view of this long, narrow body of water that stretches 18 miles north of Smithville.

The focal point of most community activities is the downtown square, which is lined with a number of lovely antiques and gift shops and a few thrift stores that are always worthy of investigation. A farmers' market operates here Saturday morning from May through October, and a number of special events keep the square lively throughout the year.

For more information, contact the Smithville Chamber of Commerce at (816) 532-0946 or visit www.smithvillemo.org.

where to go

Comanche Acres Iris Gardens. 12421 Southeast State Highway 116, Gower. Travel about 4 miles north of Smithville on U.S. Highway 169, then turn left on Missouri Highway 16 to the beautiful seventeen acres of Comanche Acres Iris Gardens. Before the land was flooded to form Smithville Lake, Jim and LeMoyne Hedgecock scoured the old homesteads for iris rhizomes, which they replanted. They've bred nearly 2,500 new types of flowers, which they sell around the world through a catalog company—and to anyone who happens by. Spring is the most impressive time for a visit. You can wander through the flowers without charge and enjoy the guinea hens, turkeys, and ducks that eat the bugs from the blooms. (816) 424-6436; www.comancheacres.com.

The Jerry L. Litton Visitor Center. Missouri Highway 92 east from Kearney or US 169 north from Kansas City to 16311 Highway DD (south end of dam), P.O. Box 428, Smithville, MO 64089. The visitor center is named after the late sixth district congressman; it offers exhibits and artifacts concerning the Missouri Valley and the Native Americans who inhabited it. There's information about the lake and dam and on the life of Litton. The center also has nature films, and you can schedule tours of the dam control tower. Free. Open 8:00 a.m. to 4:00 p.m., Monday through Saturday. (816) 532-0174.

Shatto Milk Company. 9406 North Missouri Highway 33, Osborn. Head north out of Smithville on US 169 and turn right on Highway 116, following signs to the Shatto Milk Company. This family-owned dairy produces hormone-free milk bottled in glass bottles. Enjoy a fresh-baked chocolate-chip cookie and a glass of cold milk at the end of your tour. Open daily. Fee. Check the Web site for special events, such as Easter egg hunts and family fun days at the farm. (816) 930-3862; www.shattomilkcompany.com.

Smithville Lake and Clay County Parks (Camp Branch, Little Platte Park, and Crow's Creek Area). Two miles east of US 169 on Northeast 180th Street. Located amid rolling hills and grassland, the 7,200-acre lake is just 20 miles from downtown Kansas City and is surrounded by 27 miles of walking and horseback-riding trails. Clay County operates recreation areas on the lake, leasing nearly 5,500 acres from the U.S. Army Corps of Engineers. The recreation areas include more than 777 campsites for tents and RVs, 2 swimming beaches, 200 picnic sites, 11 shelter houses, and 2 full-service marinas. Favorites with fishermen are bass, walleye, crappie, and catfish.

Golfers are offered challenging play on two par-72, award-winning eighteen-hole championship golf courses.

The Kansas City Trapshooters Association offers the public a chance to do some of the finest trap and skeet shooting in the Midwest. This well-equipped facility includes twelve trapshooting pads, two skeet houses, five-man sporting clays, and a clubhouse. In addition to all campground restrooms, Crow's Creek Area offers a wheelchair-accessible fishing dock and

> ## beauty and remembrance
>
> *The downtown square of Smithville, the location of many community activities, is a spacious plaza-style setting with picnic tables, benches, potted plants, and grand shade trees. The focal point, however, is the public stage. It is dedicated to the memory of Allie Kemp, a Leawood teenager who was tragically murdered in 2003. Kemp's father is a native of Smithville, and her grandparents live here today. The family business, Diversified Metal Fabricators, created the beautiful accent pieces that adorn the stage. As one local businessperson said, "It's a beautiful place in memory of a beautiful young woman."*

picnic shelter. Most of the walking trails have been paved in recent years. Fee. &. (816) 407-3400; www.claycogov.com.

Woodhenge. Located on the west side of Smithville Lake in Little Platte Park, this is a working replica of the only known square prehistoric Native American solar calendar. The original site was flooded when Smithville Lake was created in the late 1970s. It's an interesting place to visit if you're already at the lake. Open year-round. Free with admission to the park. (816) 407-3400.

where to eat

Lowman's Cafe. 505 South US 169. This is where the locals come for a cup of coffee and to catch up on the latest gossip. You can count on a great selection of cream pies and the Lowman's special-recipe barbecue sauce on the ham and beef sandwiches served seven days a week. $; (no cards). (816) 532-9000.

Main Cup Cafe. 103 Main Street. Stop in for a cup of gourmet coffee or tea and perhaps the best homemade baked goods north of the river. This delicate, Victorian setting includes an antique soda fountain. Whole pies and quiches are for sale to take home and enjoy later. Open for lunch Wednesday through Saturday and dinner on Friday evenings. $. (816) 532-8377.

day trip 02

northeast

jesse james country:
liberty, mo; kearney, mo; watkins mill
(lawson, mo); excelsior springs, mo;
richmond, mo

liberty, mo

One of the most famous robberies attributed to the notorious James Gang was the daylight holdup of Clay County Savings in Liberty back in 1866. The robbers took $60,000 in gold and currency, and none of the money was ever recovered. Others who put Liberty on the map are Joseph Smith, the Mormon prophet, and Alexander Doniphan, who took up the practice of law in Liberty in 1833. During his residence of thirty years, he became a leading citizen, orator, jurist, statesman, and soldier, eventually leading his famous expedition to Old Mexico in 1846–47, the longest military march ever made.

By 1820 Clay County was formed and named in honor of Henry Clay, the famed senator. Liberty, selected as the county seat, was established that same year. Two years later a college grew under the supervision of Dr. William Jewell, and today the lovely campus is still a fine center of higher learning. For more information, contact the Liberty Area Chamber of Commerce, 9 South Leonard Street; (816) 781-5200; www.libertychamber.com.

where to go

Bratcher Cooperage. 109 South Water Street. Stop in this fun shop, a former gas station, to see one of the nation's top craft artisans at work. Doug Bratcher has been handcrafting barrels, buckets, kegs, and churns in the traditional style for more than twenty years. If he's not in the shop when you come by, it's because he is at Silver Dollar City, where he is a featured

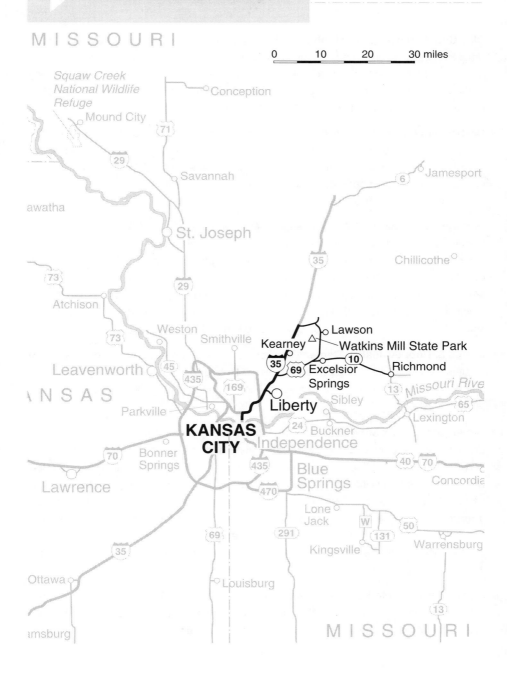

craft artisan, or on site at a movie location or Civil War reenactment. But you'll enjoy a visit with Doug's wife, Jan, who runs the gift shop filled with "Made in the USA" gifts, cards, and accessories. Open 10:00 a.m. to 5:30 p.m., Monday through Saturday. Closed Sunday. (816) 781-3988.

Clay County Museum and Historical Society. 14 North Main Street. Housed in an 1877 drugstore, the museum collection focuses on Clay County history. It features a restored doctor's office, prehistoric Native American relics, toys, tools, arrowheads, and artifacts relating to the operation of a nineteenth-century drugstore. Open Monday through Saturday, afternoons. Closed in January. Fee. (816) 792-1849.

Corbin Theatre Co. 15 North Water Street. Once the site of all entertainment in Liberty, this historic, circa-1880s theater has recently been renovated. It now hosts regular musical and theatrical performances in an intimate setting on the square. Visit the Web site for upcoming dances, plays, and concerts by some of the area's most talented entertainers. (816) 516-7373; www.corbintheatre.org.

Historic Liberty Jail and Visitors Center (Mormon Jail). 216 North Main Street. Mormon leader Joseph Smith was imprisoned here in 1838–39 for his beliefs. Built in 1833, the limestone jail eventually crumbled but was reconstructed by the Church of Jesus Christ of Latter-day Saints in 1963. The jail has cutaway walls so that visitors can see what conditions were like more than 150 years ago. The center also teaches about the unfairness of persecuting those of different faiths. Guided tours include historical highlights, exhibits, artwork, and interactive video displays. Open daily 9:00 a.m. to 9:00 p.m. Free. (816) 781-3188.

James S. Rooney Justice Center. Clay County Courthouse, 11 South Water Street. Take a self-guided tour through the courthouse, which features outdoor ceramic murals depicting the county's history. If the court is in session, children can sit in, but they must be quiet. Free. (816) 407-3900.

Jesse James Bank Museum. 103 North Water Street (the northeast corner of Courthouse Square). Frank and Jesse James were responsible for the first successful daylight bank robbery during peacetime. The James boys made a bank "withdrawal" of $60,000 from the Clay County Savings Association on February 13, 1866. A William Jewell College student who witnessed the event was shot and killed. Nobody was ever convicted. Today you can take a glimpse into the workings of a nineteenth-century bank and view a number of artifacts related to Jesse James. The original bank vault and a rare Seth Thomas calendar clock are part of the tour. The building is listed on the National Register of Historic Places. Open Monday through Saturday; closed Sunday. Fee. (816) 781-4458.

Liberty Farmers' Market. West side of Historic Liberty Square. The Saturday farmers' market is open from May through October, and you can find a variety of produce here, including fruits, vegetables, flowers, bedding plants, and honey. There is also a farmers' market on

Monday and Wednesday, located next to Crowley Furniture on Missouri Highway 291. The Saturday market opens early and closes at 1:00 p.m. The Wednesday market also closes at 1:00 p.m. Free. (816) 781-2649.

Martha Lafite Thompson Nature Sanctuary. 407 North LaFrenz Road (0.5 mile southeast of William Jewell College). This one-hundred-acre sanctuary is filled with wildlife that inhabit prairies, woodlands, meadows, and marshes. White-tailed deer, raccoons, foxes, squirrels, birds, and butterflies delight the eyes. The visitor center features educational exhibits for children and has organized activities such as wildflower and full-moon hikes. The visitor center is closed Sunday and Monday. The four miles of hiking trails are open daily from 8:30 a.m. to sunset. Free. &. (816) 781-8598; www.naturesanctuary.com.

Wynbrick Wellness Center. 1701 Wynbrick Drive. This 1930s-era home has become a location for wellness and fellowship, according to Alice Brink, whose family started the center because of an interest in caring for others. The center is popular for small gatherings, such as teas and bridal showers; has fitness and educational programs; and offers spa services. (816) 792-4325; www.wynbrickcenter.com.

where to eat

By the Book. 4 North Main Street. This locally owned bookstore is a great place to enjoy a cup of coffee or hot tea while perusing new and used books and local art, featured in the upstairs gallery. You can also get a nice milkshake or frozen fruit drink if you'd like, or come early for breakfast specials. $. (816) 792-3200.

Cajun Tony's. 18 North Main Street. Tony and Lorena Potter moved to the Kansas City area in 2005 from Lafayette, Louisiana, for another job, which didn't work out. But they loved Liberty so much they decided to stay and follow their dream of operating a Cajun restaurant. The gumbos and étouffées are made fresh daily and the frog legs, shrimp, and other seafood are flown in fresh every day as well. Tuesday night is all-you-can-eat catfish; Thursday is all-you-can-eat shrimp. You'll love the fresh crab dip appetizer and the bluegrass bands that play on Thursdays. And ask about Tony's friend in Louisiana who caught the 12-foot alligator on display. $$; (816) 222-4134. Closed Sunday and Monday.

Los Compas Mexican Restaurant. 5 East Kansas Street. For more than one hundred years, this historic building on the downtown square was home to either a hardware store or a restaurant of the same name. Today it is a very popular Mexican restaurant, but the original tin ceilings, brick walls, and hardware cabinets are reminders of the building's place in Liberty history. Try one of the house specials—Chile Colorado and Chalupa Especial. $$; (816) 415-0244.

where to stay

The Stone-Yancey House. 421 North Lightburne Street. If you struggle with high cholesterol, you'll enjoy the breakfast Carolyn Hatcher serves her guests—a hot toddy oatmeal featuring a healthful dose of demara whiskey. But you'll also enjoy her fresh-baked cookies and evening desserts, plus the magnificent antiques and stained-glass windows in this 1889-era home. Carolyn and her husband, Steve, are only the fourth owners, and they have tastefully decorated the three bedrooms with period antiques. Carolyn's own wedding dress adorns the entryway. $$$. (816) 415-1811; www.stoneyanceyhouse.com.

kearney, mo

The former home of outlaw Jesse James holds several attractions of historic importance, many of them highlighted in the 2007 movie *The Assassination of Jesse James by the Coward Robert Ford* starring Missouri native Brad Pitt. Kearney also hosts a Jesse James Festival complete with parade, rodeo, craft show, carnival, and barbecue cook-off the second and third weekends of September. For information, contact Jesse James Festival, P.O. Box 242, Kearney, MO 64060; (816) 628-4229; www.jessejamesfestival.com.

where to go

Jesse James Farm and Museum. 21216 James Farm Road (5 miles east of Kearney on Highway 92). This is the birthplace of Jesse James, where he and his brother Frank grew up during the mid-1800s. The house has been authentically restored, and the museum features the world's largest collection of James family artifacts, including guns, saddles, and boots. The quilt, handmade by Frank's wife, Annie, remains on the bed in which he died. Open year-round. Fee. (816) 628-6065; www.jessejames.org.

Jesse James Grave. Mount Olivet Cemetery, west end of Highway 92 on the way out of Kearney. Jesse's grave is located between two small evergreen trees on the cemetery's west side. Originally he was buried on the front lawn of the farm so that his family could protect his remains from grave robbers and curiosity seekers. For years Jesse's mother, Zerelda, sold pebbles off the grave to tourists. Later his body was moved to Mount Olivet. A relatively small marker identifies the grave as that of Jesse James and his wife, Zerelda. Jesse's marker reads: BORN: SEPTEMBER 5, 1847. ASSASSINATED: APRIL 3, 1882. To the left and right of Jesse's grave stand taller monuments inscribed *Samuel,* where the outlaw's mother and stepfather are buried. Also nearby is the grave of young Archie Samuel, Jesse's half-brother who was killed when Pinkerton detectives bombed the James farm in January 1875. Open daily. Free.

Mount Gilead Church and School. 15918 Plattsburg Road. This was the only school west of the Mississippi River to remain open during the Civil War. Third- and fourth-grade students are invited to take a class trip back to the 1800s, where they can experience an old-fashioned education. Lessons in history, reading, arithmetic, and spelling are taught by a schoolteacher in period attire. Experiencing school life in this one-room schoolhouse offers children a unique and unforgettable history lesson. The church is also available for weddings. Fee. Reservations required. (816) 628-6065.

Tryst Falls Park. Five miles east of Kearney on Highway 92. The Clay County Parks and Recreation Department runs this forty-acre park, which includes the area's only waterfall open to the public. It's a great place to picnic because of the many shelters and grills. Jesse James's father, a Baptist minister, baptized Walthus Watkins, owner of Watkins Mill, at Tryst Falls. Swimming is dangerous and not allowed here because of the rocks. Fishing is not allowed. The park makes a sightseeing stop in your tour of Jesse James Farm or Watkins Mill State Park. Open daily. (816) 407-3400.

watkins mill (lawson, mo)

where to go

Watkins Woolen Mill State Historic Site and Park. Located 6.5 miles north of Excelsior Springs and 7 miles east of Kearney, off Highway 92 at Highway RA, Lawson. This is the last nineteenth-century woolen mill in America with original equipment. The mill heralds the beginning of the industrial age and still contains sixty of the original machines and a steam engine. The Watkins home, smokehouse, summer kitchen, and fruit dry house, along with an octagonal school and a church, add interest. The original farm was 3,550-acres, but the park is now 1,500 acres and includes the original sawmill, gristmill, and brick kiln built by the Watkins family.

The state park features picnicking, camping, hiking, fishing, and swimming in the lake. Bring your bike along and enjoy the 3.5-mile bike/hike trail around the shoreline. Bring food and drink; there are no concessions here and water is turned off from November 1 to April 1. Open daily. &. Free (fee for historic site). (816) 580-3387; www.mostateparks.com/wwmill.

excelsior springs, mo

A drive north on U.S. Highway 69 will take you to Excelsior Springs in fewer than forty minutes. Long revered as a haven of health, Excelsior Springs has attracted thousands of people to its mineral waters since 1881 and still offers historical insight into the healing powers of the waters. A summer festival celebrates the influence of the waters in this town. For information on what there is to see and do, call the Excelsior Springs Chamber of Commerce at (816) 630-6161; www.exspgschamber.com.

where to go

Historic Hall of Waters. 201 East Broadway. The Historic Hall of Waters was the central dispersal site of the five mineral waters found here and focused on the development of equipment for the use of water in therapeutic treatment. Siloam Springs remains today as the only natural supply of iron manganese mineral water in the country and is one of five recognized in existence worldwide. Here, you can belly up to the longest mineral-water bar in the world and sample the natural calcium mineral water or take home a bottle to drink. Bring your camera to photograph the beautiful Mayan Indian and art deco architectural designs. Fee. (816) 630-0752.

where to stay

The Elms Resort and Spa. Regent Street and Elms Boulevard. Touting itself as a unique retreat and conference facility for businesses and groups, The Elms Resort and Spa features tastefully appointed guest rooms and suites that include modern amenities such as voice mail, wireless Internet, and a refreshment center. Choose from casual or fine dining options or pamper yourself at The Spa, a 10,000-square-foot facility featuring therapists who wrap you in mud, seaweed, and aloe and massage you until you're jelly. A fitness center provides a swim track, jogging track, sauna, steam rooms, and equipment. There's also an outdoor pool, heated whirlpool, and hiking and biking trails. The Challenge Course, with its climbing wall, ropes course, and Burma bridge, is not for couch potatoes. A leadership center provides principle-based training and customized workshops that enhance personal, team, and organizational effectiveness. $$$. (800) 843-3567; www.elmsresort.com.

The Inn on Crescent Lake. 1261 St. Louis Avenue. This country inn makes a great romantic getaway or a pleasant alternative for businesspeople tired of the motel shuffle.

The three-story Georgian colonial mansion is nestled on twenty-two acres and surrounded by two ponds and a lawn designed for strolling and relaxing. The innkeepers, Ed and Irene Peege, moved here from Connecticut and invite you to unwind as they have. A full breakfast might include quiche, scones, waffles, French toast, and other delights.

Each of the ten guest rooms has a private bath, including a whirlpool or claw-foot tub. The downstairs guest room is wheelchair-accessible, with its own separate entrance, and is adjacent to the kitchen. The ballroom-size third floor can be reserved as a honeymoon suite. It features a king-size bed, a separate sitting area, and a whirlpool bath and custom marble shower big enough for two.

If that's not enough, there's an outdoor swimming pool where you can practice your backstroke on warm summer days. The ponds are stocked with bass and catfish, and the inn will supply you with a fishing pole and boat. The inn is available for private parties, weddings, and corporate retreats, with enough meeting space to accommodate up to fifty people. $$$. (816) 630-6745; www.crescentlake.com.

richmond, mo

Located 11 miles north of Lexington on Missouri Highway 13, Richmond, Missouri, touts itself as "the Mushroom Capital of the World." Time your trip so that it coincides with Richmond's annual mushroom festival the first weekend in May. This is when those hard-to-find morel mushrooms pop up, begging to be sautéed in butter and wine. The mushrooms are plentiful enough around here for a celebration in their honor. Richmond hosts a parade, plenty of food and craft booths, a model train show, a carnival, a beer garden, and other activities. Richmond folks will sell you some morels to take back home, but they won't reveal their secret mushroom spots. If you want to go searching in the woods, you're on your own.

Fans of Jesse James lore come to Richmond to visit the grave of Robert Ford, the man who shot the outlaw in the back. Ford was the subject of a 2007 movie (starring Missouri native Brad Pitt) called *The Assassination of Jesse James by the Coward Robert Ford*. Bob Ford and his brother Charley, who was in on the plan to shoot James, are buried in the Sunnyslope Cemetery.

For more information, call the Richmond Chamber of Commerce at (816) 776-6916; www.richmondmissouri.com.

where to go

The Farris Theatre. 301 West Main Street. Look closely at this structure and see if it reminds you of the Folly Theatre in downtown Kansas City. Originally built in 1901 as an opera house, the Farris was modeled after the Folly. The Farris Theatre has been fully restored for use as a performance theater, movie house, and community center, by a not-for-profit group called "Friends of the Farris." Call (816) 776-6684 for a schedule of shows and events.

Ray County Museum. 901 West Royal Street. This odd-looking Y-shaped building, constructed in 1910, was designed so that all fifty-four rooms would have lots of sunshine. Today it is home to a number of artifacts that tell the story of this region, including Native American, Civil War, and Mormon history. It is open year-round, Wednesday through Saturday 10:00 a.m. to 5:00 p.m., and closed on holidays. Admission is free. (816) 776-2305.

United Methodist Church. 212 Main Street. This lovely limestone church is remarkable for its fifteen stained-glass windows of various sizes. But unique to a church in 1918 was the inclusion of an in-ground swimming pool and library, both open to the public. Although neither exists today, the public is welcomed to visit anytime to see the windows and lovely woodwork rarely found in construction projects today. (816) 776-2122.

where to eat

Mushroom Patch Restaurant. 908 East Main Street. Recently remodeled after a fire in the summer of 2007, the Mushroom Patch is more comfortable than ever. It still serves that great comfort food, such as real mashed potatoes and gravy and homemade pies, for which it has been known for years. Open seven days a week. $. (816) 776-5308.

day trip 03

northeast

amish country:
Jamesport, mo

jamesport, mo

In Jamesport, the Amish community offers a glimpse of a bygone era. These people are part of the Old Order Amish, who are direct descendants of the Mennonite Anabaptists, a group that developed during the Reformation in Germany and Switzerland. Today there are Amish settlements in at least twenty-one states and Canada. In the early 1950s the Amish immigrated to Jamesport, now the largest settlement in the state. Currently about 2,200 Amish reside on the rich farmland of the area.

They shun the use of modern conveniences and travel by means of horse-drawn vehicles. Their peaceful lifestyle revolves around a close-knit family, their faith, and farming. These people may seem quaint to outsiders but are uniquely adapted for survival today. They beat inflation by living without the things we take for granted. They use no electricity, no cars, no televisions or radios. Their education ends at the eighth grade, and they don't seem to miss it. Many of the Amish farmhouses now have indoor plumbing, and most Amish families use oil furnaces, kerosene- or wood-burning stoves, and kerosene lamps. Their primary mode of transportation, the horse and carriage, is certainly more picturesque and environmentally friendly than automobiles.

Amish men are expert farmers who still use plows pulled by horses to till their fields. They dress modestly in black broad-brimmed hats, white shirts, and black trousers.

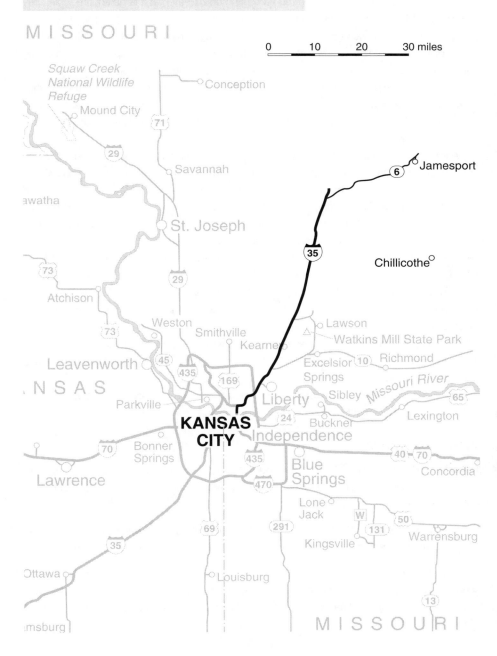

The women excel in the home arts, and anyone fortunate enough to attend an Amish quilting bee has a rare privilege in store, for every stitch sewn by these women is a perfect example of how well-made things used to be put together.

Usually a dozen Amish women attend a quilting bee. Seated at a large square table, they sew pattern blocks by hand and quilt them around a rectangular quilting frame. They wear plain, long cotton dresses held together with pins (they consider buttons worldly). On their heads they wear white prayer caps at all times. Their conversation often lapses into something called "Ferhoodled English," a combination of German, Dutch, and English.

Jamesport has prospered as a tourist attraction because of the Amish, and they, in their practical way, have taken advantage of public curiosity. If you're looking for authentic Amish foods, goods, and services, be aware that "Amish style" does not necessarily mean that something is Amish-made.

A visit to Jamesport can be fun if you tour it with the idea that there are two separate reasons for coming here. The first is to visit the Amish-owned stores, where you will find authentic Amish foods, quilts, and other items. The second reason is to enjoy the antiques, craft, and specialty shops; restaurants; and bed-and-breakfasts, most of which are *not* Amish-owned.

If you want to determine whether an establishment is Amish or Mennonite, check the days it is open; Amish shops close on Thursday and Sunday. The Amish typically do not want their pictures taken, since it violates their religious beliefs. As a courtesy, ask permission before you shoot.

You might try timing a trip to any one of a number of festivals, including the town's renowned Step Back in Time Christmas Craft Show, held the Friday and Saturday after Thanksgiving.

Free maps of the area are available at all the businesses and the Amish Country stores. Tours are available through Hook & Eye Dutch House and Tour Service, 509 North Elm Street, Jamesport, MO 64648; (660) 684-6179.

For more information, contact the Jamesport Community Association, P.O. Box 215, Jamesport, MO 64648; (660) 684-6146; www.jamesport-mo.com.

where to shop

Broadway Pavilion Mall. South of the four-way stop. The mall has a large assortment of antiques, collectibles, furniture, glassware, pottery, records, old books, and more. Open daily. (660) 684-6655.

DeVual Art Gallery. 107 South Broadway. This gallery features the work of western artist Lee Teeter, along with pottery and other handcrafted items by Missouri artists. (660) 684-6010.

The Family Tree House. 100 North Broadway. Specializing in a decorative touch for every season, this fun shop offers custom floral arrangements, water fountains, fern stands, candles, and more. You'll find this creative store just one door north of City Hall. Closed Sunday. (660) 684-6210.

Firehouse Antiques. 101 South Broadway. Located in the former firehouse that served Jamesport from the 1930s to the 1970s, this store carries a mix of old and new, including antique furniture but new western and lodge decor. Closed Mondays. (660) 684-6789.

Kramer-Yoder Country Goodies. Kramer-Yoder Farm, Route 3, Box 59 (2 miles west on County Road NN). Natural farm-raised meats, homemade goodies, and crafts are sold at this Amish-owned store. Open Monday, Wednesday, and Friday. No phone.

Pastime Carlyle's. 100 Auberry Grove. Early country furniture and decorative items, plus original painted furniture, are sold here along with old-fashioned candy and collectibles. Closed Sunday. (660) 684-6222.

This 'N That. 1 block north of the four-way stop. A little bit of everything, including furniture, jewelry, and glassware, is sold here. Closed Sunday. (660) 684-6594.

where to eat

Anna's Bake Shop. Route 1, Box 34–A (west end of town). This Amish shop sells mouth-watering fresh-baked doughnuts, pies, breads, and cinnamon and dinner rolls. Closed Christmas through February 1. According to the owner, the phone works only "when the weather is above twenty degrees." Call for hours. $; (no cards). (660) 684-6810.

Country Bakery. Located 0.5 mile south of Jamesport on Missouri Highway 190. Leave room in your tummy and your car for some delicious, authentic Amish homemade baked goods. Closed Thursday and Sunday. $; (no cards). No phone.

Gingerich Dutch Pantry. Located at the four-way stop in downtown Jamesport, this Mennonite-owned restaurant specializes in Mennonite cooking using Old Dutch recipes. Homemade pies, breads, cinnamon rolls, and other baked goods are featured. A buffet and a complete menu are available for individuals or large groups. Closed Sunday. $. (660) 684-6212.

where to stay

Country Colonial Bed & Breakfast. 106 East Main Street. Sleep tight in an original pre-Civil War rope bed, the kind that instigated the term "sleep tight," in this three-bedroom inn that is filled with antiques throughout. But don't snuggle in too tightly before enjoying a moonlight, horse-drawn carriage ride through the Amish countryside. And don't sleep too late or you'll miss Nina den Hartog's fabulous cinnamon raisin French toast. Yummmmm. $$. (660) 684-6711 or (800) 579-9248.

Grand River Inn. Junction of U.S. Highways 36 and 65, Chillicothe. Amenities here include a restaurant and lounge, along with comfortable rooms and a large pool with a sauna and hot tub. Golf packages are available. The hotel can also arrange tours of the Jamesport area. $$. (660) 646-6590; www.grandriverinn.com.

Marigolds Inn and Gift Shoppe. Three blocks west of downtown Jamesport. If you like handmade quilts, you'll enjoy a stay in one of the ten individually decorated rooms at Marigolds. Several have a garden theme; others have a western or bunkhouse look to them— all based on the bed coverings. Breakfast is on your own. $$. (660) 684-6122.

east

east day trip 01

day trip 01

east

history, a president's residence, and red delicious:
independence, mo; sibley, mo; lexington, mo; waverly, mo

independence, mo

To reach Independence from Kansas City, take Interstate 70 East to Interstate 435 North and the Truman Road exit; then take Truman Road east to Independence. Founded in 1827, Independence became known as the Queen City of the Trails, heading three dominant routes west—the Santa Fe, California, and Oregon Trails. (The Santa-Cali-Gon Festival, held annually on Labor Day weekend, commemorates the opening of these prairie pathways.)

Fortunes were made here during the westward expansion and Victorian periods, and many of the charming homes built during these times have been designated with historic markers. Today Independence is best known as the home of the thirty-third president, Harry S. Truman. Places related to his life here include his home, courtroom, and office, as well as the Harry S. Truman Museum and Library.

Just a few blocks from the Harry S. Truman National Historic Site (Truman home) is Independence Square, filled with restaurants and shops housing arts, crafts, antiques, and memorabilia. It's fun to go exploring around a historic area that has a great past. Smack in the middle of the square is the Jackson County Courthouse. Built in 1836, it was renovated in 1933 during the administration of Jackson County Judge Harry S. Truman.

On the east side of the courthouse is a full-size statue of Harry himself. *The Man from Independence,* a multimedia show highlighting Truman's life before his presidency, is shown on the hour inside the courthouse. While you're there you can visit the gift shop, which features crafts made by senior citizens.

Three walking trails are available in Independence for historically minded leisure walkers. The Swales Walking Trail at the Bingham-Waggoner Estate winds along a quarter-mile paved surface through the grounds, and nine interpretive signs focus on wagon ruts that follow the Santa Fe trade route west. The second trail begins in front of the Harry S. Truman National Historic Site Visitors Center. This 2.7-mile trail features forty-three brass plaques embedded in the sidewalks throughout the Truman neighborhood. Finally, the Missouri Mormon Walking Trail begins on the corner of Walnut and River and explores the religious history of the Mormons, illustrated by fourteen brass sidewalk markers at locations of significance in the early days of the church. Brochures for the Truman and Mormon walking tours are available from the City of Independence Tourism Department, 111 East Maple Street, Independence, MO 64050; (816) 325-7111; www.visitindependence.com.

where to go

The Auditorium. 1001 West Walnut Street. This is part of the world headquarters for the Community of Christ. The 6,000-seat chamber features a world-famous 111-rank, 6,334-pipe Aeolian-Skinner organ, one of the largest church organs in the nation. Thousands of people use the building yearly for religious, cultural, and community-centered activities. Free organ recitals are offered daily from June through August and on Sunday the remainder of the year. Guided tours are available daily to the public. (816) 833-1000, ext. 3030; www.cofchrist.org.

Bingham-Waggoner Estate. 313 West Pacific Avenue. Built in 1855, this private home eventually became the residence of Missouri artist George Caleb Bingham, who lived here with his wife, Eliza, until 1870. In 1879 the home was purchased by Peter and William Waggoner, who remodeled the original structure. The house served as the Waggoner family home until 1976. The twenty-six-room residence is open to tour from April 1 to October 31 and throughout the month of December. Fee. (816) 461-3491 or 325-7111; www.bwestate.org.

1827 Log Courthouse. 107 West Kansas Avenue. The first courthouse in Jackson County, this is the oldest historic site open to the public in Independence. Originally a county courthouse, it was used as a private residence in 1832. During the 1920s and 1930s, the structure housed the headquarters of the Community Welfare League, with Bess Truman (Harry's wife) as honorary vice-chairperson. In 1932 Jackson County Judge Harry S. Truman held court there while the main courthouse was being remodeled. Open year-round. Fee. (816) 325-7111.

1859 Jail, Marshal's Home, and Museum. 217 North Main Street. Four buildings constitute this museum operated by the Jackson County Historical Society. These include the jail that held the outlaw Frank James, the marshal's restored home, a one-room schoolhouse, and a county museum. Open daily April 1 to October 31 and in the month of December. The complex is closed in November and January through March. Fee. (816) 252-1892.

George Owens Nature Park. 1601 South Speck Road. This 85-acre gem of the Jackson County Parks system celebrated its thirtieth birthday in 2007. The park has two fishing lakes stocked with bass, channel cat, bluegill, and bullheads. A fishing license is required for people ages fifteen through sixty-four. There are 4 miles of nature trails for hiking, one of them wheelchair accessible, as well as a nature center whose outdoor habitat is filled with live deer, bats, geese, and snakes. Films are offered on Saturday once a month. Group reservations must be made at least two weeks in advance. Open year-round. Closed Monday. Free. &. (816) 325-7115.

Harry S. Truman Courtroom and Office. Independence Square Courthouse, Room 109, Main at Maple Street. This is where the thirty-third president of the United States began the political career that led him to the White House. You'll see Judge Truman's restored quarters and an audiovisual presentation about his life and courtship with Bess. Open Monday through Friday, 10:00 a.m. to 3:30 p.m. Fee. (816) 252-7454.

Harry S. Truman Museum and Library. U.S. Highway 24 and Delaware Street. One of ten presidential libraries administered by the National Archives and Records Administration, this library houses exhibits and memorabilia of the Truman years, as well as a research facility. An extraordinary Thomas Hart Benton mural greets you as you walk through the door. Permanent museum exhibits on President Truman's career include a replica of the Oval Office and a glimpse into his dramatic 1948 election victory over Thomas Dewey. Interactive exhibits allow visitors to participate in some of the difficult decisions Truman made, including dropping the atomic bomb. Temporary traveling exhibits are often augmented with special programs. The graves of President and Mrs. Truman are located in the library's courtyard. Open daily. Fee. (816) 268-8200; www.trumanlibrary.org.

Harry S. Truman National Historic Site. 219 North Delaware Street. Located in the Harry S. Truman National Landmark District, this was the home of the former president and his wife, Bess Wallace Truman, until their deaths. Informative tours include a twelve-minute slide show at the ticket center and a fifteen-minute tour of the residence. Individuals must reserve their tickets in person on a first-come, first-served basis on the day of the tour at the Truman Home Ticket and Information Center, 223 North Main Street, adjacent to Independence Square. Open daily Memorial Day through Labor Day. Closed Monday from Labor Day through Memorial Day. Fee. (816) 254-2720; www.nps.gov/hstr.

Leila's Hair Museum. 1333 South Noland Road. In fifty-one years as a hairdresser, Leila Cohoon has developed a fascination with hair and a fascinating collection. She has hundreds of pieces of hair art and jewelry, some dating to the 1680s. She is considered a leading expert on hair and has been consulted in criminal cases by the FBI. Her museum is the national headquarters for the Victorian Hairwork Society. Open Tuesday through Saturday. Fee. (816) 833-2955; www.hairwork.com/leila.

Missouri Pacific Railroad Station. Grand Street and Pacific Avenue. This depot, which figured in Truman's 1948 "Whistle Stop" campaign, is listed on the National Register of Historic Places. There's daily Amtrak service into Kansas City. Round-trip group rates are available. Free (fee for Amtrak). (816) 421-3622.

Mormon Visitors' Center. 937 West Walnut Street. Operated by The Church of Jesus Christ of Latter-day Saints (Mormon). The high-tech exhibits document the doctrines of the church. Visitors enter through a covered wagon and see the daily life of the Saints portrayed in a log cabin. Open daily. Free. (816) 836-3466.

National Frontier Trails Museum. 318 West Pacific Avenue. This acclaimed museum, library, and archival center is located at the principal jumping-off point of the Santa Fe, Oregon, and California Trails. It is the only interpretive center in the nation devoted to all three trails. The gripping story of the exploration and settlement of the American West is shown in an award-winning introductory film that prepares visitors for their interesting trip through the museum's many exhibits, which feature memorabilia and relics from the prairie pathways. The two-story Chicago and Alton Depot, restored from the 1890s, is located on the grounds. Only two such two-story depots remain in Missouri. Open daily. Fee. (816) 325-7575; www.frontier trailsmuseum.org.

Pioneer Spring Cabin. Southeast corner of Noland and Truman Roads. The austere two-room cabin was originally constructed in an Irish community known as Brady Town and moved to its present location in 1971. A spring outside the cabin has been re-created to represent the kind of welcome oasis that traders and emigrants may have found on their way west. Open daily April 1 to October 31. Free. (816) 325-7111.

The Temple. 201 South River Street. This unusual architectural structure is part of the Community of Christ World Headquarters complex. It includes two visitor theaters, a lecture hall, and classrooms, plus a museum, a bookstore, a library, and a chapel with an adjacent meditation garden, along with administrative offices. Highlighting the building is a 1,600-seat sanctuary and a 102-rank, 5,686-pipe organ built by Casavant Frères Limitée of Quebec, Canada. Fashioned after the nautilus seashell, the 150-foot spire rises from the sanctuary and can be seen from many areas of the city. The public is invited to attend the programs dedicated to peace and reconciliation, along with a daily prayer for peace, offered in the Temple sanctuary at 12:30 p.m. Public organ recitals are offered at 3:00 p.m. daily June through August and on Sunday only the remainder of the year. Free. (816) 833-1000, ext. 3030.

Vaile Mansion–DeWitt Museum. 1500 North Liberty Street. One of the best examples of Victorian architecture in the United States, this 1882 mansion has a second-floor smoking room where woodwork is painted with dozens of little faces and animals. The home also has nine beautiful fireplaces and an indoor water tower. Open daily April 1 to October 31. Also open in December. Fee. (816) 325-7111.

where to eat

Courthouse Exchange Restaurant and Lounge. 113 West Lexington Avenue. This place features a full lunch and dinner menu offering everything from prime rib to homemade cinnamon rolls. The tenderloin sandwiches here are famous. The private banquet room can be reserved for groups. $–$$. (816) 252-0344.

Ophelia's. 201 North Main Street. Located on Historic Independence Square, this trendy restaurant offers American cuisine, with the highest-quality seafood, steaks, chops, and pastas available for lunch, dinner, and Sunday brunch. $$–$$$. (816) 461-4525.

V's Italiano Ristorante. 10819 U.S. Highway 40 East. This family-owned and -operated restaurant offers an Old World ambience and friendly service. Pasta, chicken, and seafood specialties are offered along with early-bird specials, as is a modestly priced Sunday brunch. $$. (816) 353-1241; www.vsrestaurant.com.

where to stay

The Inn at Ophelia's. 201 North Main Street. Seven rooms and one suite afford the business or leisure traveler gracious accommodations, complete with private baths, voice messaging, modem capability, hotel amenities, and down comforters and pillows to make you feel at home. $$–$$$. (816) 461-4525; www.ophelias.net.

Serendipity Bed and Breakfast. 116 South Pleasant Street. Housed in an 1887 home, this bed-and-breakfast features antique furnishings along with Victorian children's books and toys, china figurines, glassware, and books for guests to peruse. The backyard garden provides a hammock and swing for peaceful relaxation. Accommodations include the carriage house, with king and twin beds, a kitchen, and a sitting room on the ground level, as well as two-room suites, one with a kitchenette. All six rooms have private baths. A full breakfast is served in the main dining room. The home also offers a Tour and Tea and antique car rides, weather permitting, for a fee. $$–$$$. (816) 833-4719; www.bbhost.com/serendipitybb.

Woodson Guest House. 1604 West Lexington Avenue. This elegant nineteenth-century home features overnight accommodations complete with a full breakfast and evening hors d'oeuvres, plus a large two-room suite and two lovely guest rooms with private baths. The home sits on an acre of ground and is tucked away in an all-natural setting filled with trees, gardens, shrubs, and herbs. $$. (816) 254-0551; www.woodsonguesthouse.com.

Woodstock Inn Bed and Breakfast. 1212 West Lexington Avenue. Located near Independence's historic sites, this inn offers ten rooms with private baths and two elegant suites. You can choose from king-, queen-, and double-bed accommodations that also include fireplaces and Jacuzzis. Breakfast is included and features gourmet waffles. $$–$$$. (816) 833-2233; www.thewoodstockinn.com.

sibley, mo

It's the weekend and you're lying in bed daydreaming about places you'd rather be. You yawn and stretch, envisioning a drive through the Old South, with its historic homes and genteel manners. An instant later you picture yourself savoring a harvest of apples in New England. But a trip like that may cost more money than you want to spend. Besides, you've only got a day to relax—and this is it.

Not to worry. You could be out right now, picking apples in Missouri. Or taking in lunch at a lovely river town crammed full of historic homes and antiques shops. All this and more are within a forty-five-minute drive east of Kansas City on US 24.

where to go

Fort Osage National Historic Landmark. 105 Osage Street. Drive 14 miles northeast of Independence and take US 24 east to Buckner. Turn north at Sibley Street and follow the signs. When the Lewis and Clark expedition passed this bluff on the Missouri River in June 1804, William Clark noted in his journal that it would be a prime location for a military outpost. In 1808 he returned to supervise the building of this, the second outpost in the Louisiana Purchase. It operated as Fort Clark for several months but then became Fort Osage until it ceased operation in 1827. An impressive new 15,000-square-foot visitor center opened in November 2007 that explores the geology, flora, and fauna of the Missouri River basin, as well as the prehistoric Hopewell Indians and the namesake Osage Indians. A wide veranda filled with rocking chairs and benches provides wonderful views of the Missouri River and a place to contemplate this spot's role in American history. Open Tuesday through Sunday year-round. Fee. The visitor center is wheelchair accessible, but many of the buildings—to retain their authenticity—are not. ⬅. (816) 650-3278; www.epsi.net/graphic/osage.html.

Sibley Orchards. 4121 California Avenue. Located 3 blocks from historic Fort Osage, the orchard offers blackberries and peaches in summer, along with sweet corn, tomatoes, and other seasonal vegetables. Peaches and apples are sold here in July. In fall apples, apple cider, and pumpkins are available. Evening hayrides that take visitors through the orchard are also offered. Open daily. (816) 650-5535.

lexington, mo

The historic town of Lexington can be reached by meandering along Missouri Highway 224, which takes you through the picturesque towns of Napoleon and Wellington, or you can zip here along US 24.

Lexington was once one of the great river ports of this state. River trade made it a fine commercial center and an outfitting point for those heading west. A U.S. land office was established in 1823, followed by a courthouse, a bank, churches, colleges, and more than 120 lovely antebellum and Victorian homes and buildings.

The cannonball embedded in one of the courthouse columns is a relic of the Confederate victory in the 1861 Battle of Lexington. The Anderson House, built in 1853 and located on the battlefield, was used as a field hospital and has been restored to its original elegance. For information: The Lexington Tourism Bureau, P.O. Box 132, Lexington, MO 64067; (660) 259-4711; www.historiclexington.com.

where to go

Anderson House. On the grounds of the Battle of Lexington Historic Site. Built in 1853 by Colonel Oliver Anderson as a private home, Anderson House has been restored and furnished with antiques of that period. The house was used as a field hospital during the Civil War, changing hands from North to South three times. Battle damage is still visible both inside and outside the home. Guided tours are given on the hour, starting at the visitor center. Open daily. Fee. For information, contact the Battle of Lexington SHS, P.O. Box 6, Lexington, MO 64067; (660) 259-4654; www.mostateparks.com/lexington.

Antebellum Homes. Lexington has four historic districts on the National Register of Historic Places, and more than 120 antebellum and Victorian homes and buildings are listed on the register. The Vintage Homes Tour, held in September of odd-numbered years, allows the public a glimpse of the interiors of these elegant historic structures. For information, contact the Lexington Tourism Bureau, P.O. Box 132, Lexington, MO 64067; (660) 259-4711; www.historic lexington.com.

Battle of Lexington State Historic Site. Northwest edge of town on Thirteenth Street. Between September 18 and 20, 1861, Union forces suffered a major defeat at Lexington when the pro-Southern Missouri State Guard, commanded by former Missouri governor Major General Sterling Price, led 12,000 men against the Union outpost at Lexington. The siege ended when the Union troops ran out of food, water, and ammunition. This is one of the few Civil War battlefields that has never been cultivated, and outlines of the trenches are still visible on the self-guided walking tour. The visitor center is open daily and has a fifteen-minute film that brings the Battle of the Hemp Bales to life. Visitor center. Open daily. Fee. &. (660) 259-4654; www.mostateparks.com/lexington.

1830s Log House Museum. West end of Main Street. This original log house was used as a home and business by several of Lexington's prominent early citizens and was also used as a tavern located on the Santa Fe Trail. Its pioneer furnishings provide a lesson in nineteenth-century life. Open Wednesday through Sunday in summer or by appointment. Free. For information: The Lexington Tourism Bureau; (660) 259-4711; www.historiclexington.com.

Lexington Historical Museum. 112 South Thirteenth Street. Built originally as the Cumberland Presbyterian Church in 1846, the museum contains an extensive exhibit on the Pony Express, along with Civil War artifacts from the Battle of Lexington, a coal-mining display, and a fine collection of early Lexington photographs. Open daily during summer; other times by appointment only. Fee. (660) 259-4711; www.historiclexington.com.

Madonna of the Trail. At the corner of Highland Avenue and Cliff Drive. This monument is one of twelve placed in every state crossed by the national Old Trails Road, the route of early settlers from Maryland to California. It honors the pioneer women who helped settle the west.

***Saluda* Memorial at Heritage Park.** In 1852 the *Saluda* steamboat's boilers exploded while it was docked at Lexington, killing approximately one hundred people. The people of Lexington responded, providing medical care, housing, and, in some cases, adopting the children of those adults killed in the accident. The memorial was dedicated in April 2002 on the 150th anniversary of the accident. (660) 259-4711; www.historiclexington.com.

where to shop

Main Street Lexington is peppered with more than a dozen interesting boutiques, specialty shops, and quality antiques stores. Come with plenty of cash in your pocket or an extended limit on your credit card because it's almost impossible to go away with your vehicle empty. A few suggestions:

Missouri River Antique Co. 912 Main Street. Straight from many old homes, barns, and businesses in rural Missouri, you'll find lots of primitives, architectural salvage items, and odds and ends. Open seven days a week. (660) 259-3097.

the williamsburg of the west

Lexington at times has been called "the Williamsburg of the West" because of its numerous historic homes and the dedicated efforts of the community to preserve the city's historic and cultural integrity. Early settlers built a performing arts school and three women's colleges to cultivate the finer elements of life.

A modern-era concert series known as "Live! in Lexington" brings renowned performers such as the Kansas City Symphony and the St. Louis Philharmonic to this small river town an hour east of downtown Kansas City.

Despite its early emphasis on culture, Main Street Lexington was once known as Block 42 because of the number of saloons that thrived here. It has been said that proper women and children never were seen on the sidewalks of Block 42, which is now home to lovely shops and restaurants that do indeed reflect the finer elements of life.

The Velvet Pumpkin. 920 Main Street. Just a few doors down the street from the Missouri River Antique Co., this inviting store carries a more refined selection of antiques and lots of fun decorative accents. Check out the creative line of greeting cards. (660) 259-4545.

where to eat

Peddler's Tea Room. 900 Main Street. This quaint tearoom offers daily specials and plenty of hearty, country-style food. Try the warm bread pudding or fruit cobblers in season. Lunch only. Closed Monday. $. (660) 259-4533.

Riley's Irish Pub and Grill. 913 Main Street. This downtown gathering spot is located in a restored 1890s building complete with original tile floors, stained-glass window, pressed-tin ceiling, and back bar. Irish specialties such as mulligan stew are offered, along with sandwiches and Southern specialties such as sweet potato fries. Open Wednesday through Saturday. $; (no cards). (660) 259-4771.

where to stay

Inn on Main Street. 920½ Main Street. Located in the downtown historic district, this 1840s building was renovated in 1998 and offers four king-size suites with private baths. Guests get a complimentary breakfast and a gift basket complete with coffee, champagne, and snacks. $$–$$$. (660) 259-3600.

The Parsonage. 1603 South Street. This large, Queen Anne–style home was built in 1894 and served as the Methodist Church parsonage for many years. It features three nicely appointed guest rooms, a full breakfast, a hot tub, and a cafe area where cappuccino, tea, and wine are served. $$; (no cards). (660) 259-2344.

waverly, mo

Missouri's Lafayette County contains numerous farms and orchards that lie along the site of the historic Santa Fe Trail. In spring, summer, and fall, roadside stands near the intersections of U.S. Highways 24 and 65 sell delicious handpicked produce to passersby.

East of Lexington on US 24 is Waverly, one of the Midwest's best fruit-producing areas, harvesting half the apple crop in Missouri. The town celebrates its fortune by holding the annual Apple Jubilee in mid-September. The jubilee features apple judging, entertainment, music, contests, and plenty of family fun. For information, call City Hall at (660) 493-2551.

The Santa Fe Trail Growers Association promotes tourism in this area and can provide you with a brochure that lists sixteen grower members that sell everything from "U-pick" and prepicked blackberries and asparagus to top-quality bedding and vegetable plants. In recent years, several vineyards have joined the agriculture community here. For a complete list of the orchards and wineries, their crops, and special events, visit www.historiclexington.com/growers.html.

Highway 24 has recently been declared a Missouri Scenic Byway, and you'll understand why when you drive this road between Lexington and Marshall. The shades of gold from fields of soybeans readying for harvest, punctuated by the hearty reds and greens of apple orchards loaded for the season, are enough to make Monet's garden at Giverny tip its hat in appreciation.

where to go

Baltimore Bend Winery. 27150 Highway 24. Harvesting more than three tons of grapes in a season, this little vineyard is quickly making a name for itself with chardonel, Cynthiana, and cabernet grapes. (The Cynthiana, by the way, is the state grape of Missouri.) The tasting room is open seven days a week. (660) 493-0258; www.baltimorebend.com.

Peters Market. Located 1.5 miles east of Waverly on US 65. Homegrown yellow and white peaches, as well as nectarines, abound here in season, along with delicious fruit butters and locally grown farm produce. Fall brings crops of Red and Golden Delicious apples, together with the popular Braeburn, Fuji, Granny Smith, and Staymen Winesap varieties. Peters holds a flea market in October that offers utility-grade apples at ridiculously low prices. During fall harvest season, free tours of the market and orchard are offered to organized groups by appointment only. (660) 493-2368; www.petersmarket.com.

Schreiman Orchards. Two miles west of Waverly on US 24. This roadside market sells peaches in summer and apples in fall, along with homemade apple butter, honey, jams, jellies, apple-wood chips, cookbooks, and Amish-made foods. The Schreiman family has been in business here for seventy-five years. Open daily from mid-June through mid-November. (660) 493-2477 (pager).

where to eat

Bridge Inn. 323 Highway 65. Admittedly, it's not much to look at from the outside, but the Bridge Inn has been serving fried catfish every day for more than forty years, so they've got to be doing something right. If nothing else, the view of the Missouri River flowing by and the traffic on the bridge are worth the time for a glass of iced tea and fresh fruit pie, courtesy of the local orchards. $. (660) 815-4039.

day trip 02

east

the katy trail and boonslick corridor:
arrow rock, mo; boonville, mo; new franklin, mo;
fayette, mo; rocheport, mo; columbia, mo;
jefferson city, mo; california, mo; sedalia, mo
worth more time: fulton, mo; hermann, mo

the katy trail corridor and boonslick country

This trip encompasses cities and hamlets along the Katy Trail and Boonslick Country. You can begin your tour at Arrow Rock and make your way east on I-70, visiting Missouri River towns along the way. You can overnight in any one of a number of places or head home the same way you came. If time permits, travel south to Jefferson City along scenic Missouri Highway 179 instead of taking a quick trip on U.S. Highway 63. From Jefferson City you can make the loop back to Kansas City on U.S. Highway 50. Fulton and Hermann are the easternmost points on the trail. Although they lie closer to St. Louis than to Kansas City, they are included here because they are part of the Katy Central Consortium, a group of six communities that have banded together to promote the Katy Trail, one of several arms of the "Rails-to-Trails" program that is part of the National Trails System Act.

It's flat, free, and fun, and it snakes across the state for more than 200 miles from Clinton to St. Charles. If you've never traveled the Katy Trail, you're missing some of the prettiest country in Missouri. The Katy Trail route can be traveled on foot, on horseback, or on wheels, and it parallels the Missouri River, with the water on one side and towering bluffs on the other.

east day trip 02

All along the way you can see glimpses of dense forests, wetlands, valleys, and rolling farm fields. In spring there are flowering dogwood and redbud trees. Fall brings crimson colors of maple and sumac, along with an abundance of wildlife that includes woodpeckers, red-tailed hawks, waterfowl, deer, and other creatures.

Trail users can meander through slices of rural history, some of which predate the Civil War. The section of trail between Boonville and St. Charles has been designated an official segment of the Lewis and Clark National Historic Trail, and the entire trail is part of the American Discovery Trail.

The Katy Trail is a common denominator that has revitalized many small towns that once flourished along the railroad. The Missouri-Kansas-Texas (MKT) Railroad, known as the Katy, ceased operation in 1986 and donated its right-of-way for the Katy Trail State Park. The Department of Natural Resources acquired the Katy Trail through the National Trails System Act—the "Rails-to-Trails" program that has helped turn inactive railroad corridors into recreational opportunities. Bed-and-breakfasts, restaurants, shops, and other services have prospered as a result.

Although the Katy Trail State Park has been designed specifically for bicyclists and hikers, campers or people on tight budgets may find themselves out in the cold, so to speak, for the small towns offer little in the way of inexpensive lodging as of this printing. One exception is the Katy Roundhouse in New Franklin, which provides camping, public restrooms, a quick-stop shop, showers, and RV hookups. Larger cities, such as Columbia, Jefferson City, and Sedalia, offer inexpensive motels if that option suits your pocketbook better.

Transportation to and from lodging isn't a widespread trailside amenity yet. Some of the bed-and-breakfast establishments are very close to the trail. Morgan Street Repose in Boonville, for example, is only a block away. To ensure that you get where you want to go, it's best to call ahead and find out whether you'll have to hike or bike to your overnight lodging, or if you can arrange for a courtesy car to pick you up when you get there.

Although the trail is mostly flat, with a grade that seldom reaches more than 5 percent, it is very possible to overextend yourself, especially on a hot day. If you aren't an experienced hiker or biker, it might be best to drive to one of the trailside jumping-off points and pick up your bike there. Almost all the Katy Trail towns have bike-rental shops, and most offer a selection of mountain bikes, tandems, and toddler trailers for a modest hourly cost.

Six communities—Arrow Rock, Rocheport, Columbia, Jefferson City, Callaway County, and Hermann—have banded together to form the Katy Central Consortium, the purpose of which is to provide visitor information about the trail. Call (888) 441-2023 for information about these six communities.

For more in-depth information on the Katy Trail State Park, get a copy of *The Katy Trail Guidebook* by Brett Dufur. An excellent resource, this book covers most of what you need to know when traveling the trail. Call (800) 576-7322 for a copy, or check your local bookstore or library. (Brett's Web site is www.pebblepublishing.com.) The Department of Natural Resources (800-334-6946) has brochures and information. Persons with hearing impairments can call (800) 379-2419 with a TDD. &, ⓐ. The Katy Trail Web site is www.mostateparks/katytrail.

boonslick country

Central Missouri's Boonslick Country was already beginning to enjoy a comeback long before the Katy Trail took shape. Happenstance would have it that the Katy Trail also passes near or through the Boonslick towns of Arrow Rock, Boonville, New Franklin, Fayette, Glasgow, Rocheport, Pilot Grove, Pleasant Green, and other communities. Something noteworthy to keep in mind is that many of the gorgeous old homes you'll find along the Katy Trail corridor and in and around Boonslick Country are listed on the National Register of Historic Places and offer bed-and-breakfast accommodations, as well as full country or continental breakfasts with all the trimmings.

As long as you're traveling the Katy Trail, you might as well visit the Boonslick region, which takes its name from a salt lick in southwestern Howard County that was worked, about 1805, by Nathan and Daniel Morgan Boone, sons of the famed pioneer and scout Daniel Boone. (The actual location of the salt springs is now part of Boone's Lick State Historic Site, located 8 miles northwest of New Franklin near Boonesboro.)

According to research provided by the Boonville Chamber of Commerce, Daniel Boone came to Missouri in 1779 at the request of the Spanish lieutenant governor. Boone was promised a grant of 1,000 *arpents* (an Old French unit of land equal to about an acre). He was to function as the commandant of the Femme Osage District as judge, jury, and sheriff. He died in Missouri in 1820 at the home of his son Nathan Boone near Defiance, Missouri.

The magic of the Boone name, plus the salt licks and fertile soil, drew early settlers to the area. There has been much speculation since that time as to why the *e* was left out of *Boonslick*. It may have been because then, as now, many people placed little importance on accurate spelling.

Boonslick Country is chock-full of history, for many of its towns brought politicians, land speculators, and entrepreneurs who later gained fame, such as painter George Caleb Bingham and frontier scout Kit Carson.

If you have the time and the inclination, you might want to take a guided tour of Boonslick Country. For a self-guided tour brochure of the area, contact the Friends of Historic Boonville, P.O. Box 1776, 614 East Morgan, Boonville, MO 65233; (660) 882-7977; www.friendsof historicboonville.org. For more information: Boonville Chamber of Commerce, Katy Depot, Spring and First Streets, Boonville, MO 65233; (660) 882-2721; www.boonvillemochamber ofcommerce.com.

For those interested in Lewis and Clark history in this area, James M. Denny of the Missouri Department of Natural Resources, in conjunction with the Boonslick Historical Society, has written the booklet *Lewis and Clark in the Boonslick.* It is for sale through the Missouri River Communities Network in Columbia. ⓐ. (573) 256-2602; www.moriver.org.

arrow rock, mo

As the state's first historic site, the Missouri River town of Arrow Rock is the western gateway to Boonslick Country. Located east of Kansas City, Arrow Rock can be reached by taking I-70 to Missouri Highway 41 North or traveling US 24 East to Highway 41 South. Founded in 1829, it was an important Santa Fe Trail rendezvous point and home of several distinguished Missourians, including three Missouri governors, painter George Caleb Bingham, and Dr. John Sappington, who pioneered the use of quinine for treating malaria.

On their epic expedition upriver in 1804, Lewis and Clark made note of the area, and later William Clark termed it a "handsome spot for a town." Just twenty-five years later, in 1829, a town was founded here. Indeed, Arrow Rock was then, as it is now, a beautiful place, and it has somehow retained its peaceful country character and managed to keep the look and feel of nineteenth-century America.

Once a bustling frontier village with a population of 1,000, it has only fifty-five year-round residents today. Each October during the annual Arrow Rock Craft Festival, that number increases as visitors come to enjoy historically authentic crafts interpreted in a period setting. The town hosts a variety of other events, including the Traditional Folk Music Festival in September and an antiques show in May.

If you're planning to overnight in Arrow Rock, be sure to make your reservations in advance at any one of a number of accommodations. Arrow Rock State Historic Site also offers several picnic places and a camping area on the limestone bluffs overlooking the Missouri River. Basic campsites and improved sites on the campground are available by reservation by calling (877) 422-6766.You can also make reservations online at www.mostateparks.com/arrow rock/camp.htm. *Note:* Though the campground is open year-round, there is no water from November to the end of March. A discount is available to seniors. Contact Arrow Rock State Historic Site, P.O. Box 1, Arrow Rock, MO 65320; (660) 837-3330.

For information on accommodations, restaurants, shops, tours, and events: Arrow Rock Merchants Association, P.O. Box 147–B, Arrow Rock, MO 65320 (660-837-3352); the Historic Arrow Rock Council, P.O. Box 23, Arrow Rock, MO 65320 (660-837-3307); and the Friends of Arrow Rock Walking Tours, P.O. Box 124, Arrow Rock, MO 65320 (660-837-3231); www.arrowrock.org.

where to go

Arrow Rock Lyceum Theatre. High Street. The Lyceum is Missouri's oldest professional regional theater and the only professional theater serving rural Missouri. Popular, professional summer theater is presented here in rotating repertory from May through August and into parts of October. Fee. (660) 837-3311; www.lyceumtheatre.org.

The Friends of Arrow Rock Information Center and the State Historic Site Interpretive Center. P.O. Box 124, Arrow Rock, MO 65320. Guides conduct tours of the village and historic structures that take in the George Caleb Bingham Home (1837), the Saline County Courthouse (1839), the Sites Home (1875) and Gun Shop (1844), and the Print Shop (1868). Fee. Tours are conducted daily Memorial Day through Labor Day and weekends in spring and fall. The interpretive center has fascinating displays that trace the westward expansion to the Boonslick region and its frontier life along the Santa Fe Trail. Tours: (660) 837-3231. Hours: (660) 837-3330; www.arrowrock.org.

River Hills Llamas. Eleven miles south of Arrow Rock (call for directions). One of the world's oldest domesticated animals, llamas are bred and raised here as show-quality animals, pack llamas, sheep guardians, and pets. The farm has a herd of seventy llamas. You can pet them and have your picture taken with them. Llama-wool gift items are for sale, and you may tour the farm's 1860s-era home. If you're into browsing for llamas, this is certainly the place to come. Call ahead for hours and fee information: (660) 846-2255; www.riverhillsllamas.com.

where to shop

Many Arrow Rock merchants and businesses operate seasonally, with hours that are frequently subject to change. It's always best to call ahead to find out what will be open the day you plan to visit.

Arrow Rock Antiques. Main Street. This shop features period furniture. Open weekends or by appointment. (660) 837-3333.

Arrow Rock Country Store. Main Street (on the boardwalk). At this shop you can choose from a variety of gifts and collectibles, including Hummels, music boxes, crystal, unusual cards, educational toys and games, and more. Open year-round. (660) 784-2441.

Arrow Rock Craft Shop. Main Street (in the Masonic Lodge Building). Wood and fabric artwork, clothing, quilts, china, jewelry, and toys are offered here, plus breads, plants, confections, and seasonal produce. Open daily May through October and weekends only December and April. (660) 784-2441.

The House of Mary B. Main Street. Find quality reproduction antiques and other gift items at this long-time establishment on Main Street. (660) 837-3305.

where to eat

The Old Arrow Rock Tavern. Main Street. Built in 1834, the tavern continues to serve the public as it served those who drove their wagons over the Santa Fe Trail. The fare includes catfish, country ham, and fried chicken. Private parties and groups are accommodated. Call for reservations. $$. (660) 837-3200.

The Vine Wine Bar and Garden. Main Street. The newest addition to the Arrow Rock experience carries all Missouri wines and other treats to enjoy indoors or under the lovely shade trees in back. Open evenings only. Closed Monday and Tuesday. (660) 837-3118.

Ye Olde Ice Cream Shoppe. On the boardwalk. This place offers a variety of ice-cream specialties, soups, sandwiches, and salads. $; (no cards). (660) 837-3364.

where to stay

Borgman's Bed & Breakfast. 706 Van Buren. This 1850s-era home offers four rooms and three shared baths. A family-style breakfast is served in the kitchen and features the owner's home-baked items. You'll love the cinnamon rolls. Open year-round. $$; (no cards). (660) 837-3350.

Bunny's Bed and Breakfast. 300 North Seventh Street. New to Arrow Rock (established in 2007) is the classic comfort of Bunny Thompson's home. With five guest rooms, each with a private bath, your accommodations here may be even more comfortable than you have at home. $$. (660) 837-3352.

DownOver Bed & Breakfast Inn. Main Street. This unusual establishment features six distinctively decorated guest rooms with private baths and a fully equipped guest cottage. A full breakfast is served daily. There are lounge areas for games and a front porch for relaxing. A bicycle built for two is available. $$–$$$. (660) 837-3268.

boonville, mo

To reach the oldest surviving Missouri River town in the region, travel on Highway 41 south from Arrow Rock to I-70 and east to Boonville. The central gateway to Boonslick Country, Boonville was settled in 1810. The town still exhibits the cultural mix of original Southern settlers, along with the influx of German immigrants who settled here in the mid-nineteenth century. Boonville's many restored historic buildings, restaurants, and bed-and-breakfasts make this a place worth visiting.

Boonville is also the county seat of Cooper County and the site of the first Civil War battle fought in Missouri (June 1861). South of Boonville are three interesting old plantation homes, including Ravenswood, Crestmead, and Pleasant Green Plantation House, that are open for tours.

Boonville was a town that made the transition from being a major river port to a booming railroad town. Many remnants of this era can still be seen in Boonville, including the restored MKT depot. You can pick up the Katy Trail State Park from Boonville eastward along the route of the Missouri River.

Named for Daniel Boone (as was the Boonslick region), Boonville prospered during the late 1820s. German immigrants arrived ten years later, and the river trade and Santa Fe Trail activity were the economic forces that sustained the town. The advent of railroads and the resulting confusion from the Civil War engagements fought in and around Boonville slowed the city's growth. Boonville today remains an important local center for transportation, tourism, and agribusiness.

The ongoing downtown revitalization program is strengthening the role of the central core as a business, cultural, and political center. Many of the buildings downtown are on the National Register of Historic Places. Indeed, Boonville contains seven National Register Districts and nineteen individual listed sites.

Boonslick Tours/Big Canoe Records offers excursions that relate to the culture, folklore, and history of central Missouri. Owned and operated by Bob Dyer, a local historian and folklorist as well as poet and musician-songwriter, Boonslick Tours offers an in-depth look at the region's history. In addition, Dyer has several music recordings that provide a satisfying glimpse into Missouri's rich and memorable past. Two Civil War recordings, "Johnny Whistletrigger" and "Rebel in the Woods," done in tandem with noted folk duo Cathy Barton and Dave Para, are masterpieces of Missouri lore. For information on tours, performances, and recordings, call (660) 882-3353; www.bartonpara.com.

For a self-guided tour brochure of the area, contact the Friends of Historic Boonville, P.O. Box 1776, 614 East Morgan, Boonville, MO 65233; (660) 882-7977; www.mo-river.net/friends. For more information: Boonville Chamber of Commerce, Katy Depot, Spring and First Streets, Boonville, MO 65233; (660) 882-2721; www.boonvillemochamberofcommerce.com.

where to go

Many of the museums, homes, and attractions in Boonville have hours that are subject to change. Call ahead to find out if these places are open on the day you plan to visit.

Cooper County Jail Museum, Jailers Residence, and Hanging Barn. Friends of Historic Boonville, P.O. Box 1776, 614 East Morgan, Boonville, MO 65233. Built in 1848, this venerable structure was the oldest continuously used county jail in Missouri until its closing in 1978. The last public hanging took place here in 1930, when a man named Lawrence Mabry was executed for a robbery and murder in Pettis County. This hanging was a factor in the elimination of capital punishment in Cooper County. The most famous prisoner held here was Frank James, brother of Jesse James. He was brought here on April 24, 1884, to answer a warrant for his arrest for a train robbery (what else?) that took place in 1876. Sympathetic citizens of Boonville raised his bond in a matter of hours, and the case was later dismissed for lack of evidence. Open daily. Fee. (660) 882-7977.

Crestmead. 7400 Highway A, Pilot Grove. Located 6 miles south of Pilot Grove, the Italianate mansion was built in 1859 by John Taylor. The three-story home has a wide central hall that runs the length of the structure and features a massive octagonal newel post and sixteen rooms with 8-foot windows and period furnishings. Outbuildings include an ice and carriage house, restored slave quarters, and an old barn. The home has been owned since 1903 by the Betteridge family, who renamed it Crestmead, meaning "high meadow." The home is open to tour by appointment. Fee. (660) 834-4140.

Katy Depot and Katy Trailhead. Spring and First Streets. The restored 1912 depot houses the Katy Trail offices and the Boonville Chamber of Commerce. Katy Trail gift items are sold here. (660) 882-8196.

Katy Trail State Park. Cooper County trailheads in Boonville, Clifton City, and Pilot Grove. This trail heads east from Boonville along some of the prettiest country in Missouri. For information and brochures about the Katy Trail from Boonville to Jefferson City, call the Department of Natural Resources. Free. ♿. (800) 334-6946.

Pleasant Green. 7045 Missouri Highway 135, Route 1, Box 81, Pilot Grove, MO 65276. Located 9 miles south of Pilot Grove, this Federal-style brick mansion is built of handmade bricks and native stone. It was begun as a one-room house, with additions added from the 1830s through the 1870s, and was once a plantation of 2,500 acres. Settled by Winston and Polly Walker of Virginia in 1818, it survived Civil War raids and years of neglect. Many original furnishings are part of the home, and the facade has been returned to its 1877 appearance. The home is listed on the National Register of Historic Places and includes outbuildings that feature an old hexagonal barn, a curing shed, and restored slave quarters. The 1870 Pleasant Green Post Office building was moved here to serve as a minigallery for local artists. The home is open to tour by appointment. Guides in antebellum dress serve coffee or tea in the dining room by advance request. Fee. (660) 834-3945.

Ravenswood Farm. Twelve miles south of Boonville on Missouri Highway 5, Bunceton. This impressive private home was built in 1880 by Captain Charles E. Leonard and his wife, Nadine. Five generations later it is still owned by Leonard descendants. Few changes have been made in the house: The furnishings and decorations are much the same as when it was built. Group and individual tours of the home are offered by appointment from March through November. Fee. (660) 882-7143.

Roslyn Heights. 821 Main Street. This 1894 Queen Anne home features Romanesque Revival structures, towers, turrets, gable dormers, and a porte-cochere with Moorish decorative elements. Paneled front doors open from the front porch into a reception hall, and the entrance hall's original tile floor is intact. The house is graced by a geometrically designed stairway with motifs that illustrate the use of machinery during the Industrial Revolution. The parlor features a hand-painted ceiling and mahogany fireplace mantel. The other rooms in the home also have ornate designs and elegant antique furnishings. Tours are by appointment only. The home is open to the public for meetings, luncheons, receptions, and special events. Fee. (660) 882-5320.

Thespian Hall. Main and Vine Streets. This restored Greek Revival opera house, built in 1857, is owned and managed by the Friends of Historic Boonville. It is the oldest theater still in use west of the Alleghenies and is on the National Register of Historic Places. If you can, time your visit to coincide with one of the music festivals held here. The Missouri River Festival of the Arts in August brings in fine performers, ranging from symphony orchestras and ballet companies to jazz, pop, and theater groups. The Big Muddy Folk Festival in April plays host to local and national musicians. Tours are available by appointment. For information: Friends of Historic Boonville, www.friendsofhistoricboonville.org; (660) 882-7977.

where to shop

Boonville has many shops that offer a variety of antiques, crafts, and collectibles. For a complete list, contact the Tourist Information Center, Boonville Area Chamber of Commerce, Katy Depot, Spring and First Streets, Boonville, MO 65233; (660) 882-2721; www.boonville mochamberofcommerce.com.

Celestial Body. 221 Main Street. Owner Annie Harmon is also a flight attendant with an international route, so she travels the world finding natural items to enhance the quality of our lives. She also produces a line of skin care products, free of chemicals or preservatives, made with organically grown plants on her nearby farm. (660) 882-0333; www.celestialbody.com.

The Sunflower Company. 414 Sixth Street. Stella the cat will greet you at this pleasant gift shop that also includes a photography studio. Home decor items, handmade jewelry, and special items for the baby are among the treats here. (660) 882-8307.

where to eat

Glenn's Cafe. 501 High Street, inside the Hotel Frederick. Those familiar with Glenn's long history in nearby Columbia will appreciate his new location and local favorites like Fried Missouri-Raised Catfish. However, for more adventurous palates, try the unusual offering of items like Chicken Tchoupitoulas, a grilled free-range chicken breast served on a bed of griddled potatoes and topped with Hollandaise sauce. For dessert, the bread pudding and Hummingbird Cake are fabulous. Closed Monday. $–$$. (660) 882-9191.

Riverside Diner. 203 Main Street. Richard and Janice Held found themselves eating at this local diner so often that in March of 2007, they bought the place for themselves. The Diner is now famous for Fried Chicken Fridays, which delight the nose of anyone within three blocks of the downtown restaurant. Richard's big contribution to the menu is a breakfast sandwich his wife named "Richard's Full of Bologna." It's an egg, cheese, and fried bologna sandwich served on Texas toast. Open seven days a week. $. (660) 882-6333.

The Settlers Inn. I-70 and Highway 135 (Arrow Rock and Pilot Grove exit), Boonville. For something very different, come and dine in this simple log home, where made-from-scratch food is cooked up in a small but mighty kitchen. The excellent family-style meals include main dishes such as beef and buffalo T-bone steaks, pheasant, country ham, game hen, buffalo brisket, smoked pork chops, and more. All dinners include salad, potato, vegetables, home-baked desserts, bread, and beverage. The cost is so reasonable you won't believe it.

Because the restaurant is small, you will need reservations. Call well in advance, especially if you have a large party. To expedite mealtime, the restaurant requests that you order your meat selection when you make your reservation. Seatings are at 5:30 and 7:30 p.m. on Friday and Saturday evenings. Special group bookings are available during the week. Closed Sunday. $$. (660) 882-3125.

where to stay

Hotel Frederick. 501 High Street. With a fabulous perch above the Missouri River, the Hotel Frederick has been welcoming guests since 1905. But after some less than glorious days, the hotel was renovated and reopened in glorious style in July 2007. The twenty-four guest rooms today are simply decorated, as they would have been one hundred years ago, but with modern and comfortable amenities such as towel warmers, freshly pressed bed linens, and complimentary WiFi. The designer soaps are by Indigo Wild in Kansas City, and the classic bathroom dividers are by Kansas City glass artists Bill Drummond and Peregrine Honig.

Many of the lobby antiques are original to the hotel. Ask the front desk about the bicycles on loan to explore the Katy Trail, or schedule an in-room massage. A continental breakfast is included, but enjoy lunch or an evening meal at Glenn's Cafe. $$–$$$, www.hotelfrederick .com; (660) 882-2828.

new franklin, mo

Campgrounds are a rarity along the Katy Trail. However, for tired travelers on tight budgets, New Franklin, 3 miles north of Boonville on Highway 5, provides an alternative to more expensive lodging. Campgrounds, public restrooms, showers, and RV hookups are located adjacent to Trail Mile Marker 189 at the Katy Roundhouse. Once you bed down for the night, it's "happy trails" to you as you catch some Zs on famous ground "where the four trails meet": the Katy, the Santa Fe, the Boonslick, and the Lewis and Clark. For information: New Franklin City Hall, 130 East Broadway, New Franklin, MO 65274; (660) 848-2288; www.newfranklin .missouri.org.

where to go

Boone's Lick State Historic Site. Eight miles northwest of New Franklin, near Boonesboro. Take Missouri Highway 87 West from the northern approach to the Missouri River Bridge on Highway 5 to Missouri Highway 187, about 1 mile north of Boonesboro. Continue 2 miles west to the site of the salt springs, worked by the sons of Daniel Boone beginning around 1805. The year before, Captains Meriwether Lewis and William Clark noted this area and its potential for development in their journals. The state of Missouri has a kiosk here with information about the Boonslick region and the salt springs. A trail with informational signs winds through the woods by the remnants of the saltworks, and there's a shelter house with picnic tables, as well as public restrooms. Free. Artifacts from the industry are displayed at the Arrow Rock State Historic Site. ♿, 🏛. (660) 837-3330.

where to eat and stay

Katy Roundhouse. 1893 Katy Drive (Katy Trail Mile Marker 189), New Franklin. Located on the grounds of a century-old restored train depot, the Katy Roundhouse stands on the site of the former MKT Railroad switching yard. The area offers a full-service campground with spacious, secluded campsites for tent camping, including picnic tables, fire rings, and bike racks. In addition, there are full RV hookups, modern shower facilities, public restrooms, a mini grocery, and tents for rent. Home-cooked dinners are served on Friday and Saturday evenings by reservation only. The steaks are fresh cut and broiled outdoors over an open grill. There are also beer and wine gardens and occasional live music for a small cover charge. $–$$. (660) 848-2232; www.katyroundhouse.com.

Rivercene Bed and Breakfast. 127 Country Road 463. Listed on the National Register of Historic Places, this fifteen-room mansion was built by Captain Joseph Kinney. The riverboat baron began construction in 1864 on the floodplain, leading locals to call the structure Kinney's Folly. Kinney was undaunted. Finding the highest flood point, he built the house 1 foot higher. Of course, he hadn't counted on the Great Flood of 1993. Jody and Ron Lenz purchased the home in 1992, only to be confronted by 4 feet of water in their living room during the flood, when Rivercene could be reached only by boat.

The couple has fully restored the mansion, incorporating the splendor of Kinney's original architectural masterpiece. The home has Italian marble for the nine fireplaces, black walnut for the front doors, and a hand-carved mahogany staircase. (A few years after Kinney completed Rivercene, the architectural plan was duplicated for the present Governor's Mansion in Jefferson City.)

Rivercene offers tours of the home, as well as overnight stays with queen-size beds and private baths, or you can take your choice of a two-room suite or a room with a whirlpool. A delicious breakfast is served in the large dining room. Group and individual tours are offered by appointment (fee). Rivercene can be rented for business retreats or meetings or for family reunions. Call for hours and reservations. $$–$$$. (800) 531-0862; www.rivercene.com.

fayette, mo

where to go

The Ashby-Hodge Gallery of American Art. On the campus of Central Methodist University, 411 Central Methodist Square. Opened in 1993, the Ashby-Hodge Gallery holds a special collection of oil paintings, lithographs, watercolors, bronzes, graphite drawings, and acrylics representing the work of American regional artists. The gallery holds rare pieces by

Swedish-born artist Birger Sandzén, lithographs by Jackson Lee Nesbitt, an ink and wash by Thomas Hart Benton, a rare egg tempera on panel by Charles Banks Wilson, and many other interesting pieces. This little gem of a place also features special exhibits throughout the year, often bringing in the artists themselves to greet guests at gallery openings. Call for a schedule of events. Open Sunday, Tuesday, Wednesday, and Thursday from 1:30 to 4:30 p.m. Free. (660) 246-6324; www.centralmethodist.edu.

rocheport, mo

Rocheport is one of those tucked-away towns that are filled with history and memorabilia. From New Franklin you can head east on US 40 to Route BB or head east from Boonville on I-70 to the Rocheport exit. The town is a perfect romantic getaway close to home, yet it also offers Katy Trail access for family outings. Antiques shops, an art gallery, cafes, a winery and bistro with a panoramic river-bluff view, and superior bed-and-breakfasts are part of its charm. Each summer the town's population swells from 225 persons to as many as 30,000 visitors, many of whom are Katy Trail travelers.

Located on the Missouri River, Rocheport was founded in 1825 and grew rapidly as steamboat transportation brought business to town. In 1849 fifty-seven steamboats made 500 landings at Rocheport. Nine years earlier the Whig Party held its convention in Rocheport and thousands of delegates arrived by carriage, wagon, steamboat, and horseback to support William Henry Harrison's presidential campaign.

Rocheport has survived disasters, including the Civil War and the Great Flood of 1993, when the 243-foot-long MKT Railroad tunnel, built in 1893, was filled with 4 feet of water.

Rocheport is on the National Register of Historic Places, and many of its residents live and work in restored nineteenth-century homes and buildings. The special blend of history and charm makes this town stand out as a great place to unwind from today's frenetic pace.

As the eastern gateway to Boonslick Country, Rocheport also affords one of the most beautiful views along the Katy Trail, parts of which wind along the river under the spectacular Moniteau Bluffs. If you would like to explore the Missouri River a little bit more closely, a number of canoe and kayak outfitters are located in Rocheport.

For more information on Rocheport, write the Rocheport Area Merchants Association, P.O. Box 44, Rocheport, MO 65279; (573) 698-2063; www.rocheport.com.

where to go

Friends of Rocheport Museum. Moniteau Street. Museum displays include historic photographs and memorabilia of Rocheport as a nineteenth-century river and railroad town. Open Saturday and Sunday from 1:00 to 4:00 p.m. (573) 698-3701.

Trailside Cafe and Bike Rental. From Katy Trail Mile Marker 179, you can literally pedal into the parking lot of the Trailside Cafe. This nice little operation began as a small sandwich shop and eventually expanded into a dining room with an adjacent bike shop. The cafe is noted for its excellent pork tenderloin sandwiches that will feed two, plus fresh homemade baked goods. It sells Gatorade for thirsty trail users, as well as spring waters and trail mix. Fresh fruit and grilled portobello-mushroom sandwiches are on the healthy side of the menu. On the other side are deep-fried Snickers bars. It also sells and rents bikes to fit everybody from a two-year-old to an adult. Child carts, tandems, and mountain bikes can be rented by the hour or by the day. Bring in your bike for tune-up or repair service. Closed in cold weather. Call for hours. $. (573) 698-2702; www.trailsidecafebike.com.

where to shop

Rocheport is filled with plenty of places to browse and shop. Here are some of the more interesting places:

Flavors of the Heartland/Rocheport Gallery. 204 Second Street. This unique store sells a variety of Missouri-made specialty and gourmet food products. You can choose from herb and fruit-infused vinegars, delicious apple and pumpkin butters, mustards, barbecue sauces, salsas, Boone County hams, and much more. The store features custom gift baskets filled with goodies like Caramel Satin and Chocolate Satin Dessert Sauces (ooooh!) and Lemon Satin Dessert Sauce (yum-yum!). The free samples are tempting. When you're through slurping and shopping, you can visit the adjoining gallery and ogle the original art. An artist reception is held the first day of each exhibit, and exhibits change every four to six weeks. (573) 698-2063.

White Horse Antiques. 505 Third Street. This long-time favorite in Rocheport is located in the historic 1840 Waddell House, where the nineteenth-century antique country furniture, quilts, and primitives for sale come to life in their natural setting. You can also find a great selection of modern decorating accessories. Open Wednesday through Sunday. (573) 698-2088.

where to eat

Abigail's. 206 Central. This restaurant offers wholesome fare in a restored downtown building. The menu changes daily. Open for lunch Wednesday through Sunday; dinner by reservation. $–$$. (573) 698-3000.

Les Bourgeois Vineyards, Winery, and Bistro. 14020 West Highway BB (1 mile north of I-70 on Route BB). This unique restaurant and winery makes a great place to unwind and enjoy a spectacular sunset from atop a river bluff. The land here offers rich soil and a microclimate that is ideal for grape production. Les Bourgeois produces red, white, and blush table wines from French hybrid grapes and native cultivars. The restaurant offers an outdoor wine garden and indoor dining featuring a variety of nicely prepared fish, chicken, and steak dinners, plus great desserts. $$–$$$. (573) 698-2300; www.missouriwine.com.

where to stay

The small town of Rocheport offers some of the finest bed-and-breakfast accommodations to be found anywhere in Missouri, including the following:

Katy Trail Bed and Bikefest. 101 Lewis Street. This modest Victorian home was built in 1880 and is on the National Register of Historic Places. The Katy offers four rooms, including a converted railroad boxcar in the backyard that sleeps up to five and has a private bath, refrigerator, and cable television. The upstairs of the main house offers a family suite with a private bath, queen-size bed, and futon. There is a smaller bedroom downstairs with one double bed. Above the garage is a large rustic room with two beds and a sleeper sofa, which serves as a bunkhouse for cost-conscious travelers. $. (573) 698-2453; www.katytrailbb.com.

Schoolhouse Bed and Breakfast. Third and Clark Streets. Touted as one of the country's top ten romantic inns, the Schoolhouse has been the subject of greeting cards and magazine articles. Large framed prints of the famous Dick and Jane primer grace the walls of this former schoolhouse. Elegantly refurbished, it now offers ten bedrooms with private baths, two of which have a "sweetheart" Jacuzzi. Each of the nicely appointed guest rooms is decorated in beautiful antiques. An upstairs dining room offers a full breakfast of coffee, fresh fruit compote, baked bread or muffins, and egg strata. $$–$$$. (573) 698-2022; www.schoolhouse bandb.com.

The Yates House. 305 Second Street. Completed in 1991, the Yates House is a pretty reproduction of an 1850 roadside inn. Guests have a choice of two bedrooms and a suite, all with private baths. A back porch, a courtyard patio, and flower and herb gardens are yours to enjoy. The garden house next door has two bedrooms with private baths and a suite with a fireplace and jetted tub. $$–$$$. (573) 698-2129; www.yateshouse.com.

columbia, mo

Leave your "girth control" pills at home and head east from Rocheport on I-70 to this college town.

Columbia is the place to come for thick, hand-cut Angus steaks, blue-plate specials, fine wines, and eclectic and cross-cultural cuisine. Plan a "dine-around" day at restaurants that offer unusual items ranging from satay quesadilla to pizza with cilantro, pesto, and artichokes. Dessert might be a double-dip cone of fresh, homemade Tiger Stripe ice cream, or pear strudel with Gewürztraminer caramel sauce (don't worry if you can't pronounce it; you can still eat it). If this is too rich for your blood, you might like a 1950s-style diner where you can get good home-style meals and great malts, or a venerable establishment that still serves everything from filet mignon to yellowfin tuna—at yesteryear's prices.

Columbia is home to the University of Missouri-Columbia, Stephens College, and Columbia College. However, you don't have to be a college student to enjoy yourself in this town.

On any given summer night, you can listen to live jazz and blues outdoors or catch a concert by noted artists such as Wilco, Ray LaMontaine, or Hot Tuna at the Blue Note, one of the best live-entertainment venues in the state.

If you're looking for one-of-a-kind finds, visit downtown Columbia's arts-and-crafts shops, which sell everything from handmade Brazilian tables, regional art, and rare books to items that reflect social, political, and environmental issues.

Within a 50-mile radius around Columbia are historic Missouri River towns, the nationally acclaimed Katy Trail, state parks, historic sites, antebellum mansions, and other Missouri treasures. The free *Columbia Visitors Guide* brochure lists several tours, as well as things to do, lodging, dining, nightlife, and other information. Contact the Columbia Convention and Visitors Bureau, 300 South Providence, Columbia, MO 65203; (573) 875-1231 or (800) 652-0987; www.visitcolumbiamo.com.

where to go

The Blue Note. 17 North Ninth Street. For more than a quarter-century, one of central Missouri's best live-entertainment venues has been located in this restored vaudeville theater that features renowned blues, reggae, rock, and folk artists. Two full cocktail bars and an espresso bar are located on the premises. The popular College Trivia Challenge, a fundraiser for Special Olympics each October, is an opportunity for parents to see what their kids are (*not!*) learning at school. For tickets and information, call (573) 874-1944; www.thebluenote.com.

Columbia College. 1001 Rogers Street. This was the first institution of higher education for women chartered by a state legislature west of the Mississippi River. Founded in 1851, the coeducational school offers undergraduate degrees in liberal arts, sciences, and the professions. Located on twenty-six acres in the midst of the city, it features day and evening courses on the main campus and through its branch campuses located throughout the United States and Puerto Rico. Tours are free. (800) 231-2391; www.ccis.edu.

MKT Trail. Fourth and Cherry Streets (downtown) to Scott Boulevard (Route TT). Walk, jog, or bike on this 8.9-mile wheelchair-accessible trail, which varies from an urban walkway to a densely wooded passageway. Parking is available at Stadium, Forum, and Scott Boulevard accesses. The MKT is Columbia's spur connection to the Katy Trail. The Martin Luther King Jr. outdoor amphitheater is located at the Stadium access. Free. &, 🏕. (573) 874-7460.

Rock Bridge Memorial State Park. 5901 South Highway 163. This 2,273-acre park takes its name from the area where a stream flows beneath a natural rock bridge formation. The park offers hiking trails, picnic areas, and a wilderness discovery area in both wooded area and restored prairies. But the park is best known for the Devil's Icebox Cave, the sixth-longest cave in Missouri, with more than 6 miles of passages. Twice a year, for a month each spring and two months each fall, the Devil's Icebox Wild Cave Tour allows you to explore these wet, dark places.

You'll get to stoop, squat, crawl, and climb through teeny, tiny passages that could be rather confining, paddle and portage canoes, and hang out with a colony of gray bats. Call the park office to arrange a tour. The park is free; fee for cave tour. Open daily. (573) 449-7402; www.mostateparks.com/rockbridge.htm.

Shelter Gardens. 1817 West Broadway. Here's an insurance tip for you: This company has an award-winning, five-acre garden in the heart of town, with more than 300 varieties of trees and shrubs, as well as 15,000 annuals and perennials.

Particularly impressive is the outstanding architectural landscaping that fills the entire garden with sweeping color and beauty. Shelter Gardens is a place of repose within a busy metropolis. You can take your lunch on the lawn or enjoy a quiet walk through the tree-shaded paths. Public concerts are held on designated Sunday evenings in June and July.

What makes this garden particularly unique is the thinking and planning that went into it. It is wheelchair-accessible and features an outstanding "Sensory Garden" that can be experienced by both sighted and visually impaired visitors. The plants have been carefully laid out to allow you to smell, touch, and feel them. There's nothing like the sweet fragrance of a geranium leaf or the velvety softness of lamb's ears to impart nature's meaning.

The grounds also include a one-room schoolhouse relocated from Brunswick, Missouri. There is also a rose garden, with more than sixty varieties of grandifloras, floribundas, and standard tea roses, along with a massive sundial. In addition, there are a shaded pool and a stream featuring a waterfall—the sound alone is enough to calm you down after a rough day. Free. (573) 214-4715; www.shelterinsurance.com.

Stephens College. 1200 East Broadway. Founded in 1833, Stephens College is the second-oldest women's college in the nation. It offers programs in the arts, business, professional studies, and liberal arts and sciences. Its continuing education division offers weekend and independent study and short-format courses. The performing arts department is well respected for its productions and summer stock throughout the Midwest. The Firestone Baars Chapel features a unique four-foyer design created by Eero Saarinen, who also designed the St. Louis Gateway Arch. (800) 876-7207; www.stephens.edu.

Twin Lakes Recreation Area. 2500 Chapel Hill Road. This family-oriented facility offers swimming, boating, fishing, hiking, and nature study. The six-acre swimming lake has a deck, a diving platform, water slides, and a large sand beach. There's a water playground separate from the lake for small children and paddleboats available for rent. Fee. (573) 874-7460.

University of Missouri-Columbia. The first public university west of the Mississippi River, UMC was founded in 1839. The 1,340-acre campus has an enrollment of nearly 28,000 students. UMC is one of the few institutions in the country that houses journalism, law, medicine, agriculture, engineering, and veterinary medicine on a single campus. The journalism school of UMC was the first such school in the world.

The center of the campus is the historic Francis Quadrangle, at the entrance of Eighth and Elm Streets. This is the site of the Chancellor's Residence. Its eighteen surrounding buildings are on the National Register of Historic Places. The row of six Ionic columns that adorn the center of the Francis Quadrangle once supported the portico of Academic Hall, the first building erected on campus. The open area around the columns is the center of the cluster of red-brick buildings known as the Red Campus. It is modeled after Thomas Jefferson's design for the University of Virginia. Walking through those columns into the quad is a freshman class orientation rite, and passing through the columns, back into the world, is a treasured memory at graduation.

UMC houses the first monument erected for the grave of Thomas Jefferson. When Virginia decided to erect a new monument for Jefferson's grave and give the original away, UMC was first in line to grab the valuable castoff. Since President Jefferson was instrumental in acquiring UMC as the first state university in the Louisiana Purchase Territory, "Old Mizzou," as it is nostalgically called, was the logical choice to house the prized stone slab. (Virginia has since regretted its decision to give up the original grave marker, but UMC has no intention of returning it.)

UMC is spread out around Columbia and has several phone numbers and ZIP codes. If you are not interested in the academics and just want a tour of campus, call (800) 856-2181 or go to www.visitus.missouri.edu. For intercollegiate athletics schedule and ticket information: (573) 882-6501. To charge tickets: (800) CAT-PAWS. Some places you may want to visit on campus include the following:

Buck's. Eckles Hall, East Rollins and College Streets, UMC Campus (see listing under Where to Eat).

Mizzou Arena. 600 Stadium Boulevard. The Mizzou Arena, officially opened in 2004, seats 13,000 people for basketball, volleyball, and concerts. For ticket and show information: (573) 884-PAWS.

Museum of Anthropology. 100 Swallow Hall, University of Missouri-Columbia. The Museum of Anthropology is one of those tucked-away-and-taken-for-granted places that doesn't get much fanfare. As early as 1885 UMC began accepting gifts of ethnographic materials, finally organizing them into a cohesive collection in 1902. The only anthropology museum in the state and one of the few in the Midwest, its archaeological collection is the largest holding of prehistoric Missouri artifacts in the world, including those dating from 9000 B.C. to modern times. In addition, the museum curates objects from many Native American cultures.

The Grayson Archery Collection housed here is probably one of the largest and most comprehensive collections of its kind in the world. Unusual thumb rings of carved jade used by Chinese archers represent only a fraction of the materials that are showcased in the museum's exhibit hall; the remainder lie in the Museum Support Center on Rock Quarry Road. Collections of archaeological and ethnological materials are available for use by qualified researchers, as well as students and faculty.

There are a number of Native American exhibits, dating from 11,000 years ago to the present. Works by Hopi artist Iris Nampeyo, plus Santa Clara pottery and authentic Hopi kachinas, are showcased. There is also a prehistoric section of Native American work that features Hohokam and Anasazi pottery. Another unusual display offers a glimpse into life on the plains after the Europeans introduced horses, guns, and glass beads. Imported primarily from Venice and Czechoslovakia, the beads were used by Native Americans in their art. Cloth ribbon, also introduced by Europeans, eventually replaced porcupine and bird quills. Both the museum exhibit hall and the exhibits in the Museum Support Center are open to the public. Tours are available by appointment. Open Monday through Friday. Free. (573) 882-3764.

The Museum of Art and Archaeology. Pickard Hall, University of Missouri-Columbia. One of the best-kept secrets in the Midwest, this gem of a museum is worth the drive to Columbia. It houses 13,000 pieces of art and artifacts from six continents and is the third-largest collection of its kind in Missouri. The Saul and Gladys Weinberg Gallery of Ancient Art is one of the most comprehensive in the state and features exhibits from ancient Egypt, Palestine, the Near East, Greece, Italy, and the Roman world. Religion, myth and art, and cultural connections are represented here and reflect the everyday life and teaching of ancient peoples from prehistory to the present. Pottery, metalwork, terra-cotta, glass vessels, coins, and stone sculptures are also featured.

Particularly noteworthy is the oldest piece in the museum, a 250,000-year-old ax handle that belonged to somebody's forefather, as well as a 4,000-year-old cuneiform tablet and case that afford a glimpse into an early form of human communication before computers and faxes. A Cypro-Archaic vessel, thrown before 600 B.C., is a reminder that the venerable craft of pottery is blessed with longevity, while coins and gaming pieces from Egypt, Alexandria, and Rome tell the story of leisure-time spending sprees long before riverboat casinos.

Other areas of the museum feature European and American paintings, sculptures, drawings, prints, and photographs from the fifteenth to the twentieth centuries. Lectures, symposia, gallery talks, film series, and educational programs are offered throughout the year. The museum encourages persons with disabilities to participate in its programs and activities. Don't forget to check out the gift shop. Closed Monday and Tuesday. Free. (573) 882-3591.

The Walters–Boone County Historical Museum and Visitors Center and Maplewood Home. 3801 Ponderosa Street. Located 3 miles south of the junction of State Highway 63 and I-70, the visitor center is housed in a traditional family farmhouse. The museum contains the history of the area from prehistoric to present day in its 16,000 square feet of exhibition space. The Montminy Art Gallery located on-site showcases the talents of mid-Missouri artists as well as the outstanding collection of half a million photographic images that are part of the Boone County Historical Society Photo Archives, which date from the late 1800s to the mid-twentieth century. The museum also can be used for banquets, meetings, workshops, weddings, and receptions.

Just north of the museum is the Maplewood Home, a historic Victorian residence built in 1877. The original furnishings include the latest innovations of the period. The home is listed on the National Register of Historic Places.

Boone Junction Village, a historic town, has been added in recent years. Consisting of an 1820s era log cabin, a Victorian home, and a 1920s era general store, the village is expected to include a one-room schoolhouse and other buildings in the near future. Open Wednesday through Sunday, 12:30 to 4:30 p.m. The museum is free, but a $4 charge is necessary for guided tours of the historic village. (573) 443-8936.

where to shop

There's not enough room to list all of Columbia's shopping venues here. Major centers include Columbia Mall, Crossroads West, and the Forum Shopping Center, which features anchor stores as well as boutiques, shops, restaurants, eateries, and theaters. The thriving community also has many antiques shops that cater to every taste and budget.

Columbia's downtown district is filled with fine restaurants, shops, galleries, bookstores, museums, and one-of-a-kind specialty stores that cover 45 square blocks surrounding Broadway. Some of the downtown establishments interconnect, making them easily accessible during inclement weather. For a free map and visitor's guide of downtown Columbia, contact Central Columbia Association Special Business District, 11 South Tenth Street, Columbia, MO 65201; (573) 442-6816; www.discoverthedistrict.com. Below are just a few of the places you can visit:

A La Campagne. 918 East Broadway. This interesting concept in building space features interior design ideas and furnishings for residences and businesses. Upstairs is a gallery featuring the work of Missouri artists. Downstairs holds fabrics, fine art, antiques, and other furnishings that showcase bold, unusual styles. Closed Sunday. Free to tour. (573) 815-9464.

Bluestem Missouri Crafts. 13 South Ninth Street. This unusual store is actually a partnership of craftspeople who feature their own ceramic jewelry, weaving, pottery, and batik work. In addition, Bluestem is a showcase for an extensive collection of handmade functional and decorative work by other artists. Pottery, glass, wood, metal, and fiber art are represented here. Baskets, wooden boxes, toys, cards, and clothing made in Missouri are part of the colorful displays. The "Neighboring States Gallery" features the work of equally talented artisans from the states that border Missouri and includes a large selection of pieces by Decorah, Iowa, artist Brian Andreas. Bluestem Missouri Crafts was named the number-one retailer of American crafts in 2005 by *Niche* magazine. Open daily. (573) 442-0211.

The Candy Factory. 701 Cherry East Street. This bright and cheery candy store is renowned for its delicious handmade chocolates, including chocolate-covered strawberries and scrumptious truffles. For real chocoholics, there's always "The Ultimate Pizza," a gourmet treat featuring one and a half pounds of deep-dish chocolate topped with fresh pecans, cashews, walnuts, cherries, and marshmallows, and drizzled with white chocolate. Open daily. (573) 443-8222.

Columbia Art League Gallery. 111 South Ninth Street. Art lovers will find real treasures at this cozy and intimate gallery, which features the work of local members, professionals, and nationally acclaimed artists. The league's annual "Sparkling Arts" exhibit, held from mid-November through early January, features one-of-a-kind art finds. Closed Sunday and Monday. Free. (573) 443-8838.

Columbia Books. 309 South Providence Road. If your idea of a bookstore is a laid-back, one-owner place in which to browse and buy, this bookstore may fit your needs. It offers a mix of 60,000 new and used books that includes everything from rare publications dating back four centuries to the latest best-sellers. The store has a wealth of children's illustrated books, gardening tomes, and first editions. Open daily. (573) 449-7417.

Cool Stuff. 808 East Broadway. Globe-trotting owner Arnie Fagan has a great sense of humor and an eye for the unusual. By his own definition, he seeks all things "cool, unusual, practical, and fun"—much of it from Africa, Asia, Central and South America, and parts of Europe and the Middle East. The place offers an eclectic mix of ethnic items that range from Southwestern sage smudges to Israeli dreidels. There are more than 4,000 varieties of beads and thousands of candles, plus toys, jewelry, accessories, and clothing. Unless he sells it prior to this book's publication, there's a one-of-a-kind Indonesian ricksha for sale with an asking price (don't ask) of $5,000. Open daily. (573) 875-5225.

Ice Chalet Antique Mall. 1100 Business Loop 70 East. More than 200 dealers, selling everything from antiques and collectibles to primitives and "junque," can be found here. Open daily. (573) 443-1970.

Poppy. 920 East Broadway. Nominated as a Top 100 Retailer of American Crafts in the United States, this shop offers an excellent collection of contemporary artwork in clay, fiber, metal, wood, glass, and jewelry. A fine art addition includes two-dimensional art, sculpture, and mixed media. Open daily. (573) 442-3223; www.poppyarts.com.

Orchids and Art. 10 West Nifong Boulevard. Displays by local and regional artists are surrounded by flowering orchids, which are also for sale. The gallery collection rotates often and includes prints, mixed media, paintings, drawings, and photography. Closed Sunday. (573) 875-5989.

where to eat

Nation's Restaurant News has touted Columbia as the best up-and-coming place to open a dining establishment. Several youthful restaurateurs have taken it upon themselves to impart fresh and vigorous menus that have boosted the city's image as a restaurant town. Columbia now has a wide variety of choices that range from low-priced cafes to upscale eateries.

Espresso and cappuccino are found almost everywhere. So great is the demand for good wine and brews that you can find alcoholic beverages served at pizza houses, luncheonettes, sub shops, and inexpensive diners. Competition has spurred the upgrading of menus and ambience to keep pace with demand. Some of the best bets include the following:

Boone Tavern. 811 East Walnut Street. Prime rib, fresh seafood, steak, pasta, sandwiches, and salads are served at this popular establishment, which also offers outdoor dining. Located next to downtown's Boone County Courthouse, the restaurant features large banquet rooms and has driver and escort service available for groups of forty persons or more. Open daily for lunch and dinner. $$. (573) 442-5123.

Broadway Diner. 22 South Fourth Street. *USA Today* touted this venerable restaurant as "one of the ten great places to eat" in America. The working-class establishment opened in 1949 and is the only remaining diner of its style in Missouri. It features breakfast anytime and daily lunch specials for under $5. Come here for real hash browns and freshly mashed potatoes. Open daily for breakfast, lunch, and dinner. $. ⅋. (573) 875-1173.

Buckingham Smokehouse Bar-B-Q. 213 Business Loop 70. You smell this no-frills spot, named for rock guitarist Lindsey Buckingham, long before you arrive at it. Owner Mark Brown spent several years on the road with rock bands, including Fleetwood Mac. Today Brown specializes in hickory-smoked beef brisket, pork loin ham, and turkey. The horseradish cole slaw is guaranteed to burn on the way down. $. (573) 449-7782.

Buck's Ice Cream Place. Eckles Hall, East Rollins and College Streets (on the UMC Campus). Under the supervision of UMC's Department of Food Science and College of Agriculture, Buck's is a student-run research, teaching, and service operation. It's also a gathering spot for aficionados of good ice cream. Old Mizzou's "Truman the Tiger" mascot is the inspiration for Buck's Tiger Stripe ice cream, a mixture of vanilla and chocolate, with some orange coloring thrown in to account for the tigerlike hue. It contains 12 percent milkfat, which is not as rich as butterfat, so maybe your thighs will be a little thinner from eating it. All ice cream is freshly made, is available in dipped and packaged forms, and weighs about 30 percent more per serving than most commercial products. Closed Sunday. $; (no cards). (573) 882-0591.

C.C.'s City Broiler. 131 South Tenth Street. This excellent steakhouse is renowned for its corn-fed Black Angus beef, hand-cut daily on the premises and cooked exactly as you like it. The signature item is a filet mignon, a mini mountain of meat about 3 inches high, tender enough to cut with a fork, and accented with a special seasoning that makes the flavor sing. If you want something even bigger, there's a whopping twenty-two-ounce porterhouse that can fill you up fast. All steaks come with the restaurant's famous jalapeño twice-baked potato, burgundy mushrooms, salad or soup, and fresh, hot sourdough bread. On the lighter side, the chargrilled seafood is always fresh, and you can mix and match a meal of steak and shrimp, steak and oysters, or steak and lobster tail. The prime rib, served only on Friday and Saturday, sells out fast. There's a wall-to-wall wait on weekends, so come early. Dinner is served seven nights a week. $$–$$$. (573) 875-2282.

Cherry Street Artisan. 111 Ninth Street. Part coffeehouse, part deli, part art gallery, and part performing arts venue, this hot spot in the downtown district is popular with college students and downtown employees. Everything is made fresh in kitchen, like spinach and feta quiche, or apple dumplings that are big enough for you and a couple of friends. Pizza and paninis are served with coffee, beer, and specialty drinks. All sandwiches come with chips and homemade hummus. Free wireless Internet is a bonus. Check out the Web site for the latest in poetry readings and dance performances. (573) 817-3274; www.cherrystreetartisans.com.

Ernie's. 1005 Walnut Street. This venerable art deco storefront establishment has been in business since 1934 and was recently upgraded from a greasy spoon to a not-so-greasy spoon that even features a short wine list. It still serves up good food at great prices. Hearty breakfasts, classic sandwiches, and luncheon specials are offered here, as are espresso, cappuccino, and lattes. One of the best things about Ernie's is the ambience. The eclectic assortment of patrons ranges from babies to bearded octogenarians. Blue-collar workers elbow in side by side at the counters with college students and faculty. Open daily until 3:00 p.m. $. (573) 874-7804.

Lakota Coffee Company. 24 South Ninth Street. This popular coffee roastery, located in the heart of downtown, is the only Columbia coffee shop to roast its own beans daily. The owner named the place for the Lakota Sioux, who loved the taste and smell of hot, strong coffee and who would, in their caffeine quest, raid wagon trains and steal the beans for their own coffee klatches. The establishment's lattes and cappuccinos are served in enormous Alice in Wonderland–size cups. You can have your choice of scones, croissants, biscotti, lox and bagels, and other edibles for dipping and sipping. The comfy chairs and laid-back ambience make the Lakota a perfect place to relax. The Lakota also sells coffee to take home and is especially proud of its hard-to-find varieties. Open daily. $. (573) 874-2852.

The Main Squeeze. 28 South Ninth Street. Have you run out of energy? Then come here to jump-start your battery. Start your morning with a sixteen-ounce "Elvis Parsley"—a mixture made with beets, spinach, parsley, celery, carrots, and garlic—which provides the equivalent of five servings of vegetables. Have a smoothie or go for the homemade soups, hearty sandwiches, salads, or fresh baked goods. There are no preservatives or artificial colors or flavors in anything you'll eat here. Breakfast can be free-range organic eggs, whole-grain pancakes, organic roasted potatoes, scrambled tofu, breakfast burritos, or biscuits with soy sausage gravy. There are also wheat-free nondairy entrees for vegans. Open daily 7:00 a.m. to 4:00 p.m. and for Saturday brunch. Closed Sunday. $. (573) 817-5616.

63 Diner. 5801 State Route 763. Remember the old neighborhood diner with its good food and soda fountain where you could always get super shakes and malts? Well, it's come back in the form of this 1950s-style diner, featuring neon lights, jukebox music, and the art and architecture of the era. The 63 Diner touts itself as a place that's "a little behind the times . . . when . . . grass was mowed, coke was a cold drink, and pot was a cooking utensil." Specialties include open-face roast beef and mashed potatoes, homemade ham and beans with grilled corn cakes, country-fried pork fillets, and country-fried chicken or pork cutlets with home-style gravy, mashed potatoes, and green beans. There's also a broccoli walnut casserole for those who swoon at the thought of ingesting too many calories. Sandwiches include almost any variety of burger known this side of Mars. Save room for homemade breads, rolls, pies, cobblers, and a hot fudge brownie sundae, complete with whipped cream and a cherry. Closed Sunday and Monday. $. (573) 443-2331.

Sophia's. 3915 South Providence Road. This popular restaurant has a laid-back, cosmopolitan ambience that goes well with its southern European fare that includes tapas, pastas, fresh seafood, steaks, and more. For after-dinner sport, there's always the boccie-ball court located next to the outdoor patio. There is usually a thirty- to forty-minute wait to get in, but early birds could luck out. For late-night owls, Sophia's stays open until 11:00 p.m. during the week and until midnight on weekends for the restaurant; until 1:00 a.m. for the bar. $$–$$$. (573) 874-8009.

Trattoria Strada Nova. 21 North Ninth Street. This downtown eatery is popular with the business crowd, which comes for the northern Italian cuisine of seafood and steaks. You may wish to call for reservations. The wine list is also impressive. Closed Sunday. $$–$$$. (573) 442-8992.

Village Wine and Cheese Shoppe. 929 East Broadway. As soon as you walk in the door of this long-time Columbia business, the enticing aromas from the kitchen let you know that this is more than a wine and cheese store. The wine selection includes labels from California, Australia, Italy, and beyond, with cheeses from equally far and wide. Samples are always available to help you make your selection. Open for lunch every day, the store offers specials that include hot pastrami or Mediterranean chicken salad. Dinner is offered Wednesday through Saturday with menu items such as Dijon-crusted pork chop or hazelnut-encrusted mahi-mahi. Reservations accepted for dinner. Closed Sunday. Special events and wine tastings offered throughout the year. $$$. (573) 442-1010.

The Wine Cellar & Bistro. 505 Cherry Street. Connoisseurs of fine wine and good food will enjoy a meal at this quiet, intimate bistro that features an ever-changing menu of eclectic and cross-cultural cuisine. You can choose from an interesting array of appetizers, entrees, and desserts, sample wines by the glass, or select from a number of superior bottled labels from around the world. The restaurant's "Flights of Wines" is a popular activity wherein patrons are offered three half-glasses of wine to sample with their meal. Depending on the day and the disposition of the chef, dinner can be a gravlax appetizer of cured salmon with pressed crackers, onions soaked in cranberry juice, capers, and a mustard dill sauce. Entrees like roast pork with honey bourbon glaze served with orange mashed potatoes and a corn cobette with sun-dried tomato butter, or bouillabaisse—a fresh seafood stew of shellfish, fish, onions, tomatoes, wine, olive oil, garlic, saffron, and herbs—are not to be missed. Desserts are absolutely decadent. Call ahead to find out what's on the daily menu. Reservations recommended. Closed Sunday. $$–$$$. (573) 442-7281.

where to stay

Columbia is filled with hotels and motels to suit every budget. Best Western, Days Inn, Budget, Comfort Inn, Drury Inn, Econo Lodge, Holiday Inn, Ramada, and Motel 6 are just a few of the better-known accommodations. Bed-and-breakfasts, although not as plentiful, include:

University Bed and Breakfast. 1315 University Avenue. Close to downtown and within walking distance of UMC's campus, this turn-of-the-twentieth-century home offers midwestern hospitality and delicious gourmet breakfasts served in the dining room. The four guest rooms are nicely appointed and come with their own private baths. Special rates are available for rental of the whole house. $$. (573) 499-1920; www.universityavenuebnb.com.

jefferson city, mo

From Columbia you have a couple of ways to reach Jefferson City. Heading back west on I-70 to Highway 179, the road takes you through some pretty countryside that passes the Runge Nature Center on the way to Jefferson City. US 63 South is faster and connects with U.S. Highway 54, the mid-Missouri gateway to the Lake of the Ozarks region.

Like two sides of a coin, Columbia and Jefferson City are separated by fewer than 30 miles, yet there's a world of difference between them. Located south of Columbia on US 63, Jefferson City is exactly opposite of Columbia with regard to atmosphere and ambience. Columbia is a liberal and laid-back college town with a high degree of tolerance for unconventional appearances and beliefs. Jefferson City is an old, conservative city that thrives on influence, politics, and power lunches, most likely taken at acceptable restaurants with acquaintances grouped according to social behavior and dress code. In Jefferson City moderate nonconformists fit in as long as no boats are seriously rocked.

Jefferson City is full of lovely residences and old refurbished homes, and a genteel, rather Southern influence permeates the town, which touts itself as a great place to raise a family. While Columbia places its emphasis on fun, food, and shopping, Jefferson City views history, architecture, and tradition as its most important assets. Travelers on the Lewis and Clark Trail will find several points of interest here.

Jefferson City's unique art and architecture are not to be found elsewhere. As the state capital, it holds the magnificent State Capitol Building, where the Missouri legislature convenes. The Governor's Mansion and Governor's Garden, Jefferson Landing State Historic Site, Cole County Museum, and other historic points of interest are also worth visiting.

Visitors can come to town along the Katy Trail. Binder Park campgrounds are the closest camping spot to the trailhead on US 54 and State Road West. However, it still is a 10-mile ride by bike through traffic to the heart of the city.

If you decide to spend the night, you'll find a number of accommodations that cater to business and leisure travelers alike, as well as a smattering of good restaurants. Leave time for a visit to the Runge Nature Center and Missouri's most delicious secret, the Central Dairy. For information: Jefferson City Convention and Visitors Bureau, 100 East High Street, P.O. Box 2227, Jefferson City, MO 65101-2227; (800) 769-4183 or (573) 632-2820; www.visit jeffersoncity.com.

where to go

The Benton Mural. House Lounge, on the third floor, west wing of the Missouri State Capitol. One of the most important and best reasons to visit the Missouri State Capitol is for the Thomas Hart Benton Mural, an expansive, stunning masterpiece that reflects the enormous genius behind it. You are welcome to return after the tour and sit in the lounge for a while and contemplate the painting from all angles.

At one time the mural was seriously in danger of being destroyed by the very legislators who commissioned it. Painted in 1936, the work covers four walls with a breadth and scope that reflect the legends, history, landmarks, industry, and people of Missouri. According to the Missouri Department of Natural Resources brochure on the State Capitol, the Benton Mural, entitled *A Social History of the State of Missouri,* offended many people because of its "lack of refinement." Refined, Benton was not, since he wanted to portray "activities that did not require being polite." His mural, in addition to its niceties, also depicts racist actions, hangings, and other messy and corrupt things that human beings—even Missourians—did in their zeal to build a state.

So enraged were the legislators by Benton's masterpiece that they deliberately defaced the mural, dashing out lighted cigars on it. They were about to whitewash it altogether when Benton's famous temper erupted. He took his case to the media and to the Missouri people, who backed him. The politicians relented and the painting stayed. There is no charge to see the restored work. Benton would have liked that. (573) 751-4127.

Clark's Hill/Norton State Historic Site. This unit of the Missouri State Park System is near Osage City just east of Jefferson City. This thirteen-acre property, donated to the state by William and Carol Norton of Jefferson City, is believed to be where William Clark camped on June 1, 1804, at the mouth of the Osage River. The area also includes Native American archaeology that will be preserved in an interpretive center. Call for hours and directions. &, 🏛. (573) 449-7402.

Cole County Historical Museum. 109 Madison Street. Located across from the Governor's Mansion, the museum is housed in an 1871 building that features a collection of inaugural ball gowns of the former First Ladies of the state, along with other vintage clothing and

Victorian furnishings. One floor of the four-story building is devoted to the Civil War in Missouri. Open for tours Tuesday through Saturday, or by appointment. Call for hours. Fee. (573) 635-1850.

Governor's Mansion. 100 Madison Street. This is the official residence for Missouri's First Family. Built in 1871, the mansion has an interior that is authentically restored to the Renaissance Revival period and includes a winding stairway, marble fireplaces, elaborate ceiling stenciling, and period furnishings. Portraits of Missouri's First Ladies are showcased on the walls. Docents in period costumes conduct tours of the first floor Tuesday through Thursday from 10:00 a.m. to noon and from 1:00 to 3:00 p.m. except during August and December. The grounds also hold the Carnahan Memorial Garden, a beautiful location for weddings. Constructed in the late 1930s, it is filled with flowers, pools, and walkways and can be reserved for special events. Christmas Candelight Tours are held at the mansion two evenings in December. Free. The garden is also free to tour. (573) 751-7929.

Jefferson Landing State Historic Site (Lohman Building and Union Hotel). Jefferson and Water Streets. The three-story Lohman Building, constructed of limestone in 1839, is thought to be the oldest structure in Jefferson City. It served steamboat passengers during the city's heyday as a busy river town. Charles Lohman, a native of Germany, operated an inn here at that time. A small museum on the premises depicts the history of the area. Adjacent to the Lohman Building is the Union Hotel. It was built in the 1850s, when the community was a busy center for rail and river traffic; it operated as a hotel following the Civil War and continued to do business until the decline of steamboating. The Elizabeth Rozier Gallery in the building is open for exhibits featuring Missouri's arts, artists, and cultures. An Amtrak station is located on the first floor of the Union Hotel. Both buildings are open Tuesday through Saturday. Call ahead for hours and information. Free. (573) 751-2854; www.mostateparks.com/jeffersonland.com.

Lincoln University. 820 Chestnut Street. Established in 1866, the university is situated on fifty-two rolling acres and is a source for cultural events, sports activities, and continuing education. The Soldiers Memorial at the center of campus is an impressive bronze sculpture that pays homage to the soldiers of the Civil War who eventually established Lincoln University. Free tours are available. (573) 681-5599; www.lincolnu.edu.

Missouri State Capitol Building. West High Street. Ranked number two among the nation's capitols for its art and architecture, the Missouri State Capitol sits on three acres of ground and rises 262 feet to the top of its dome. Completed in 1918, the Renaissance-style building is where Missouri's state senators and representatives meet from January through May to enact laws that govern the state. On Tuesday, Wednesday, or Thursday morning, you can watch the political process unfold from the visitors' gallery. The Missouri Museum, located on the first floor, features exhibits of outstanding historical significance, including portraits of Meriwether Lewis and William Clark. The large state seal in the center of the first-floor rotunda is wrought in bronze and can be viewed from a higher location during a tour of the building. The guided tours, conducted by docents, take in the legislators' chambers, architecture and design, some unusual murals painted in such a way that they present an optical illusion for the viewer, and the Benton Mural. A color guide to the capitol and a booklet on the Benton Mural can be purchased at the information desk on the first floor. Tours are given daily, every hour on the hour from 8:00 a.m. to 4:00 p.m. except holidays. A Christmas concert is held annually the second Tuesday of December. Free. 🏛. (573) 751-4127; www.visitjeffersoncity.com.

Missouri State Highway Patrol Museum. 1510 East Elm Street. Part education/safety center and part museum, this museum includes patrol cars, uniforms, weapons, and other equipment dating to the department's inception in 1931. Kids will love Otto, the talking car. Open Monday through Friday, 8:00 a.m. to 5:00 p.m. Free. (573) 526-6149.

Native Stone Vineyard and Bull Rock Brewery. 4301 Native Stone Road. This 300-acre family farm and business on the river bluff northwest of Jefferson City includes a tasting room, microbrewery, gift shop, and antiques. The farmhouse dates to the 1800s, and special occasion meals are available. Take a hike along a wood-chip path to a scenic overlook on the Missouri River to see Bull Rock, noted by Lewis and Clark in their journals as they passed this way in 1804. 🏛. (573) 584-8600; www.nativestonewinery.com.

Runge Nature Center. Highway 179, c/o Missouri Department of Conservation, P.O. Box 180, Jefferson City, MO 65102. This 3,000-square-foot facility west of downtown is the Department of Conservation's showpiece. Missouri's habitats are explored in a variety of exhibits and dioramas that feature the state's wetlands, agricultural lands, rivers and streams, ponds and lakes, prairies, glades, forests, and caves. Hiking trails, outdoor demonstrations, and naturalist-guided programs are offered over 112 acres seven days a week. Free. ♿. (573) 526-5544; www.mdc.mo.gov/areas/cnc/runge/.

where to eat

Central Dairy. 610 Madison Street. In Jefferson City the milkman still makes deliveries to your door twice a week, courtesy of Central Dairy, a mid-Missouri operation that sells products made in its plant from locally produced milk. The owner keeps his prices low at the ice-cream store as a goodwill gesture to the community, so everybody can afford to come here. Cones still sell for around a dollar, including sales tax, and prices are minuscule for colossal blockbuster sundaes and splits so top-heavy with triple dips of ice cream, marshmallow, and hot fudge toppings and nuts that you'll need several napkins just to clean up. Try the Rock & Roll sundae, one of humanity's finest inventions, featuring vanilla, chocolate, strawberry, and black walnut ice cream, crowned with banana, marshmallow, pineapple, and strawberry toppings and nuts. Worry about cholesterol later. Central Dairy sells fifty flavors of ice cream, including spumoni, Texas pecan, black walnut, cinnamon, caramel caribou, and other delights. Hand-packed pints and quarts are so affordable that serious aficionados will want to bring a cooler and plenty of dry ice to take some back home. The place never advertises: It doesn't need to. Call for hours. $; (no cards). (573) 635-6148.

Das Stein Haus Restaurant and Lounge. 1436 Southridge Drive (off US 54, next to the Ramada Inn). German specialties here include beef rouladen, Wiener schnitzel, smoked pork chops with sauerkraut, sauerbraten, and bratwurst. Dinners also feature chateaubriand for two, veal medallions, frog legs, and Long Island Duckling Flambé, topped with orange sauce and served with spiced rice and red cabbage. The lounge features live music on Sunday evening. $$–$$$. (573) 634-3869.

Domenico's. 3702 West Truman Boulevard. Located near the Capital Mall, this family-owned business has been a favorite of Jefferson City diners for nearly fifteen years. This is the fourth location for the Arcobasso family, which also operates restaurants in St. Charles and Florissant near St. Louis and at the Lake of the Ozarks. Pictures of the extended Arcobasso family line the walls, and family antiques contribute to the decor. While you can dine on a wide selection of steaks, seafood, and pasta, the meatball sandwich with Provel cheese is worth trying. For dessert, any of the three cheesecakes are great. Open for dinner only. Closed Sunday. $$. (573) 893-5454.

Ecco Lounge. 703 Jefferson Street. In 1838 the land on the corner of Jefferson and Dunklin was purchased for $32; in 1840 the back parking lot was bought for $26 more. The building was erected in 1858 and served as a "beer saloon." *Lounge* has replaced the word *saloon,* but beer is beer, and Ecco serves it up along with giant beer-battered onion rings and hefty burgers made from ground chuck and topped with blue cheese. Specialties are hot spiced shrimp, prime rib, and steak. The funky, working-class surroundings are fun. $. (573) 636-8751.

where to stay

Capitol Plaza Hotel and Convention Center. 415 West McCarty (US 50 and Missouri Boulevard). The nine-story atrium setting and five-story waterfall set the scene for this pleasant hotel located in the heart of downtown. Nicely appointed rooms and suites open to the atrium, and there are king suite rooms for hosting meetings and interviews. Hospitality suites, banquet service for up to 1,200, state-of-the-art audiovisual equipment, and many other services are available for business guests. The hotel also offers a fully equipped exercise room, as well as restaurants featuring an array of items for breakfast, lunch, and dinner. $$–$$$. (800) 338-8088 or (573) 635-1234; www.capitolplazajeffersoncity.com.

Hotel DeVille. 319 West Miller Street. This small, moderately priced downtown hotel offers shuttle service to and from the Katy Trail. There are ninety-eight guest rooms equipped with coffeemaker, refrigerator, high-speed wireless Internet, and other amenities. $$. (800) 392-3366 or (573) 636-5231; www.devillehotel.com.

california, mo

where to go

Burgers' Smokehouse. Department 57–L, Highway 87 South. From US 50 go south on Highway 87 a short distance to Burgers' Smokehouse. The eighteenth-century art of meat preservation is still used by this family-owned operation to smoke and cure turkeys, chickens, and meats the old-fashioned way. You can pig out on pork in the form of country-cured bacon and naturally aged smoked ham. The visitor center contains some interesting displays. There is a covered bridge, as well as dioramas with educational themes that point out the importance of the changing seasons as they relate to natural curing, drying, and aging of country-cured ham. Open Monday through Friday and on Saturday from mid-September through December. (800) 705-2323 (tours) or (800) 624-5426; www.smokehouse.com.

sedalia, mo

From California head west on US 50 to Sedalia. The MKT (Katy) Depot was built in 1896 and used to house railroad offices and restaurants. Today the building is owned by the Department of Natural Resources and listed on the National Register of Historic Places.

Sedalia's history dates back to 1857, when General George R. Smith decided to found a new town amid the prairie grasses. He envisioned a prosperous railroad city and named it Sedville, after his daughter's nickname. Friends eventually persuaded him to use the more mellifluous "Sedalia" to commemorate his progeny.

When the Civil War erupted, Sedalia was in the thick of the fighting. Missouri, though a slave state, did not secede from the Union as did other slave states. Sedalia was captured and held by the Confederates, and later was made the seat of Pettis County.

The railroad, as Smith foresaw, did indeed play an important role in the town's growth. Sedalia flourished and drew people with talent, such as Scott Joplin, who became known as the King of Ragtime. His sound spread across the country with compositions like the "Maple Leaf Rag," one of the finest pieces of ragtime music ever written. A historical monument was built at the Maple Leaf Club site in the 100 block of East Main Street, where Joplin lived and worked.

The Scott Joplin Ragtime Festival is held annually the first full weekend in June in Sedalia. The four-day event is the only classical ragtime festival in the world and commemorates the noted composer's work, bringing musicians and visitors from around the globe to the birthplace of ragtime. Food, crafts, and free performances on the Maple Leaf Club grounds are part of the fun.

Aside from its musical past, beautiful architecture can also be found in Sedalia. Take a nostalgic scenic tour of historic downtown Sedalia in a horse-drawn carriage. Call Any Occasion Surrey Co. at (660) 827-3515. The old homes that line Broadway (US 50), the buildings on the

State Fairgrounds, and the downtown area are all of interest. Brochures for walking tours are available from the chamber of commerce (located on the north side of the courthouse), 600 East Third Street, Katy Depot Historic Site, Sedalia, MO 65301; (800) 827-5295; www.visit sedaliamo.com.

where to go

Art Impressions. 412 South Ohio Street. More than thirty local and regional artists are represented in the light and airy gallery in the historic district. Glass works, fiber art, and oil and acrylic paintings are for sale along with soaps, jewelry, and decorative notecards. On occasion an artist will demonstrate his or her technique, such as a glassblowing demonstration on the street in front of the gallery. Matting and framing services are also available. Open Tuesday through Saturday or by appointment. (660) 826-4343.

Bothwell Lodge Historic Site. 19349 Bothwell Park Road. Located 6 miles north of Sedalia on US 65, this 180-acre park offers visitors scenic bluffs and wooded trails. It features picnic areas and Bothwell Lodge, a century-old lodge open for tours year-round. Fee to enter the lodge. (660) 827-0510.

Daum Contemporary Art Museum. 3201 West Sixteenth Street. Located on the campus of State Fair Community College, these nine galleries exhibit paintings, drawings, prints, photographs, and sculptures by midwestern artists. A focal point is a chandelier in the atrium created by glass artist Dale Chihuly. The museum rotates exhibits four times a year. Guided tours are available. Free. Closed Monday. (660) 530-5888; www.daummuseum.org.

Historic Katy Depot. 600 East Third Street. This 1896 depot has been fully restored and includes a museum of the early days of Sedalia history, as well as an interactive train station, including the flashing lights and rumbling of the building as an imaginary train passes by. A children's area allows kids to dress up as an engineer and manually operate a wooden train along its tracks. Katy Trail souvenirs and Missouri gift items are for sale in a well-stocked gift shop. The Sedalia Convention and Visitors Bureau makes its home here and has information on anything you need in Sedalia. (800) 827-5295.

Liberty Center Association for the Arts. 111 West Fifth Street. This renovated 1920s theater in downtown serves as the center for performing and cultural arts in the area. Visual artists display their work at Gallery 111, and the Sedalia Community Theatre's all-volunteer troupe stages three productions a year. Stop in for a cup of coffee at The Bean Coffee Shop, located on the premises. (660) 827-3228. A calendar of performances is listed at www.visitsedalia.com.

Maple Leaf Room. State Fair Community College Library, 3201 West Sixteenth Street. The bar and stained-glass window from the Maple Leaf Club, frequented by Scott Joplin, are housed here. Ragtime buffs will enjoy browsing through letters, music, and other Scott Joplin memorabilia. Free. (660) 530-5842.

Missouri State Fair. State Fairgrounds, 2503 West Sixteenth Street. The 397-acre showplace for agriculture and industry comes alive with color and excitement in late August for ten days of shows, exhibits, and competitions, drawing nearly 400,000 people every year. Fee. (800) 422-FAIR or (660) 530-5600; www.mostatefair.com.

Paint Brush Prairie Conservation Area. Nine miles south of Sedalia, off US 65 (watch for signs). This natural area captures the historic atmosphere at the time of homesteading. Unique plant species have been restored to the area, encouraging the return of native animals like prairie chickens, upland sandpipers, and Henslows' sparrows. Hiking trails wind throughout the area. &. (660) 530-5500.

Sedalia Heritage Trail. 600 East Third Street, Katy Depot Historic Site. Stop by the chamber office downtown and get a copy of a free walking tour brochure that highlights fifty-seven historic buildings in Sedalia. Many of the architecturally significant buildings house antiques and specialty shops. (800) 827-5295.

where to eat

Eddie's Drive-In. 115 Broadway. If you own a classic car, on warm summer evenings you'll often find others of your kind gathered in the parking lot of this 1930s-era diner. But even if you drive a twenty-first century vehicle, you'll enjoy the classic burgers, fries, and old-fashioned malts. $; (no cards). (660) 826-0155.

Wheel Inn. 1800 West Broadway. If you like peanuts, you'll love the Wheel Inn. In business for more than fifty years, the Wheel Inn touts its claim to fame on its menu as a "Guberburger." This is a hamburger topped with melted peanut butter and garnished with fresh lettuce, tomatoes, and your choice of mayo, catsup, mustard, and onions. Some sage advice: Don't knock it before you try it. Why not be bold and surprise your taste buds with a Guberburger and a thick, rich peanut butter milk shake? Too much overstimulation? Not to worry: There are other popular items, such as fresh-squeezed limeades and lemonades, homemade chili, and the best foot-long chili dog in town. The Wheel Inn is the last of a dying breed—one of those rare and admirable restaurants that still have carhops, giving patrons the opportunity to dine inside or in the privacy of their cars. $; (no cards). (660) 826-5177.

where to stay

Hotel Bothwell. 103 East Fourth Street. This National Historic Landmark hotel originally opened to the public in June 1927 and over the years hosted such names as Harry S. Truman, Bette Davis, and Clint Eastwood. Renovated in 2001, the Hotel Bothwell preserves much of the original class and charm that drew thousands through its doors for more than seventy-five years. Original telephone booths in one corner of the lobby and a six-story mail

drive-through déjà vu

Fans of Winstead's hamburgers in Kansas City may experience déjà vu as they dine at Eddie's Drive-In in Sedalia. Built in 1937, three years before Kathryn and Nelle Winstead set up shop at 1200 Main Street in Kansas City, Eddie's was also a Winstead family endeavor.

Kathryn and Nelle began their restaurant experience with a root beer stand in Springfield, Illinois. Their youngest sister, Fannie, married a gentleman named A.C. Garst and moved to Sedalia in 1937.

Fannie and her husband opened and operated Garst's Drive-In, the first drive-in restaurant in the state of Missouri. Business records show that monthly rent was paid to Kathryn and Nelle, who had since moved to Kansas City. You'll notice the art deco–style building of Eddie's is identical to Winstead's in Kansas City.

The business operated as Garst's Drive-In until 1970, when Fannie's brother-in-law Eddie purchased the business and changed the name. The current owner, George Geotz, purchased the property in 1983. Many old-timers in Sedalia still call the restaurant Garst's and have encouraged George to change the name back. Others, who knew Eddie, insist that he keep the name the same.

No matter what the name, Eddie's Drive-In serves the same style steakburger, onion rings, and malts that have drawn crowds to Winstead's in Kansas City for generations.

chute contribute to the feeling of yesteryear, as do original marble floors, walnut woodwork, and a lower-level "speakeasy." The hotel has forty-eight rooms, each unique in its furnishings and decor. Some of the rooms have been renovated into suites and long-term apartments, and six have been remodeled to their exact appearance in 1927. A coffee shop, restaurant, and gift shop add plenty of pizzazz to this familiar face in downtown Sedalia. $. (660) 826-5588; www.hotelbothwell.com.

Sedalia House Bed and Breakfast. 26097 County Road HH (2 miles east of US 65). This elegant two-story colonial-style home is situated in the midst of a 300-acre cattle ranch surrounded by ponds, woods, and rolling hills. You can relax on the beautiful pillared front porch or walk the trails to see bountiful wildlife. The accommodations offer four rooms, including two suites with private baths. A full country breakfast is served. Closed in winter. $$. (660) 826-6615; www.sedaliahouse.com.

worth more time: fulton, mo and hermann, mo

fulton, mo

Fulton, Missouri, is located east of Columbia on US 54 within the "Kingdom of Callaway County." Fulton's distance from Kansas City is longer than a usual day trip, but as one of the communities in the Katy Central Consortium, it is included here. Callaway County calls itself a kingdom because of a Civil War treaty whereby Callaway County forces signed an agreement with Union troops that neither of them would invade the other. Since that day, when the sovereign United States dealt with Callaway County as an equal, Callaway County has been designated a kingdom by those who live there. At one point, Callaway County was known as the Mule Capital of the World. Building on that heritage, planners of the annual Fulton Street Fair in June include a mule auction and a mule race as well as food, music, crafts, and other fun activities. For information on bed-and-breakfasts, dining, and other attractions: Kingdom of Callaway Chamber of Commerce, 409 Court Street, Fulton, MO 65251; (800) 257-3554; www.callawaychamber.com.

where to go

Heart of America Tourism Center and Firefighters Memorial. Located at the I-70 exit to Fulton, exit 148, the Heart of America Tourism Center offers thousands of brochures and other sources of information on things to do in mid-Missouri, as well as Missouri-made products. As you enter the center's parking lot, you will notice the Firefighters Association of Missouri Memorial. This bronze monument was created by a sculptor located in the World Trade Center in Manhattan. It had just been loaded on a truck to be shipped to Missouri when the tragedies of September 11, 2001, took the lives of so many Americans and firefighters. The Firefighters Association of Missouri gifted that original memorial to the people of New York. The one on display at Fulton is a reproduction. (573) 642-7692.

Winston Churchill Memorial and Library. Westminster College. Listed on the National Register of Historic Places, this is the site where Sir Winston Churchill gave his 1946 "Sinews of Peace" (Iron Curtain) speech. The memorial is the only museum of its kind in the world. However, there is a hefty admission fee for a self-guided visit that leaves much to be desired. If you've never been here before and know little about Churchill, it may be best to call ahead and arrange a tour with someone knowledgeable enough to discuss this famous church and British prime minister in depth.

The museum is housed inside the Sir Christopher Wren Church of St. Mary the Virgin, Aldermanbury, which was brought over to the United States stone by stone and rebuilt on the grounds of the college. There are exhibits that mostly feature old photographs and newspaper articles relating to Churchill, along with stories about Gorbachev's 1992 visit to the college. Also housed here are some of Churchill's paintings, books, and other memorabilia. Located on the museum grounds is a sculpture created by Churchill's granddaughter from eight sections of the Berlin Wall to symbolize the fall of the Iron Curtain. The memorial is also home to the Missouri Watercolor Society's ongoing exhibits, which have received national recognition. The group's Web site address is www.mowsart.com. Open daily. Fee. (573) 642-6648; www.wcmo.edu.

hermann, mo

Located on picturesque Missouri Highway 19 just south of I-70, Hermann is outside the usual day-trip time frame, but it's included here because it is part of the Katy Central Consortium communities. Hermann is best known for having the state's oldest wineries, lots of antiques shops, and dozens of nineteenth-century homes, many of which have been converted to great bed-and-breakfasts.

Two historic homes—the Pommer-Gentner House on Market Street and the Strehly House on West Second Street—reflect the town's early German traditions. Hermann's popular wineries include Stone Hill, Adam Puchta, and Hermannhof, all offering tours and award-winning wines to sample. Hermann has a host of other attractions, including the Showboat Community Theater, open for live entertainment and tours; the Show-Stopper Revue, featuring a mix of Broadway and vaudeville fare; and the Historic Hermann Museum and Information Center, housed in an 1871 German school and featuring a number of educational displays.

Hermann also holds several renowned festivals and celebrations throughout the year. These include the Hermann Maifest, a May celebration of spring, complete with parades, German food, drink, arts, crafts, and music, and Octoberfest in fall, which offers music, food, and fun. There are daily Amtrak stops to and from Hermann. For more information on bed-and-breakfasts, attractions, restaurants, shopping, and festivals: Hermann Tourism Group, 312 Schiller Street, P.O. Box 104, Hermann, MO 65041; (800) 932-8687; www.hermannmo.com.

day trip 03

east

brass bands, beer, and birds:
blue springs, mo;
concordia, mo

blue springs, mo

This Kansas City suburb offers a high standard of living, good schools, and popular parks and wildlife areas that bring people from around the region to this part of town.

where to go

Burr Oak Woods Conservation Nature Center. 1401 Park Road (Missouri Highway 7 North and Park Road). The center is nestled within 1,100 acres of mixed hardwood forest, prairies, glades, and limestone outcrops. Exhibits include hands-on displays of Missouri's fish, forest, and wildlife resources, including live animals. In addition, there are a 3,000-gallon aquarium stocked with native fish and reptiles, a 155-seat auditorium, and an indoor wildlife viewing area. Four outdoor hiking trails and wildlife food plots afford a glimpse of deer, turkeys, and raccoons. Two trails are wood-chipped, and two are paved. Picnic areas are available. Free. (816) 228-3766; www.mdc.mo.gov/areas/cnc/burroak.

Burrough's Audubon Center and Library. Fleming Park (off Woods Chapel Road, near Lake Jacomo Marina). You can learn all about nature at the five-acre center, which contains exhibits of birds' nests, insects, and butterflies and hiking trails through the wildflower gardens. Outdoor feeders bring in a variety of birds to watch. The natural history library on site allows visitors to check books and videos out for four weeks. A gift shop on the premises

Jamesport

0   10   20   30 miles

M I S S O U R I

35

29

Smithville   Kearney   Lawson
                          Watkins Mill State Park
435   10   Richmond
     169   Excelsior   Missouri River
            Springs   13
     Liberty   Sibley   65
                              Waverly
KANSAS   24   Lexington
CITY   Buckner
Independence   70 — 40
435   40
     Blue   Concordia
470 Springs

     Lone
69   Jack   W
     291   131   50
     Kingsville   Warrensburg
Louisburg

                    13

Marais des Cygnes   Clinton
Wildlife Area

sells birdseed, feeders, bird guides, and related items. Closed Monday, Wednesday, and Sunday. Free. (816) 795-8177.

Missouri Town 1855. Fleming Park. Head east on I-70, then south on Missouri Highway 291; take a left at the Colbern Road exit to Cyclone School Road, then go left and follow the signs. This reconstructed 1850s farming community comprises more than thirty original structures that make up a charming village. Barnyard animals such as free-ranging chickens, sheep, and horses add an authentic touch. The volunteer staff, dressed in period attire, demonstrates chores done by frontier Americans. Fee. Closed Monday. (816) 503-4800.

concordia, mo

Located 53 miles east of Kansas City on I-70, Concordia is a sleepy little hamlet most of the time. Every September the town comes alive when it hosts a three-day celebration of its German heritage, complete with German brass bands, parades, cattle shows, and arts and crafts, along with plenty of German-style foods and imported German beers. Tourists come from around the state, swelling the population from 2,000 to as many as 5,000 in a single evening. For dates and times check newspaper ads or contact the Concordia Chamber of Commerce, 802 South Gordon Street, Concordia, MO 64020; (660) 463-2454; www.concordiamo.com.

where to stay

Mrs. G's B&B. One South East Fourteenth Street. This ranch-style home affords a homestay experience and offers two rooms, each with private bath. One room is on the main floor and features a full-size bed; the other is located in the loft and has a full-size bed and rollaway. A deluxe breakfast is served. Open weekends during the school year and full-time in summer. $; (no cards). (660) 463-2160.

day trip 04

east

from garden getaway to capital city:
lone jack, mo; kingsville, mo;
warrensburg, mo; sedalia, mo;
jefferson city, mo

lone jack, mo

A historic Civil War battlefield, one of the largest botanical gardens between Kansas City and Denver, a first-class bed-and-breakfast, and a dog that made national history back in 1870 are part of this unusual Day Trip that will acquaint you with this fascinating yet relatively undiscovered region.

where to go

Bynum Winery. 13520 South Sam Moore Road (3 miles east of Lone Jack at the intersection of US 50 and Sam Moore Road). Sweet and dry varieties of Seyval Blanc, Villard Blanc, and Chancellor Noir are made here, along with apple, cherry, and other fruit wines in season. Fresh fruits and vegetables are also for sale in season. Open daily; call for hours. (816) 566-2240.

Lone Jack Civil War Battlefield and Cemetery. 301 South Bynum Road (1 block south of US 50 at Lone Jack exit). This is the site of the August 16, 1862, Battle of Lone Jack, where five hours of bloody, hand-to-hand fighting ensued. The event is depicted in dioramas, artifacts, and other displays that showcase what happened on this Civil War battleground. An annual commemoration is held the weekend closest to the original battle date. Open daily April

through October; weekends November through March (donations suggested). (816) 697-8833.

kingsville, mo

where to go

Powell Gardens. 1609 Northwest US 50. Located 35 miles east of Kansas City, Powell Gardens is a not-for-profit, 915-acre botanical garden dedicated to beautifying and preserving the natural environment. Established in 1984 through a generous gift from the Powell Family Foundation, Powell Gardens is an outdoor paradise for gardeners and nature lovers, offering a changing palette of colorful flowers and plants throughout the year.

Powell Gardens utilizes horticultural displays, education, and research to serve the Kansas City community and surrounding areas. Gardens of annuals, perennials, native plants, ornamental grasses, and other seasonal plantings make up this spectacular facility.

Visitors may enjoy strolling through the Perennial Garden, Rock and Waterfall Garden, the Island Garden, and the Terrace Gardens at the Visitor Education Center. Other highlights include the magnificent structures designed by architects Fay Jones and Maurice Jennings. These include the Marjorie Powell Allen Chapel, the Visitor Education Center, and the Wildflower Pavilion.

Powell Gardens offers year-round special events, educational classes and environmental programs for children and adults, a lovely gift shop, and an excellent cafe where you can refresh and relax before or after your visit. Open daily. &. Fee. (816) 697-2600; www.powell gardens.org.

warrensburg, mo

Located east of Powell Gardens at the intersection of US 50 and Highway 13, Warrensburg has plenty of antiques stores, specialty shops, restaurants, and cafes to visit. The town is the home of the University of Central Missouri, known for its outstanding technology and aviation programs. For information: Warrensburg Chamber of Commerce, 100 South Holden Street, Warrensburg, MO 64093; (877) OLD-DRUM or (660) 747-3168; www.warrensburg.org.

where to go

Blind Boone Park. 402 West Pine Street. Once representative of segregation in Warrensburg, this long-forgotten park has been restored and is now the pride of the city. The park is named for former Warrensburg resident Willie Boone, the son of an escaped slave, who lost his eyesight at six months but grew to be an accomplished concert pianist. Today's park includes a statue of Boone along with other sculptures, a gazebo, and a sensory garden, all designed around the needs of the visually impaired. There's also a shuffleboard court, horseshoe pits, and a great picnic area. The park is the location for a music festival each June. (660) 747-3268; www.blindboonepark.org.

Downtown Warrensburg. c/o Main Street, Inc., 109 North Holden Street. Spend a morning browsing along Main Street shops, services, and businesses, many of which are housed in venerable structures that are being restored and refurbished, thanks to the Warrensburg Main Street Program. The revitalization plan is helping to maintain the city's center through the context of historic preservation. (660) 429-3988.

Missouri Pacific Railroad Depot. 100 South Holden Street. This century-old former railroad depot was rescued from physical decline and renovated for multiple uses. It houses the Warrensburg Chamber of Commerce and also serves as an Amtrak station. Two eastbound and two westbound passenger trains pass through here daily. You can take the Amtrak from Kansas City to Warrensburg and back, or head out to other locations, such as Jefferson City, Sedalia, Hermann, and St. Louis. You can purchase your ticket through a local travel agency or call (800) USA-RAIL for information on departure times and prices. (660) 747-3168.

Old Drum Monument. Market and Holden Streets (on the grounds of the Johnson County Courthouse). In 1870 Senator George Graham Vest won a court battle and the hearts of dog lovers when he paid his famous tribute to the dog during the *Burden v. Hornsby* court case in 1870. That eulogy won the case for Charles Burden, whose favorite hound, Drum, was shot by Leonidas Hornsby, a neighbor. Burden sued for damages, and the trial became the focus of national attention, as each man became determined to win. After several appeals the case reached the Missouri supreme court. Vest's eulogy, which he made in his final appeal to the jury, became a classic speech that reached the hearts of dog lovers around the world. He said, "The one absolutely unselfish friend that a man can have in this selfish world, the one that never deserts him, the one that never proves ungrateful or treacherous, is his dog." Who could resist a speech like that? Burden was subsequently awarded $50 in damages for the loss of this favorite dog. Free. (660) 747-3168.

University of Central Missouri. Office of Admissions, Administration Building 104. Founded in 1871, UCM, still commonly referred to as Central Missouri State University, despite legislative efforts otherwise, offers a wide range of academic programs in applied sciences and technology, arts and sciences, business and economics, and education and human services. The 1,050-acre campus offers opportunities to attend events and exhibitions of fine and performing arts, including those featuring celebrities in the entertainment and musical fields. The James L. Highlander Theater offers two main-stage or dinner-theater productions each semester. The UCM Archives and Museum, located in the James C. Kirkpatrick Library, houses a diverse display of artifacts that changes themes monthly. The campus is free to tour. (660) 543-4111; www.cmsu.edu.

where to eat

Heroes Restaurant and Pub. 107 Pine Street. Popular with college students and local businesspeople for lunch, this spacious pub in the downtown district is famous for its huge helpings of onion rings and cheese fries. Other than that, you might catch a Mules or Jennies sporting event on TV while enjoying your choice of salads, burgers, steaks, and pastas. The homemade desserts, such as carrot cake, are the best! (660) 747–3162.

where to stay

Cedarcroft Farm Bed & Breakfast. 431 Southeast Y Highway. Located on the 1867 John A. Adams Farmstead, now on the National Register of Historic Places, Cedarcroft has been beautifully renovated with modern comforts. The farm is surrounded by eighty acres of woods, creeks, and meadows. Wildlife—such as deer and wild turkey—abounds. The hosts provide guests with plenty of information about the area, including where to shop and how to find antiques and bargains galore. Guest quarters feature a two-room private suite with private bath or a guest cottage with wood-burning fireplace. There's also a parlor and gathering room. A large evening snack and a full country breakfast are included with your stay. $$$. (800) 368-4944 or (660) 747-5728; www.cedarcroft.com.

sedalia, mo
(See East from Kansas City, Day Trip 2.)

jefferson city, mo
(See East from Kansas City, Day Trip 2.)

southeast

0   10   20   30 miles

Conception Junction

Savannah

Jamesport

MISSOURI

35

29

Smithville   Lawson
        Kearney   Watkins Mill State Park
                        10
Excelsior
Springs   Richmond
435   Liberty   Sibley   Missouri River
169   65
KANSAS   Independence   Lexington   Waverly
CITY   Buckner   41   Fayelle   124
        435   Blue   Arrow Rock   New   Rocheport   Columbia
                Springs   Franklin   40   70
470   Concordia   Boonville
        Lone   40   70
69   Jack   W   63   Fulton
        291   131   50   Sedalia   California   34
        Kingsville   Warrensburg   5   50
Louisburg   Jefferson City
                        13   Versailles
Marais des Cygnes   5   52   Eldon
Wildlife Area   54
Pleasanton   Clinton   Laurie   Lakeland
                                                Lake Ozark
                                        HMM   Osage Beach
                        The Lake of the Ozarks   Lake of the Ozarks
                                                5   State Park
                                                42   134
Ft. Scott National   Camdenton
Historic Site and
Museum
69   71
Frontenac
Pittsburg

Carthage

day trip 01

southeast

water, water everywhere:
clinton, mo

worth more time: the lake of the ozarks, mo

clinton, mo

Travel south out of Warrensburg on Highway13 to the community of Clinton to the western-most trailhead of the Katy Trail. Located approximately halfway between Kansas City and Springfield at the intersection of Highway 13 and U.S. Highway 7, Clinton is popular for boaters and fishermen who enjoy the quiet pace of Truman Lake's 55,000 acres. Hunting is popular in the area as well.

Clinton was one of only ten cities to be named an All-American City in 2000, in part because of the exciting work that the Main Street USA program is doing to preserve and renovate the downtown business district. Today, you'll find more than one hundred shops, restaurants, and businesses thriving in the four blocks of Main Street, including seven antique shops. If you're looking for unusual collectibles from Missouri communities, a miniature village consisting of the Courthouse, the Katy Trail Depot, and the other buildings are for sale at area businesses. The downtown square comes alive for Old Glory Days, a four-day festival surrounding July 4. For more information, contact the Clinton Chamber of Commerce, 200 S. Main Street, Clinton, MO 64735; (660) 885-8166 or (800) 222-5251; www.chambermoclinton.com.

where to go

Dorman House. 302 West Franklin Street. When this house was built in the 1850s, it was all the gossip for being the first two-story brick house in Clinton. Owned by Jerubial Dorman and his wife Udolpha, the home was a hideout and resting place for both Union and Confederate soldiers during the Civil War. Many of the furnishings are original to the family. Tours by appointment. (660) 885-2121.

Henry County Museum and Cultural Arts Center. 203 West Franklin Street. A fully restored Anheuser-Busch distribution center (built in 1886) serves as the main building of the museum. The annex features building facades that would have been found here in the late 1800s. The museum includes the former Henry County Bank, built in 1887, which now serves as a performing arts center. (660) 885-8414; www.henrycountymomuseum.org.

Kiddn' Around. 104 South Main Street. Whether you are into knitting and weaving or not, you should stop in this fun shop for a look at the antique spinning wheels. Owner Lois Schuck has nine spinning wheels on display (more at her home) that date all the way to the 1600s. One is a rare trolley wheel spinning wheel that dates to 1811. Also ask to see her antique hand spindles from around the world.

The building in which Lois sells yarn and weaving supplies dates to 1848 and was Simes Shoe store in Clinton for more than a hundred years. Lois carries supplies for bobbin lace, teaches quilting classes, and takes custom orders for woven rugs. Some of the yarns she sells are made from fibers from corn, soybeans, and bamboo, but most of her yarn comes from the one hundred goats she raises on a farm outside of town (thus the name of her shop, Kiddn' Around). Open Tuesday through Saturday, 10:00 a.m. to 5:00 p.m. (660) 885-6614.

Wagoner Park. Sedalia Avenue and 52 Highway. Depending on how you look at it, Missouri's magnificent Katy Trail begins or ends in Clinton at this nineteen-acre park. There's plenty of parking if you want to hike or bike a few miles of the trail from here. Or stop by the baseball complex and check out some of the fine Little League action in town.

Yesterday's Costume Shop. 134 South Main Street. If you're looking for a truly one-of-a-kind Halloween costume, this is the place to come. Carol Murray loves Halloween, but she makes costumes all year, as she's been doing for almost eighteen years now. But don't expect to walk in the door in September or October to place an order. Be thinking about your Halloween costume in January. And even if you don't want a costume, stop by her shop in October to see the elaborate window decorations she creates. (660) 890-2299.

where to eat

Ben Franklin Coffee House. 106 Main Street. Once a Ben Franklin Dime Store, this coffee shop rivals anything that Starbucks can brew up. In addition to whole bean or ground coffee that you can take home with you, and any whipped-up latte or mocha combination you could ask for, the fruit smoothies are wonderful on a hot summer day. Come in early for Belgian waffles with nuts and whipped cream ($3) or lunch sandwiches (starting at $4) named after Ben Franklin and his contemporaries. Enjoy your treats and free WiFi at one of the many antique tables, which are for sale along with other primitive antiques. Closed Sunday. (660) 890-2021.

> ## clinton's checkered past

> *In 1923 Lawrence Brown opened a manufacturing company in Clinton that many credit with inventing the game of Chinese checkers. In reality, the game was invented in Germany in the 1830s, but Brown was the first to create the colored, star-patterned board that we associate with Chinese checkers. The boards were hand-made and painted by the thousands from the 1920s to the 1950s in Clinton. Today they are highly collectible and sell on eBay for up to $50 a board, living up to Lawrence Brown's trademark that it is "a game for all ages."*

> *A collection of these boards and other inventions by Lawrence Brown are on display at the Henry County Museum.*

worth more time: the lake of the ozarks, mo

the lake of the ozarks, mo

Located 165 miles from Kansas City, The Lake of the Ozarks is one of the Midwest's premier playgrounds. The largest lake in Missouri, it offers 1,150 miles of shoreline (more than the Pacific Coast of California).

The lake covers 59,600 acres, surrounded by one hundred marinas, dozens of waterfront restaurants and watering holes, and hundreds of shops, services, and businesses. Water activities abound from April through October. Off-season is a good time to go to the lake because it's less crowded. Even winter provides things to do, from holiday festivities to romantic cold-weather getaways at large resorts that stay open at this time of year.

There are plenty of places to camp, with more than 1,800 private campground sites, ranging from rugged, wooded locations at the water's edge to paved parks with full hookups.

In addition, The Lake of the Ozarks is a prime fishing and golf destination, hosting prestigious tournaments such as Bass Masters and the PGA Club Pro Championship.

When it was created back in 1931, The Lake of the Ozarks was considered the world's largest man-made body of water. The construction of Bagnell Dam by the Union Electric Company was hailed as the most skillful engineering feat of its day. The 2,543-foot-long dam's reservoir holds 650 billion gallons of water, covering parts of Miller, Camden, Morgan, and Benton Counties.

On the lake's eastern edge above the dam are the tiny towns of Lakeside and Lakeland. Below the dam, on the Osage River, is the village of Bagnell, for which the dam is named. The first mile south of the dam is known to tourists as the Strip, which houses shops, arcades, amusements, and restaurants, along with family resorts, motels, and hotels.

South of the Strip are U.S. Highway 54 and State Road HH. They lead to Horseshoe Bend's lush golf courses, resorts, restaurants, condominiums, and residential subdivisions. South of here is Lake Ozark, followed by Osage Beach, a popular 8-mile-long community of shopping malls, outlet stores, restaurants, country sampler shops, and many other attractions.

Following US 54 south leads you across the Grand Glaize Bridge to State Road KK, the pathway to Turkey Bend. Here you'll find more golf, luxury estates, homes, condominiums, resorts, restaurants, and marinas.

Past State Road KK is Linn Creek, a residential community that is home to the Camden County Museum and Big Surf Water Park. South on US 54 is Camdenton, the hub city of the area. It's bustling and crowded in the summer and offers shopping, restaurants, and plenty of family accommodations.

Camdenton is the dividing point between the west and east sides of the lake, where the small towns of Sunrise Beach, Laurie, and Gravois Mills provide a growing number of resorts, motels, campgrounds, and shopping and dining places.

North from here, at the crossroads of Missouri Highway 5 and Missouri Highway 52, is Versailles (pronounced *ver-sayles* by residents). It holds the Morgan County Historical Museum, retail shops, and the Hilty Inn, a bed-and-breakfast establishment.

Eldon—east of Versailles on Highway 52 as you drive southeast toward Osage Beach—boasts shops, antiques stores, and eateries.

Most of the lakeshore is privately owned, and there is little public access to boating, swimming, or fishing. There are two public beaches, campgrounds, and boat-rental facilities at Lake of the Ozarks State Park. Both Osage Beach and Lake Ozark provide entrance to the park, the largest in Missouri. Ha Ha Tonka State Park, west of Camdenton off US 54, includes unusual rock formations, castle ruins, and wheelchair-accessible trails.

The *Lake of the Ozarks Vacation and Service Guide,* available from the Lake of the Ozarks Convention and Visitor Bureau, can lead you to most of the better-known resorts, restaurants, and attractions. For information: Lake of the Ozarks Convention and Visitor Bureau, P.O. Box 1498, Osage Beach, MO 65065; (800) 386-5253; www.funlake.com; or request a self-guided car tour brochure from the Camdenton Area Chamber of Commerce, 1191 North Highway 5, Camdenton, MO 65020; (800) 769-1004.

where to go

boat rentals, marinas, and scenic cruises

One way to enjoy the lake is on a boat. With more than one hundred marinas, it's impossible to list all the facilities here. Most of the resorts and campgrounds have their own boat rentals and marinas. Houseboating is also an option (see Where to Stay). For a complete rundown, get a copy of the latest edition of the *Lake of the Ozarks Vacation and Service Guide,* available from the Lake of the Ozarks Convention and Visitor Bureau, P.O. Box 1498, Osage Beach, MO 65065; (800) 386-5253; www.funlake.com.

Celebration. Physical address: Kirkwood Lodge, 1192 Lakeshore Drive, Osage Beach, MO 65065. Mailing address: P.O. Box 2086, Lake Ozark, MO 65049. If you prefer to have someone else take the stern, you might try a ride aboard the *Celebration,* the most elegant cruise ship on the lake. The 80-foot yacht features open-air decks and climate-controlled interior salons. Dinner excursions are available, as are special private charters for corporate functions, weddings, and groups. Reservations required. Fee. (573) 302-0023 or (573) 480-3212; www.celebrationlakeozark.com.

Tropic Island Cruises. The Lodge of Four Seasons, State Road HH, Lake Ozark, MO 65049. This 75-foot luxury motor yacht offers daily scenic cruises. It can also be rented for special events, such as family reunions, weddings, business meetings, and parties. It holds 150 passengers, and catered food service is available for groups. Fee. (573) 348-0083; www.tropicis landcruises.com.

caves

Renowned as the Cave State, Missouri has more than 5,000 registered and mapped caves, with 300 "wild" caves in the three counties surrounding The Lake of the Ozarks. There are three show caves located within 30 miles of one another. A 93-mile triangular drive around the lake takes you from cave to cave through tree-lined roads. The caves are open to the public for tours and feature paved walkways, handrails, and lights. They include the following:

Bridal Cave. Thunder Mountain Park, 526 Bridal Cave Road, Camdenton. Located north of Camdenton off Highway 5 on Lake Road 5-88, this forty-six-million-year-old cave is the oldest in the area and one of the three most scenic in America. It is the site of a legendary Indian wedding ceremony held in the early 1800s. More than 2,000 couples have been married in the cave's breathtaking Bridal Chapel. The cave is accessible by car or boat. Open daily year-round; hours vary. Fee. (573) 346-2676; www.bridalcave.com.

Jacob's Cave. 23114 Highway TT, Versailles. Off Route TT, north of Gravois Mills, this is the largest cave in the area and the only walk-through cave in Missouri that is wheelchair-accessible. The cave, known for its depth illusion, features the world's largest geode, reflective pools, musical stalactites, prehistoric mastodon bones, and unusual strawlike formations. The rock shop on the premises features a black-light rock display, along with native minerals, crystals, and geodes for sale. Open daily year-round. ♿. Fee. (573) 378-4374; www.jacobscave.com.

Ozark Caverns. Lake of the Ozarks State Park, 823 Ozark Caverns Road, Linn Creek, MO 65052. This state-owned cave is located inside the park, off US 54 on Route A. Visitors receive handheld lanterns as guides take groups through the spectacular highlighted sights, which include Angel's Shower, a continual flow of water that falls from the rock ceiling into two mas-

steering the titanic

I felt like the captain of the Titanic trying to avoid an iceberg, except that it was 85 degrees, under a perfect blue sky, and I was in the middle of The Lake of the Ozarks.

My friends and I had the pleasure of spending a few summer days on a house-boat at the lake. And not just any houseboat, mind you, but a 65-foot-long, 14-foot-wide VIP boat from Forever Resorts, one of the largest vessels to ply the waters of central Missouri. We had grown up on the waterways of the Midwest, my friends and I, and were comfortable with ski boats, Jet Skis, and watercraft that could turn on a dime—but perhaps not as adept as we thought with a larger vessel.

We had just gotten under way from The Lake of the Ozarks Marina when we had our first Titanic experience. The massive pillars of the Niangua Bridge loomed ahead like an iceberg, and no matter how hard I turned the wheel, nothing seemed to happen. Then ever so slowly, the nose of our freighter began to swing starboard, until we were safely away from danger. With my stomach clenched, I realized imme-diately that this would be no powerboat race. Instead, we were in for a slow-paced, five-mile-an-hour tour of the shoreline.

The point of my story is two-fold: First, no matter how many times you visit The Lake of the Ozarks, there's always a new way to enjoy the beauty of the region. Our lazy tour turned out to be refreshing and relaxing, allowing us to appreciate scenery that we had only zipped past before. Later, snuggled in a cove at Lake of the Ozarks State Park, we screamed down the boat's two-story slide into the cool lake waters. And that night, we sipped wine under a starlit sky while enjoying the pleasures of our top-deck hot tub.

Second lesson: Look out for other boats and don't assume they are going to move out of your way. Whether you are the boat or the iceberg, the consequences of a crash are not much fun.

sive stone basins below. Closed in winter. Hours vary. Fee. (573) 346-2500; www.mostate parks.com/lakeozark/cave.htm.

music shows

Main Street Music Hall. 1048 Main Street, The Landing on Main Street. Toe-tapping coun-try music and sentimental favorites from the 1950s and 1960s are performed here. Open May through October; hours vary. Also open in late November to the Saturday before Christmas with a special Christmas show; hours vary. Reservations. Fee. (573) 348-9500; www.lakemusic hall.com.

golf courses

The Lake of the Ozarks offers excellent and affordable places to hit the links. In excess of 260 holes and sixteen courses varying in length, degree of difficulty, elevation changes, water hazards, and strategic layouts make the courses appealing for all levels.

Major players, including Arnold Palmer, Lee Trevino, and Tom Watson, have lent their skills to numerous tournaments. The Junior Golf Program gives girls and boys the opportunity to participate in various golf clinics; and golf tournaments, sponsored by Wilson Golf and a PGA grant, are held June through August. Reduced rates are offered at participating courses.

Most of the lake's courses are open daily year-round, weather permitting. Call for hours. Courses include the following:

The Lodge of Four Seasons Championship Golf Resort & Spa. Lake Ozark. The Lodge's Witch's Cove Course is a classic Robert Trent Jones Sr. design that features rolling fairways, large greens, and spectacular par 3s. The design of this eighteen-hole, 6,567-yard, par-71 course utilizes land that juts out into the lake, creating challenging golf and some of the most beautiful scenery in the Midwest. Seasons Ridge Course, ranked by *Golf Week* as the fifth best course in Missouri, is one of the top public courses in the state. (800) THE-LAKE or (573) 365-3000; www.4seasonsresort.com.

Old Kinderhook Golf and Marina Community. Lake Road 54–80, Camdenton. This 638-acre recreational community includes a Tom Weiskopf championship golf course complete with undulating zoysia fairways, large bent-grass greens, four elevated tee boxes on each hole, and natural rock waterfalls. The 6,855-yard, eighteen-hole, par-71 design makes this one of the best crafted and most uniquely playable courses in the Midwest. (573) 346-4444; www.oldkinderhook.com.

Osage National Golf Resort. Lake Ozark. Nestled between the lake and the lush Osage River Valley, the first Arnold Palmer–designed course in Missouri boasts a lovely course that incorporates wandering creeks, several lakes, and greens ranging from 29 to 47 yards in depth. The par-72, twenty-seven-hole, 7,150-yard layout is challenging for all skill levels and offers three possible eighteen-hole combinations. (573) 365-1950; www.osagenational.com.

Sycamore Creek Golf Club. Lake Road 54–56, 1270 Nichols Road, Osage Beach. Fish-filled ponds serve as combination golf course water hazards and spawning pools for catfish! The eighteen-hole golf course and fishery are located on a wooded, 300-acre valley surrounded by gorgeous upscale homes. Amenities include a snack bar, a lounge, and rental clubs. There are zoysia tees, midiron Bermuda fairways, Crenshaw bent-grass greens, and, of course, catfish. (573) 348-9593; www.sycamorecreekgolfclub.com.

Tan-Tar-A Resort, Golf Club, Marina, and Indoor Waterpark. State Road KK, Osage Beach. The Oaks Course, designed by Bruce Devlin and Robert Von Hagge, is a masterful eighteen-hole, par-71 layout, with 6,432 yards of demanding approaches, nine water hazards, and breathtaking elevation changes along a tight terrain. In 1994 this was the host head-quarters course for the PGA Club Pro Championship. Another course, Hidden Lakes, offers nine holes, par 35, and fairways set amid stunning lake views and difficult sand traps. (800) 826-8272 or (573) 348-3131; www.tan-tar-a.com.

Other courses in the area include Lake Valley Country Club, Dogwood Hills Resort and Golf Club, and Bear Creek Valley Golf Club in Osage Beach; Eldon Country Club in Eldon; Bay View Golf Course and the Golf Club at Deer Chase in Linn Creek; Indian Rock Golf Club in Laurie; and Rolling Hills Country Club in Versailles. For a complete list and golf package information, contact the Lake of the Ozarks Golf Council at (800) 490-8474; www.golfingmissouri .com.

museums

Morgan County Historical Museum. Old Martin Hotel, Versailles. As the seat of Morgan County, Versailles has a history that dates to 1833. Much of the town's memorabilia has been preserved by members of the Morgan County Historical Society, who staff the museum inside the old Martin Hotel. Historical treasures found here include a library with bound volumes of Morgan County newspapers from 1877, a century-old square grand piano, and an old beauty shop with artifacts from yesteryear, plus a barbershop, a weaving room, a war relics room, and more. Closed Sunday and Monday. Fee. (573) 378-5530 or (573) 378-4401.

shrines

National Shrine of Mary, Mother of the Church. Highway 5 between Versailles and Camdenton, on the grounds of St. Patrick's Church, Laurie. Dedicated to Mary, Mother of the Church, this remarkable shrine is housed in a natural grotto on the premises of St. Patrick's Church. The shrine is surrounded by a terraced amphitheater that seats several thousand worshippers and features the Mother's Wall of Life of polished black granite. The project was designed by Frank Grimaldi of Kansas City, and the epic statue that personifies Mary is by sculptor Don Wiegand. Available for viewing daily year-round. Free. (573) 374-6279; www.mothersshrine.org.

Willmore Lodge. Business Highway 54, Lake Ozark. Just northeast of Bagnell Dam, Willmore Lodge was completed in 1930 for Union Electric during the construction of the dam. The Adirondack-style 6,500-square-foot lodge, built of white pine logs from Oregon, has been refurbished as a visitor center and museum operated by the Lake Area Chamber of Commerce. In addition to receiving brochures on lake area attractions, visitors can tour exhibits on the area's pre-lake history. The huge picture window provides a spectacular view of the Gravois Arm of the lake. Open daily; hours vary. Free. (573) 964-1008; www.willmorelodge.com.

state parks

Ha Ha Tonka State Park. Route 1, Box 113–M, Camdenton, MO 65020. Accessible by water or land; located between mile markers 14 and 15 in the Big Niangua Arm. By car it's just west of Camdenton off US 54 on State Road D. By boat, be aware that the park's famous ruins are up a 300-step staircase from the docks below. The ruins are of an early 1900s castle and estate, conceived and developed by Robert McClure Snyder, a Kansas City businessman who acquired 2,500 acres of land and built his private retreat, importing Scottish stonemasons to ensure authentic construction techniques. In 1942 Ha Ha Tonka burned, the fire caused by a spark from one of its many fireplaces. The castle was gutted, and what remains today are the outside walls. The state of Missouri purchased the estate in 1978 and opened it to the public as a state park. The 3,527-acre grounds feature scenic trails, and there are natural bridges, caves, and other geologic wonders to be found here. Open for day use only, year-round, dawn to dusk. Free admission; no camping. &. (573) 346-2986; www.mostate parks.com/hahatonka.htm.

Lake of the Ozarks State Park. US 54 to Missouri Highway 42, east to Missouri Highway 134, Kaiser. Missouri's largest state park offers 17,000 acres and 85 miles of shoreline. The park provides rare public access to two beaches, plus boat-launching areas. There's even an on-site airport, with a 6,500-by-100-foot runway, plus terminal building, parallel taxiway, and fuel and tie-down service. Hiking trails, horseback riding, and four organized youth camps are offered. The free sand beaches provide swimming opportunities, and nearby picnicking and hiking areas are available. You can also reserve a picnic shelter here for large groups. Open daily, dawn to dusk, year-round.

Along the park's lakeshore is the Ozarks Aquatic Trail, designed for boaters, with stops marked by buoys. A free booklet keyed to the buoys is available at the park office. Naturalists present programs in an open-air amphitheater during the summer; the park also provides guided hikes and a variety of other programs. Information is available on site about the park and its nine trails. Free admission. Fee for reserving picnic shelter. Fee for camping; reservations required. &. (573) 348-2694; www.mostateparks.com.

where to shop

The Lake of the Ozarks has hundreds of shops, ranging from a factory outlet mall to strip malls, antiques and craft shops, and specialty stores. The places at which to browse and buy are too numerous to list here, but we've included a few unique shops that are worth a visit.

unusual boutiques, shops, and galleries

Casa de Loco Winery. 16952 North State Highway 5, Sunrise Beach. The unusual name for this winery comes from its stint in the 1950s and '60s as a home for mentally ill patients. A small museum at the winery—which was originally built as a private vacation getaway, not a mental institution—tells the story of the facility. It's a lovely spot to enjoy a glass of wine on the patio or a walk through the trails along the river bluff, and to pick up a few bottles of the more than fifty varieties offered here. (573) 374-8801; www.casadelocowinery.com.

Country Crossroads. 1 Palisades Village, US 54 and State Road KK, Osage Beach. The store is a Gold Key Dealer for Department 56 treasures and has current additions to collectibles, such as Heritage Village, Dickens Village, and other selections, as well as accessory pieces that go with them. Candles, quilts, afghans, and nautically themed gifts are also featured. Open daily year-round. (573) 348-0606; www.gifts-usa.com.

Ozark Bar-B-Que and Boutique. Highway 5 to State Road F to State Road TT, Sunrise Beach. Devour plates of excellent ribs, fries, and pies at the adjacent barbecue eatery and then go shopping at this unique store that sells a variety of clothing, sun gear, and souvenirs. There's everything from glitzy sequined caps to comical berets such as the "Carmen Miranda," complete with bananas and other assorted fruit. The upstairs and downstairs provide buyers with a wide array of beautiful handmade clothing, soft and gauzy dresses from Indonesia, and swimsuits to fit every figure. Open April through October. Hours vary. (573) 374-7769.

Victoria Station. 5465 Highway 54 (1.5 miles west of the Grand Glaize Bridge), Osage Beach. The selection here includes everything for your home and lots of gift items, such as cookbooks, note cards, and candles. If you like the nautical theme, you'll find a huge array of practical and whimsical items that bring the feel of the lake back home. The original flower arrangements are created by Misti Atkisson, the owners' daughter. Open year-round. (573) 348-2416.

where to eat

More than one hundred restaurants are located on the lake, and some have access by both water and land. The fare ranges from fast food to gourmet, from Italian and Mexican to French and American, along with Ozark-style delicacies such as catfish, trout, and barbecue. Sunday brunch is served at several restaurants, and many establishments offer hearty breakfasts and refreshing drinks. For a complete rundown of local eateries, check the *Lake of the Ozarks Restaurant Guide,* available from the Lake of the Ozarks Convention and Visitor Bureau, (800) 386-5253; www.funlake.com.

Andre's. 1622 Horseshoe Bend Parkway, Lake Ozark. Upscale dining with a view is the specialty at this cozy restaurant. Andre's is the only restaurant on the lake to specialize in Mediterranean cuisine. Chef/owner Andre Torres and his wife bring expertise acquired in Japan, Kenya, Tunisia, Switzerland, and France. Open daily for dinner year-round. $$$. (573) 365-2800; www.andreslakeoz.com.

Black Bear Lodge. Tan-Tar-A Resort, Golf Club, Marina, and Indoor Waterpark, State Road KK, Osage Beach. The lodge offers casual family dining in a hunt-club atmosphere for breakfast, lunch, dinner, and Sunday brunch. You can dine outdoors in warm weather. $$. (573) 348-3131; www.tan-tar-a.com.

Captain's Galley. Lake Road 5–89 at mile marker 31, Camdenton. Open for breakfast, lunch, and dinner, this floating restaurant is accessible by boat or car. The lunch and dinner menu features an assortment of nicely prepared sandwiches, salads, steaks, and fish. Breakfast can be omelets, homemade biscuits and gravy, pancakes, or waffles. Days/hours vary seasonally. $–$$. (573) 873-5227.

54 Diner. 4357 Highway 54, Osage Beach. Leave the twenty-first century behind when you step through the neon-pink and chrome doors of this truly 1950s establishment. Old 45 records line the walls while Bobby Vinton, Elvis, and other crooners of the era fill the airwaves. Breakfast is served all day. Lunch offers great items like The Big Bopper, a half-pound hamburger. $$. (573) 302-7261.

HK's Steak House. The Lodge of Four Seasons Championship Golf Resort and Spa, Lake Ozark. Rated one of the top steakhouses in the state by the Missouri Beef Industry Council Beef Backers, this restaurant prepares fine cuts of certified Angus beef over an elevated charcoal grill. $$$. (800) THE-LAKE or (573) 365-3000; www.4seasonsresort.com.

On the Rise Bakery & Bistro. 5439 Highway 54, Osage Beach. This classy European-style eatery is a momentary step away from the Ozarks. Try the European flatbread sandwiches that come on wood-fired, oven-roasted sourdough in five flavors, including Tuscan, Napa, Margherita, vegetable, and, of course, Ozark. For a refreshing treat on a hot afternoon, have a glass of Monkey Juice—bananas, strawberries, and orange juice served frozen with whipped cream. The homemade potato chips, served with Parmesan and peppercorn seasonings, are as memorable as the huge cinnamon rolls and other bakery items for carry-out. Open daily. $. (573) 348-4224; www.ontherisebakery.com.

Traditionally Stewart's Restaurant. 1151 Bagnell Dam Boulevard (US Business 54), Lake Ozark. If you're looking for a place that isn't upscale, trendy, or themed, this is the spot.

For breakfast try two biscuits and gravy for under four bucks. The "biscuits" are mammoth-size, mouthwatering, miniloaves that weigh about a pound each. If they didn't taste so good, you could probably use them for ballast.

While you're stuffing yourself, the person you're with can feast on an elephant-size cinnamon roll big enough for three or perhaps snarf down a "Number 6"—country pork tenderloin, two eggs, hash browns, and, yes, a biscuit and gravy.

Return for lunch. Then you can choose from simple, tasty offerings such as salads, sandwiches, and entrees like fried catfish and Ozark sugar-cured ham. Open year-round for breakfast and lunch. $–$$. (573) 365-2400.

Vista Grande. 4579 Highway 54, Osage Beach. The Schell family has owned this California-style Mexican restaurant at the lake since 1984. For those who like a milder salsa, the original recipe is smooth and gentle on the stomach. Of the many fun items on the menu, which also includes chicken and spinach chimichangas, is an unusual dish called La Mot. One half of this large burrito is smothered in salsa verde, the other half in salsa roja. Although it sounds French, La Mot is simply named for its creator Tom Schell. Mot is Tom spelled backwards. Open daily. $$. (573) 348-1231.

where to stay

There are numerous places to stay at the Lake of the Ozarks—from no-frills fishing cottages and motel rooms to upscale family resorts, houseboats, and beautiful condominiums with a view. Many places are family owned and offer waterfront housekeeping units and playgrounds for the kids. The east side of the lake is the more frequented, with plenty of places to stay and resorts large enough to hold huge conferences. The west side is less crowded, with fewer places to stay but with more natural beauty to see. Here's a sampling of some accommodations you may find to your liking:

Country Club Hotel and Spa. State Road HH and Carol Road, Lake Ozark. This world-class resort and racquet club offers luxurious amenities, unique services, and European decor that appeals to upscale tastes. Guests are treated to scenic views from their spacious rooms, suites, or villas. They can take advantage of amenities such as an excellent health club and fitness facility, indoor and outdoor swimming pools, indoor and outdoor tennis courts, racquetball courts, a restaurant and lounge with live New Orleans–style jazz, and more. $$$. (800) 964-6698 or (573) 964-2200; www.countryclubhotel.com.

Forever Resorts. Lake of the Ozarks Marina, Highway 5 North at the Niangua Bridge (north side of bridge and west side of Highway 5), Camdenton. If you're thinking about staying aboard a houseboat, you can rent one here. These floating homes range from 56 to 65 feet long and are equipped with everything you'll need, including four staterooms, a sofa bed, a dining area, a full kitchen with two refrigerators, a gas stove, and a microwave. There's even a television equipped with a VCR in case you get bored. All houseboats come with full-size sundecks, built-in waterslide, and gas barbecue grill. Your kitchen equipment, towels, and linens are provided. There are two bathrooms in case you bring along the whole family. A houseboat costs a bit more than a hotel but can sleep up to twelve people, so you can split the cost.

For the most peace and privacy, come during the week or in the off-season. Open daily March through November, weather permitting. $$$. (800) 255-5561; www.foreverresorts.com.

Hilty Inn Bed and Breakfast. 206 East Jasper, Versailles. This elegant, historic Victorian home offers a change from resort condominiums and cabins. Accommodations include four guest rooms with private baths and a special bridal suite. A full breakfast is served. A tearoom offers English high tea and gourmet dinners by reservation Monday through Friday. Open year-round. $$. (800) 667-8093 or (573) 378-2020; www.bbim.org/hilty.

Inn at Grand Glaize. Lake Road 54–40, Osage Beach. Located in the heart of Osage Beach, it offers 150 guest rooms and suites, a pool, a fitness center, and 13,000 square feet of meeting space under one roof. A marina, complimentary boat slips, and a restaurant and lounge with live entertainment are available to guests, along with a prime rib buffet and Sunday brunch. Open year-round. $$–$$$. (800) 348-4731 or (573) 348-4731; www.innatgrand glaize.com.

The Lodge of Four Seasons. Horseshoe Bend Parkway, Lake Ozark. Named one of *Condé Nast Traveler's* 50 Best Golf Resorts and ranked as a Connoisseur's Choice Resort by *Resort and Great Hotels Magazine,* the lodge is one of only four resorts in the Midwest to be so designated. The lodge's elegant Spa Shiki, which means *four seasons* in Japanese, has been featured on the *Today* show and is recognized as a "Best Value" spa in the Midwest by *Spa Magazine.* The resort also has a full-service marina, four swimming pools, children's programs, and a cinema. There are a variety of shops and beautifully landscaped Japanese gardens to stroll through. Several restaurants on the premises feature wines, fresh specialties, and scenic views. Open year-round. $$$. (800) THE-LAKE or (573) 365-3000; www.4seasons resort.com.

Lone Oak Point Resort. 25 Lone Oak Court, Sunrise Beach. The nicest resort on the west side of the lake can be reached by taking Highway 5 south from Versailles to Route F; then go left on State Road TT and follow the signs. Located on a wooded, nine-acre peninsula with a superb lake view, Lone Oak Point is owned by an environmentally aware couple who have maintained its architectural integrity by preserving the land around it and not overbuilding. The resort has an enclosed fitness spa with indoor pool, sauna, and exercise room. Other amenities are an outdoor pool, a wading pool, an enclosed fishing area, and covered boat stalls. Open March through November. $$–$$$. (573) 374-7992; www.funlake.com.

Tan-Tar-A Resort, Golf Club, Marina, and Indoor Waterpark. P.O. Box 188TT, State Road KK, Osage Beach, MO 65065. Open for more than forty years, Tan-Tar-A is a 420-acre resort with more than 950 guest rooms, 185 suites, and meeting space totaling 93,000 square feet. Tan-Tar-A has two championship golf courses and a full-service marina that includes parasailing, a fishing guide service, and boat rentals. Relax at the Arrowhead Pool, an outdoor pool complex with a 125-foot waterslide, toddler splash pool, and whirlpool. Other amenities include an indoor pool area with a fitness center and tanning beds, the Windjammer Spa & Salon, Timber Falls indoor waterpark, bowling, horseback riding, miniature golf, and tennis. The Black Bear Lodge offers a hunting lodge setting with hearty Ozark favorites. Enjoy fine dining and a beautiful sunset at the Windrose. Amenities for children include in-room babysitting and a kid's camp. Open year-round. $$–$$$. (800) 826-8272 or (573) 348-3131; www.tan-tar-a .com.

south

day trip 01

south

precious moments:
carthage, mo

carthage, mo

Founded in 1842, Carthage (drive south on U.S. Highway 71) was the site of the first major land battle of the Civil War after the U.S. Congress formally declared war against the South on July 5, 1861. Events of the battle are highlighted at the Battle of Carthage State Historic Site. The town was destroyed by guerrilla warfare in 1864. After the Civil War, Carthage drew investors and entrepreneurs, and by the end of the nineteenth century, it is reported to have had more millionaires per capita than any other U.S. city. Much of the wealth came from mining. There were rich deposits of lead, zinc, and a gray marble for which Carthage is famous. Elaborate Victorian architecture still stands to mark the heyday when the town had unlimited prosperity.

Today the Precious Moments Chapel brings thousands of visitors here annually. The Maple Leaf Festival, held in October, is another draw; it features a car show, a dog show, crafts, food, entertainment, a homes tour, a parade, a petting zoo, a quilt show, and the biggest parade in southwest Missouri.

You can take a driving tour of several of the Victorian homes in the area, all erected between 1870 and 1910. Many of them were built using Carthage marble, and a number of them have been converted to bed-and-breakfast accommodations. A free walking-tour brochure of the Courthouse Square Historic District is available from the Carthage Convention and Visitors Bureau. For a complete listing of things to see and do, contact the Bureau at 402 South

Garrison Street, Carthage, MO 64836; (417) 359-8181 or (866) 357-8687; www.visit-carthage
.com.

where to go

"Battle of Carthage" Civil War Museum. 205 North Grant Street. The museum features authentic artifacts and information about the battle at Carthage, as well as other skirmishes
around southwest Missouri. An elaborate, detailed mural of the event, painted by local artist
Andy Thomas, and a diorama depicting the battle are showcased here. There's also an enter-
taining exhibit on Carthage native Belle Star, the notorious female outlaw who rode with the
Jesse James gang. Open daily. Free. (417) 237-7060.

Battle of Carthage State Historic Site. Near East Chestnut and River Streets, east of downtown Carthage. This small park, less than eight acres, remains relatively untouched since the
battle here in 1861. A simple walking tour takes you over the grounds where both Union and
Confederate troops camped, fought, and died. Open daily. Free. (417) 682-2279; www.mo
stateparks.com/carthage.htm.

George Washington Carver National Monument. 5646 Carver Road, Diamond. The original cabin where this great African-American was born no longer stands, although a plaque
marks the spot. This 240-acre park pays tribute to Carver's achievements and distinctions as
one of America's great scientists, educators, and humanitarians. A visitor center and museum
tell the story of Dr. Carver's remarkable life, and a walking trail through the woods allows visitors to explore the natural world that Carver studied. It's open every day. Free. (417) 325-
4151.

Jasper County Courthouse. Between Third and Fourth Streets, 2 blocks east of Garrison
Street. Designed in 1894 by Maximilian Orlopp of New Orleans, the Romanesque Revival
structure was constructed of native stone quarried by the Carthage Stone Company. It was
completed in 1895 at a cost of $100,000 and is on the National Register of Historic Places.
Inside, visitors can see several displays of Civil War artifacts and a mural by local artist Low-
ell Davis entitled "Forged by Fire." (417) 358-0421 or (800) 404-0421; www.visit-carthage
.com.

The Mud Puddle. 311 South Main Street. Located inside the Emporium on the west side of
the courthouse square, this artist studio highlights the work of potter Helen Ryan and her son
Graham. You will often find mother and son dueling it out on the two potter's wheels inside.
Take time to talk with them while they work. They know more about Carthage than just about
anyone around. Closed Sunday. (417) 358-5620.

Powers Museum. 1617 West Oak. Made possible through a gift from one of Carthage's
most prominent citizens, this museum explores the history of southwest Missouri and hosts

numerous touring exhibits. An adjacent library houses genealogical records and archives, and a gift shop offers a great selection of regional books and gift items. Maps for Route 66 and other tourism brochures are available. Open mid-March through December. Closed Monday. Free. (417) 358-2667.

Precious Moments Chapel. 480 Chapel Road. This is Samuel J. Butcher's "gift of thanksgiving to the Lord." Murals covering 5,000 square feet depict scenes from the Old and New Testaments. The Precious Moments Art Gallery showcases the history behind Precious Moments, original pieces of art by local artists, and personal family memorabilia. The visitor center is patterned after a European village. Cottage- and castle-like structures within the village house several shops. Gospel and bluegrass music shows are presented several times daily. The Fountain of Angels show is a water display choreographed to music and light. The Precious Moments Collectors Christmas Weekend, held the first weekend in December, features a candlelight service, dinner, classes, and tours of the Butcher home. Open daily. Free to tour Chapel. (800) 543-7975; www.preciousmoments.com.

where to eat

Rose Garden Tea Room. 319 South Main Street. Located inside A Little More Pizzazz, this friendly tearoom serves homemade lunches and desserts Monday through Friday. $. (417) 358-1200.

where to stay

Grand Avenue Bed and Breakfast. 1615 Grand Avenue. This Queen Anne Victorian home features spacious and elegant rooms with amenities that range from rooms with queen-size beds and private baths to a room with king-size bed and large private bath with Jacuzzi. A full breakfast is served in the formal dining room. There's also a pool available for guests. Group discounts are available with the rental of four or more rooms. Special packages and murder mystery weekends are also offered. $$. (888) 380-6786 or (417) 358-7265; www .grand-avenue.com.

The Leggett House. 1106 Grand Avenue. Completed in 1901, this Victorian Carthage stone house offers five large rooms, an elevator, private or shared bath, and full breakfast in the formal dining room. The decor features beveled and leaded curved windows, an open staircase, paneled entry hall, and mosaic-tiled solarium with marble fountain. $$. (417) 358-0683; www.leggetthousebb.com.

southwest

day trip 01

southwest

apple cider, wildlife, and history:
louisburg, ks; marais des cygnes
wildlife area (la cygne, ks);
fort scott, ks; pittsburg, ks

When sojourning in southeast Kansas, remember that people here like things simple, especially food. Fried chicken or chicken-fried is the featured cuisine in many places. If you simply
surrender yourself to iceberg lettuce rather than radicchio and don't expect Chez Panisse
cuisine, you'll be quite happy here.

Southeast Kansas is filled with stores that tout themselves as antiques shops but in actual-
ity are crammed wall to wall with flea-market "junque." Just as long as you know what to expect,
it's fun to browse and you might discover an occasional treasure, but don't expect a Sotheby-
style find.

Southeast Kansas does have unexpected charm. In small towns, such as Chanute, tree-
lined cobblestone streets, gorgeous old homes, and whole city blocks have been preserved.
Southeast Kansans take pride in their historic heritage, and the area holds many architecturally significant structures—including one of singularly weighty importance called Big Brutus.

louisburg, ks

where to go

Louisburg Cider Mill. Take U.S. Highway 69 to Kansas Highway 68, then travel west for
4 miles. If the idea of cold apple cider, fresh-baked bread, and homemade cider doughnuts intrigues you, this is the place to go for a quick getaway. The store displays cider

products and natural foods in old-time barrels and cases to give the feeling of a country emporium. The warm, friendly atmosphere makes you want to linger all day. While you're there, don't forget to sample the doughnuts. These cakelike goodies, made with cider, have a marvelous texture. You can watch the doughnuts being made and then take home the results.

The cider mill is also the home of the Lost Trail Root Beer Company. This special root-beer brew is refined in eastern Kansas from a family recipe passed down through generations to the present owners. The soft drink is a real thirst quencher on a Kansas scorcher. Also try the Lost Trail Sasparilla, introduced for the bicentennial of the Lewis and Clark Expedition, which passed about 50 miles north of Louisburg.

Apples are pressed every day except Friday and Sunday from September through November. The store is open from 9:00 a.m. to 6:00 p.m. seven days a week except Thanksgiving and Christmas. Free tours are available in fall. (800) 748-7765 or (913) 837-5202; www.louisburgcidermill.com.

Powell Observatory. Just off 263rd Street and US 69 (3 miles northwest of Louisburg). Run by the Astronomical Society of Kansas City, Powell Observatory houses a 30-inch computer-controlled telescope for public viewing of the night skies from May to October. Located in Lewis-Young Park, the facility has a heated classroom (with restrooms) attached to the 20-foot domed observatory, where star-observing parties are held twice a month. There is also a Junior Astronomers Group for kids ten to seventeen. Children should be at least 36 inches tall to use the big scope and old enough to understand what they're seeing. Free. (913) 438-3825; www.askconline.org.

marais des cygnes wildlife area (la cygne, ks)

Those who have an eye for the unexpected can find wonder in the beauty of the Marais des Cygnes Wildlife Area. Located outside La Cygne in the picturesque floodplain of eastern Kansas, the refuge occupies more than 7,000 acres of man-made marshes rippling with natural lakes and laced with miles of rivers and creeks.

The most wonderful thing about Marais des Cygnes, other than its natural beauty, is that it is only an hour south of Kansas City on US 69. The area is a resting place for migratory waterfowl and other birds. Primitive camping is available, as well as hunting and fishing with the proper license.

The refuge takes it name from the Marais des Cygnes River, meaning "marsh of the swans," a title bestowed by the early French trappers who discovered it. Ironically, there is a good chance that what the trappers saw were not swans, but white pelicans that migrate through the area each spring. Flocks of these graceful, long-billed creatures can be seen floating in the water in early May, and their presence in the marsh pool, tinted a rosy amber by the setting sun, creates a surrealistic splendor not unlike that found in the marshes and swamps of the southern United States.

Ducks, geese, herons, egrets, and birds of prey can be spotted in the marshy area. During spring and fall migration, the temporary population of migrating ducks may reach 150,000. So far, 300 species of birds have been sighted at Marais des Cygnes, and about 115 species, including mallards, blue- and green-winged teal, and Canada geese, nest here.

As for fishing, it's plentiful in spring when crappies and catfish abound. At this time of year, you can often see huge spawning carp leaping out of the water, courting each other in happy twosomes. They're wonderful to watch but not so good for angling—they're so wrapped up in each other that dangling bait holds little appeal.

The fishing draws people who stand along the marsh banks for much of the day, hoping to catch their evening meal. Those driving campers park alongside the water and sit in lawn chairs, casting in their lines at twilight.

Across from the refuge on US 69 is Trading Post, a spot that played an important role as a rendezvous for a pro-slavery gang in the 1850s. In fact, the entire Marais des Cygnes area figured prominently in the Kansas struggle for statehood from 1851 to 1861. Here the pro- and antislavery forces fought over whether the territory should enter the Union as a free or slave state. In 1858 a gang of pro-slavers massacred eleven free-state men near Trading Post. The men became martyrs to the abolitionist cause, and the site of their deaths is a registered National Historic Landmark called the Marais des Cygnes Massacre Memorial Park. It's 5 miles east of US 69 at Trading Post in Linn County.

Marais Des Cygnes Wildlife Area is free to tour and is open daily. It's managed by the Kansas Department of Wildlife and Parks, 16382 US 69, Pleasanton, KS 66075. The Marais Des Cygnes Refuge office number is (913) 352-8941; call ahead for the bird count before you go.

Adjacent to the state wildlife area is the Marais des Cygnes National Wildlife Refuge. Managed by the U.S. Fish and Wildlife Service, it's unique for its abundance of large tracts of bottomland hardwood forest. Common species are pin and burr oak, pecan, walnut, and hickory. More than thirty-five species of warblers have been documented during the spring migration. The best viewing is usually in May in forested areas. Open daily. Free. (913) 352-8956; www .fws.gov/maraisdescygnes.

where to go

Somerset Ridge Vineyard. Off K–68, between Louisburg and Paolo. Licensed in 2001, this boutique winery has about ten labels produced from the 5,000 vines that the Reynolds family planted in 1998. They invite guests to their tasting room Wednesday through Sunday all year round, but especially during Oktoberfest weekends. (913) 491-0038; www.somersetridge.com.

where to stay

Cedar Crest Lodge. Pleasanton. If you can't get enough of the natural beauty of the great outdoors of this region, spend the night with Matt and Laura Cunningham at Cedar Crest

Lodge. Their 7,000-square-foot home is situated on 113 acres of rolling hills, trees, and ponds. Their eleven guest rooms reflect their love of travel, and Laura is a great cook, preparing a breakfast you will remember for a long time. If you like to paint and decorate, ask them about their painting seminars. Or, if you need a massage or other spa treatment, they can make arrangements for that as well. Matt and Laura have children, and they will welcome your well-behaved children as well. $–$$. (913) 352-6533 or (866) 233-2700; www.cedarcrestlodge.com.

fort scott, ks

All along the Overland Trails, U.S. Cavalry forts, such as Fort Scott, sprang up to defend western settlement. Between 1838 and 1845 a military road was constructed through the Indian Territory to connect Fort Leavenworth in Kansas and Fort Gibson in Oklahoma. Throughout the years the road was traveled by soldiers, immigrants, Native Americans, outlaws, and traders.

Today the old military road no longer exists, but modern US 69 and other connecting pathways located near its original route have been designated the Frontier Military Scenic Byway. Fort Leavenworth and Fort Scott, two of the remaining historic Kansas forts that lie along that route, are open to tour today.

From April to December the restored military fort hosts a series of special events featuring activities that portray a vivid picture of life on a frontier post during the nineteenth century. In June the annual Good Ol' Days hosts a whirlwind of activities for the entire family, with plenty of food, fun, crafts, and entertainment.

One of Fort Scott's most famous residents was internationally acclaimed photographer, filmmaker, and poet Gordon Parks, born here in 1912. Not until 2003 did the city of Fort Scott finally pay tribute to this accomplished African American, first with a permanent exhibit in the gallery space of Mercy Health Center and more recently with the Gordon Parks Center for Cultural Diversity at Fort Scott Community College. An annual celebration in October honors his contribution to the city of Fort Scott and the world.

From April 1 through mid-December, the Fort Scott Tourist Information Center (located off the US 69 bypass adjacent to the fort) offers refreshments, along with information about theme weekends, special living history programs, and seasonal celebrations. It also features Dolly the Trolley tours, which take visitors through the historic city, including Fort Scott National Cemetery. The tours are completely narrated and leave hourly from the center, beginning at 10:00 a.m. Haunted tours are offered in October. You can also inquire about bus tours for schools, churches, and youth or civic organizations. For information: Fort Scott Chamber of Commerce, P.O. Box 205, Fort Scott, KS 66701; (800) 245-FORT; www.fortscott.com.

where to go

Fort Scott Jubilee. Memorial Hall, Third Street and National Avenue. Regional and national performers take the stage every Saturday night for an exciting, fun show that is great country music entertainment. Bus tours are welcome. (800) 245-FORT.

Fort Scott National Historic Site. Old Fort Boulevard. The restored 1842 Frontier Military Fort was built to keep peace between the Indians and the settlers. The troops wound up policing the plains, supplying Union armies during the Civil War, and protecting railroad workers in the 1870s. A major tourist attraction that brings visitors from around the world, Fort Scott is the only completely restored frontier fort of the pre–Civil War period in the United States. Now designated a National Historic Site, the fort is located right in the center of the city, within walking distance of many shops and dining establishments.

Fort Scott's eighteen structures, including a hospital, a guardhouse, a bakery, and barracks, tell the story of the mounted Dragoons, "bleeding Kansas," and the Civil War. Open for self-guided tours year-round; closed Thanksgiving, Christmas, and New Year's Day. &. Fee. (620) 223-0310; www.nps.gov/fosc.

The Gordon Parks Center for Culture and Diversity. Fort Scott Community College. 2108 South Horton. Honoring one of the city's most accomplished residents and one of the world's leading photographers, writers, and filmmakers, this facility on the campus of Fort Scott Community College is a resource for those who wish to explore social issues such as racism and poverty and understood how those issues influence the arts. Programs throughout the year delve into these subjects, and exhibits include the results of an annual photo contest and materials from Parks's private collection. Open Monday through Friday. Free. (800) 874-3722, ext. 515; www.gordonparkscenter.org.

Gordon Parks Photo Exhibit. Mercy Health Center Foundation, 401 Woodland Hills Boulevard. Famed photographer Gordon Parks, a native of Fort Scott, donated twenty-seven photographs and five poems to the Mercy Health Center Foundation upon the opening of a new wing in 2002. His work has appeared in *Life* and *Vogue* magazines, focusing on social injustice, poverty, and civil rights. A walking tour brochure of the Parks collection is available at the information desk. Free. (620) 223-7026.

Historic Trolley Tour. Fort Scott Tourist Information Center, off US 69 adjacent to the fort. You can start your sightseeing here with the guided Trolley Tour, which leaves every hour on the hour, 10:00 a.m. to 4:00 p.m. except at noon. The tour takes you past historic attractions, striking architecture, and landmarks. The trolley runs from mid-March through mid-November. Fee. (800) 245-FORT.

National Cemetery. Get directions to the cemetery from the Fort Scott Tourist Information Center, off US 69 adjacent to the fort. The National Cemetery is older than Arlington and just as historically important. Indian scouts buried here include many with memorable names and histories. Soldiers interred on these grounds include black infantrymen from the country's first Colored Volunteer Infantry. Free. (800) 245-FORT.

Victorian Downtown. From Old Fort Boulevard to Sixth Street. Walking-tour information is available from the Fort Scott Tourist Information Center, off US 69 adjacent to the fort. The 6-block downtown area is on the National Register of Historic Places. Buildings from the period

1860 to 1919 have been restored and are the architectural showpiece of the city. Many homes feature ornate woodwork designs of gingerbread, stained and leaded glass, turrets, hitching posts, and stepping-stones for carriages. (800) 245-FORT.

where to shop

The Country Cupboard. 12 North Main Street. The largest gift and craft shop in the area, this store sells country crafts, collectibles, and gift items. The adjacent Victorian Charm annex features new Victorian-inspired merchandise. Closed Sunday. (620) 223-5980.

Sekan Occasion Shops. 2210 South Main Street. Gifts galore can be found here, from wedding gifts and Cherished Teddies to Precious Moments memorabilia and flowers. Closed Sunday. (620) 223-5190.

where to eat

Mayberry's Restaurant. 101 State Street. Home-style cuisine is served here, with menu offerings that vary from stacked sandwiches and barbecue items to salads, steaks, and specialty entrees. Daily specials and senior specials are also featured. Open daily. $. (620) 223-1995.

where to stay

The Lyons' Victorian Mansion and Spa. 742 South National Avenue. Gracious hospitality is the hallmark here. Guest suites can accommodate couples, families, business travelers, and anyone looking for a home away from home. Seven guest rooms, some with claw-foot whirlpool tubs, are spacious. A full breakfast is served complete with country-fresh eggs, garden herbs, and produce. Other amenities include an in-room telephone with dataport, dedicated computer lines, a fax, a copier, and an answering service.

Behind the mansion, accessed via a lovely flower garden, is a guest house with three additional rooms as well as spa services. A hot tub may be reserved for special occasions.

The "Sweet Suite Retreat" features two nights, a complimentary bottle of champagne, a bag of fine chocolates, and a bouquet of long-stemmed roses. It includes a breakfast basket in your room, or you can join guests in the dining room.

The Lyons' Victorian Mansion specializes in event planning for business and social occasions, ranging from birthday parties and teas to sumptuous nine-course Victorian feasts for groups of up to fifty. Business retreats, murder mystery weekends, an on-site spa, and educational tours are also offered. $$–$$$. (800) 78-GUEST or (620) 223-3644; www.lyons mansion.com.

pittsburg, ks

The "Fried Chicken Capital of Southeast Kansas," Pittsburg has several chicken emporiums from which to choose. It is also famous for being the jumping-off point for the attraction known as Big Brutus, a sixteen-story-high, one-of-a-kind mining shovel located just southwest of Pittsburg near West Mineral, Kansas.

Pittsburg is also known as the "Gateway to the Ozarks" and is located south of Fort Scott on US 69. At first glance you might not know that this town has a lot of Old World drama behind it. Pittsburg was actually an early-twentieth-century settlement of Europeans who came to work in the coal mines. Those who live here today are the descendants of people who traveled to this part of Crawford County from Sicily, Austria, and Bohemia.

Pittsburg, along with the tiny town of Frontenac, which borders it to the north, were Crawford County mining communities that appealed to those who wanted to escape poverty, oppression, and political injustice. Lured by the promise of work, the immigrants who toiled in the mines brought an unusual mix of cultural and ethnic backgrounds to southeast Kansas. Between 1880 and 1940 more than 31,000 people from fifty-two countries flocked here to begin deep-shaft mining, the most dangerous method of digging coal out of the earth.

It was hard work, with little pay, but those who endured caught the attention of the Socialist Party in the early 1900s. The European miners, who tended to be pro-labor, vigorously supported the unions, strikes, and socialism that became closely tied to the coal industry. Eventually the area became known as the Little Balkans region because of the number of Europeans who settled here.

Crawford County's colorful past is celebrated with a number of festivals. Little Balkans Days, held on Labor Day weekend, features boccie ball, a parade, polka music, arts-and-crafts booths, and ethnic foods. For information: Crawford County Convention and Visitors Bureau, 117 West Fourth Street, P.O. Box 1115, Pittsburg, KS 66762. (800) 879-1112 or (620) 231-1212; www.visitcrawfordcounty.com.

where to go

Big Brutus. Six miles west of the junction of Kansas Highway 7 and Kansas Highway 102 and 0.25 mile south, West Mineral. You, too, can host a wedding, reception, private party, or family reunion outside—or inside—an eleven-million-pound Bucyrus Erie 1850 B mining shovel called Big Brutus. Just imagine how many hors d'oeuvres might fit inside Big Brutus's dipper, which is large enough to hold 150 tons! The behemoth reaches a height of sixteen stories and is the second-largest electric shovel in the world.

New technology in 1960 made surface mining economical. The Pittsburg & Midway Coal Mining Company purchased Big Brutus at a cost of $6.5 million—not to dig coal but to remove the dirt and rocks covering the coal seams. From 1962 to 1974, more than nine million tons of coal was gouged out of the dirt, laying bare the land and leaving hundreds of "strip pits" behind. In 1974, when it was no longer cost-effective to operate Big Brutus, the steam shovel was shut down.

The legacy of Big Brutus could have been an environmental disaster; instead, it is a rare instance of a mined land reclamation success story. The Pittsburg & Midway Coal Mining Company donated the area surrounding Big Brutus to the Kansas Department of Wildlife and

Parks, which, in turn, has reclaimed the 14,250 acres of land as a haven for hunting and fishing.

The Big Brutus Visitors Center has displays and information surrounding the colorful history and heritage of the region. You can take a self-guided tour or climb up Big Brutus's boom, but you have to be at least thirteen years old. There are primitive camping facilities and RV hookups on site, plus picnic tables and hot showers to meet the needs of campers and visitors. Open daily. Fee. (620) 827-6177; www.bigbrutus.org.

Crawford County Historical Museum. Atkinson Road and Twentieth Street on US 69. The colorful history of Crawford County is featured in interesting exhibits that include vintage clothing, coal-mining and farming artifacts, photographs, and horse-drawn vehicles. Miss America 1968 was from this area, and her handmade dress with thirty pounds of sequins is also on display. Outdoor displays include a one-room schoolhouse, an authentic neighborhood grocery store, and a coal-mining steam shovel. Open Thursday through Sunday afternoons or by appointment. Free. (620) 231-1440 or (620) 231-4145.

Hickory Creek Farms. McCune, KS. You're going to have to call for directions on this or print the map from the Web site, but it's worth the effort to spend a lovely fall afternoon lost in the hay maze, picking out pumpkins, or taking a hay ride. Each year the Zimmerman family, who has lived here for five generations, adds new and different things. Admission charged. (620) 632-4294; www.hickorycreekfarms.com.

Hotel Stilwell. Seventh Street and Broadway. Built in 1880, the historic hotel has hosted guests who have included William Jennings Bryan, Eugene Debs, Susan B. Anthony, and Theodore Roosevelt. The building was restored in 1997 by the Stilwell Heritage and Educational Foundation in partnership with MetroPlains Development, Inc., and is on the National Register of Historic Places. The architectural design features a grand stone entry flanked by brick columns on the first floor, wide bay windows, a circular leaded skylight, generous ornate plasterwork, and stained-glass windows. The upper floors have been converted to apartments for senior citizens, while the first-floor historic common areas are open to the public to tour. Open weekdays and weekends by appointment. Free to tour. (620) 231-1907.

Mined Land Wildlife Area. Several hundred water-filled former strip pits dot the Mined Land Wildlife Area, a 14,000-acre region with about 1,500 acres of public waters near the communities of West Mineral and Pittsburg. More than 200 lakes in the area are managed for fishing. Lakes range in size up to fifty acres. Sport fish are abundant here, with largemouth bass, spotted bass, channel catfish, walleye, and a specially stocked lake trout being favorites of anglers.

Native grasses have been reintroduced here, along with a variety of wildlife. Several marshes have been constructed to attract ducks and geese.

With its diversity of terrain and animal life, the Mined Land Wildlife Area is becoming popular with photographers and wildlife observers, as well as hunters. Quail, white-tailed deer, and wild turkey are found in abundance, as are raccoons, muskrats, bobcats, coyotes, and a herd of rather photogenic buffalo. Call for location and directions. (620) 231-1212 or (620) 231-3173 (Department of Wildlife and Parks); www.kdwp.state.ks.us.

Pittsburg State University (PSU)/Kansas Technology Center. 1701 South Broadway. This campus of 6,600 students on the south end of town has extensive landscaping, outdoor sculptures, a hike/bike trail, and other impressive features. The newest attraction on campus is the Veterans Memorial Amphitheatre, which features a number of patriotic bronzes, a half-scale replica of the Vietnam Veterans Memorial in Washington, D.C., and seating for 250. PSU sponsors a Visiting Writers Series, a Performing Arts and Lecture Series, and a Solo and Chamber Music Series. For information on upcoming events: (620) 235-4122; www.pitt state.edu.

where to eat

As the "Fried Chicken Capital of Southeast Kansas," Pittsburg is home to ethnic-influenced restaurants that serve fried chicken with German potato salad, coleslaw with garlic dressing, and peppers, tomatoes, and bread. This custom began in 1934, when Anne Pichler's husband was injured in the mines. Born near Budapest, the woman best known as Chicken Annie had a family to raise and started selling her fried chicken out of her home to make a living. Eventually Chicken Annie opened her restaurant, which became so famous that it began to draw competitors. In 1943 Mary Zerngast opened her fried chicken restaurant across the road from Chicken Annie's. Chicken Mary and Chicken Annie went head to head as the famous southeast Kansas chicken wars heated up. Today, these and other family-owned restaurants still compete for business as the fowl play continues. The chicken places open at 4:00 p.m. for dinner only on weekdays; those open on Sunday offer dinner from 11:00 a.m. to 8:00 p.m. They include the following:

Barto's Idle Hour. 201 South Santa Fe, Frontenac. Closed Sunday and Monday. $$. (620) 232-9834.

Chicken Annie's of Girard. Kansas Highway 5 east of Girard. Closed Monday and Tuesday. $$. (620) 724-4090.

Chicken Annie's Original. 1143 East 600th Avenue, Pittsburg. Closed Monday. $$. (620) 231-9460.

Chicken Mary's. 1133 East 600th Avenue, Pittsburg. Closed Monday. $$. (620) 231-9510.

Gebhardt Chicken Dinners. 124 North 260th Street, Mulberry. Open Friday through Monday. $$. (620) 764-3451.

Pichler's Chicken Annie's®. 1271 South 220th Street, Pittsburg. Closed Monday. $$. (620) 232-9260.

other restaurants of interest

Jim's Steak House. 1912 North Broadway. Established in 1938, this third-generation family-owned and -operated restaurant has been in the same location for seventy years. Renowned in the area for its juicy steaks, the restaurant also offers chicken and seafood specialties. Jim's serves dinner only, starting at 4:00 p.m. Closed Sunday. $$–$$$. (620) 231-5770.

Otto's Cafe. 711 North Broadway. Built in 1945 as an annex to old Hotel Stilwell, this dining establishment is a throwback to the days when coffee shops were plentiful. Simple food, prepared well, is what you'll find here. Breakfast features everything from omelets and waffles to French toast and biscuits and gravy. If you're in the mood for Otto's excellent version of fried chicken, you can have it for lunch or dinner. Leave room for homemade dessert. Open for breakfast, and lunch. Closed Sunday. $–$$; (no cards). (620) 231-6110.

where to shop

Frontenac Bakery. 211 North Crawford, Frontenac. Established in 1900, this bakery has had only four owners in more than 100 years. Bryan and Jolynne Hite recently purchased the community landmark, where Jolynne remembers coming as a child for the Italian breads and bread sticks that are famous in this part of the state. The Hites have remodeled the building and welcome retail buyers on Saturday and Sunday. (620) 231-7908.

Pallucca & Son. 207 East McKay, Frontenac. This off-the-beaten-path find is a fun place to stop and shop. Opened in 1912, Pallucca's is family-owned and -operated and specializes in imported Italian foods. The meat department carries everything you need for making a great Italian sandwich, from large imported Italian hams to handmade Italian sausage. Fine pasta, dessert items, candies, and sauces from Italy line the shelves, along with American-made products. Open daily. (620) 231-7700.

where to stay

The Old Miner's Guest House. 324 East 126 Highway. This former coal camp house from the 1890s has been moved to the site overlooking a former strip pit that's now filled with water and hundreds of fish. A Flat John boat and paddleboat are available for your use. The two-bedroom home has a queen-size bed made from hundred-year-old barn beams. Next door is a 1940s milking barn that holds dried herbs and flowers grown on site. Antiques, candles, and bath salts are also for sale here. $. (620) 231-2155; www.bbonline.com/ks/oldminer.

day trip 02

southwest

safaris and suppers:
ottawa, ks; garnett, ks;
chanute, ks

Don't head out on this trip expecting blockbuster attractions. The towns listed here all have shady, tree-lined streets and historic old homes and buildings that have been lovingly preserved. In this part of Kansas, pharmacies are still called drugstores, and most of them have real soda fountains that serve limeades and lemonades made from fresh-squeezed fruit. Two of the biggest reasons to head this way are a unique bed-and-breakfast that is a collectors' extravaganza and a museum that is the only one of its kind in America.

ottawa, ks

From Kansas City head south on Interstate 35 to Ottawa, where you'll find everything from flea-market merchandise and old-fashioned soda fountains to historic sites commemorating "Naked Voters."

Ottawa University, established in 1883, boasts architectural assets, as does the Franklin County Courthouse and the restored 200 block of the central business district, listed on the National Register of Historic Places.

Ottawa has plenty of shops that specialize in furniture, collectibles, primitives, and "junque." You may want to time your visit with Skunk Run Days, the second weekend in June. Or if you're more inclined to head for the water, you might want to visit the town on your way to Pomona or Melvern Reservoir.

southwest day trip 02

Now, about the "Naked Voters." This is a stop along the way on Franklin County Historical Society's Northeast Tour through Peoria, Wellsville, and other areas around Ottawa. This site commemorates forty-three free-state men who were so desperate to cast their ballots against slavery in 1858 that they skinny-dipped their way to the polls.

Granted, there's not much to see there now, but just imagine forty-three zealous voters fording three turbulent creeks to vote. Ponder, if you will, whether Americans today would go to such lengths. Would they strip off all their clothing, drop it on the bank, and plunge into a creek—just to enact a new law? Would they show up naked at the polls, letting their birthday suits drip dry in the open air? Of course not: They'd be arrested. Yet in 1858 the free-staters who made it to the polls defeated the pro-slavery issue by a "bare" minimum. A kind neighbor, who did not require that they dress for dinner, fed them before they returned home. For information: Franklin County Convention and Tourism Bureau, 2011 East Logan Street, P.O. Box 203, Ottawa, KS 66067; (785) 242-1411; www.visitottawakansas.com.

where to go

Dietrich Cabin. South of the Ottawa Library in Ottawa's City Park (Fifth and Main Streets). The 1859 cabin is a memorial to a courageous couple who suffered hardships on the Kansas frontier. It has been moved from its original location to the park and is open to tour on weekends. Free. (785) 242-1232 or (785) 242-1411.

Elizabeth "Grandma" Layton Exhibit. Wellsville City Library, 115 West Sixth Street, Wellsville. Elizabeth Layton was a remarkable artist whose work gained recognition in her later years. Having been through years of therapy, shock treatment, and drugs to find relief from depression, she tried drawing self-portraits to lift her emotional spirits. So effective was the relief that "Grandma" Layton went on to become a painter. Her work has been represented in numerous galleries and museums around the country, including the Smithsonian's American Art Museum in Washington, D.C. Through her artwork Grandma Layton spoke out against racism, commercialism, and nuclear war. Free. Closed Sunday. (785) 883-2870.

Franklin County Courthouse. Third and Main Streets. Built in 1893 by noted architect George P. Washburn, the courthouse features a complex, steep-pitched hip roof with intersecting gables and four square corner towers. It has a four-sided clock, bell tower, and a statue of Justice that stands over the west gable. Tours are available from the Franklin County Historical Society. Free. (785) 242-1232.

Midland Railway Excursion Train. P.O. Box 412, Baldwin City, KS 66006-0412. The Midland Railway is located just north of Ottawa on U.S. Highway 59. It operates an authentic re-creation of an American local passenger train and makes a 7-mile round-trip through scenic farmland and woods, using early-twentieth-century vintage coaches. Open mid-May through November. Call for hours and reservations. Fee. In Kansas City call (913) 371-3410. Otherwise call (800) 651-0388 or (785) 594-6982; www.midland-ry.org.

Old Depot Museum. One block west of Main Street on Tecumseh Street. Operated by the Franklin County Historical Society, the two-story limestone building was constructed in 1888 as a depot for the Kansas City, Lawrence, and Southern Kansas Railway. Exhibits here include a model railroad and displays highlighting a number of Franklin County historical events. Fee. Open daily. (785) 242-1250; www.old.depot.museum.

Ottawa Suzuki Strings. P.O. Box 99, Ottawa, KS 66067. Students from throughout the area learn to play stringed instruments via this internationally renowned teaching method at the Carnegie Cultural Center in Ottawa and play at any number of community events. Nightly performances are held in June and July as professional musicians travel from across the country to work with these local students. Concerts are offered free or for a nominal fee, providing a phenomenal opportunity to experience world-class musical performances in a small town. Check the Web site for concert dates and program details. (785) 242-0242; www.ottawa suzukistrings.org.

where to shop

Ottawa Antique Mall and Restaurant. 202 Walnut. Housed in a former soft-drink bottling plant, the mall features aisles of collectibles and furniture, plus lots of flea market–style merchandise. There is also a full-service restaurant and soda fountain that serves homemade mashed potatoes and fresh-cut french fries. Closed Monday. (785) 242-1078.

where to eat

Allegre Pharmacy, Soda Fountain, and Luncheonette. 304 South Main Street. You can get nostrums for your nose or grab a quick bite before you hit the road. The soda fountain itself isn't the old-fashioned kind, but you can still get creamy malts, shakes, and sundaes that will fill you up. Closed Sunday. $. (785) 242-3092.

J&D Family Pharmacy. 601 Main Street, Wellsville. Sodas, malts, limeades, freezes, and hand-dipped ice cream can be enjoyed at the pharmacy's old-fashioned soda fountain, complete with a wonderful wooden-back bar featuring art nouveau stained glass. Closed Sunday. $. (785) 883-2462.

Potter's Wheel Coffeehouse. 2005 South Main Street, Ottawa. This is the place to come for great drinks, desserts, or a lunchtime snack, and also to pick up some pottery or jewelry by local artists; listen to live music of all genres; and enjoy a laugh with owner/artist Scott Dawson, whose comic strips about life in a coffeehouse decorate the walls. Open seven days a week from early to late. $. (785) 242-0900; www.thepotterswheelcoffeehouse.com.

garnett, ks

From Ottawa head south on US 59 to Garnett. This small community features three lakes, more than 1,000 acres of parks, a hiking/biking trail, an unusual bed-and-breakfast, and a small but interesting museum that displays works of regional artists and more. For more information: The Garnett Chamber of Commerce, 419 South Oak Street, Garnett, KS 66032; (785) 448-6767; www.garnettchamber.org.

where to go

Anderson County Courthouse. Garnett Town Square. Designed by prominent architect George P. Washburn, the courthouse was dedicated in 1902 and is listed on the National Register of Historic Places. A classic example of Romanesque architecture, it features a restored courtroom with stained-glass windows. Open weekdays. Free. (785) 448-6767.

Cedar Valley Reservoir. 7.5 miles west of Garnett, on Kentucky Road. The beautiful scenery here provides the perfect getaway, with floating docks, boat loading ramps, picnic areas, and wilderness and RV camping facilities. Free. Boating, fishing, and camping permits required. (785) 448-5496.

Crystal Lake, Veterans Memorial Park. South US 59, Garnett. This small lake features a quiet, shady park, complete with ducks and geese for feeding. Bird-watching, picnicking, and fishing are favorite pastimes of residents. Trout season is January through March, when fishing is permitted and prizes are given. Free. Fishing and camping permits required. (785) 448-5496.

Lake Garnett. North Lake Road, Garnett. The fifty-five-acre lake offers recreational facilities that include a golf course, campsites, sporting clay range, swimming pool, and much more. Free. Boating, fishing, and camping permits required. (785) 448-5496.

Mary Bridget McAuliffe Walker Art Collection. Garnett Public Library, 125 West Fourth Avenue. A rare collection of paintings, sculptures, prints, and drawings donated to Garnett by Maynard Walker features works by John Steuart Curry, Edouard Manet, and Jean Baptiste Corot. A special wing built on the library in 2001 showcases the work in a first-class setting. The conservators from Kansas City's Nelson-Atkins Museum of Art have restored many of the paintings. Docent tours are available by reservation. Free. Closed Sunday. (785) 448-3388.

Prairie Spirit Rail Trail. Kansas Department of Wildlife and Parks, 419 South Oak Street. This 50-mile trail from Ottawa to Iola passes through Garnett on what was once the Santa Fe Railroad right-of-way. It provides a picturesque hiking and biking excursion in and around the city. Motorized wheelchairs are welcome. Trail permits are not required inside city limits but are needed for youngsters under sixteen who venture outside town. Open daily during daylight hours. Free. &. (785) 448-6767; www.prairiespirittrail.org.

> ## supper with friends
>
> *There's probably no better place to dine on good, home-cooked food than at a church supper. Ottawa's churches and civic clubs are always open to visitors, who are invited to partake of weekly offerings like chicken and noodles, chili, ham and beans, beef stew, turkey, and fried chicken. The tab runs under $6 per person; children's meals are half price. That money often helps build libraries, provide for scholarships, or contribute to other community needs. And you'll join friends you never knew you had, elbow to elbow at the dinner table, while experiencing one of the true joys of living in small-town America.*
>
> *To get a schedule of suppers, visit the city Web site at www.visitottawakansas .com or call (785) 242–1411.*

Santa Fe Depot. Main Street and Eighth Avenue. Built during the Depression years, this depot saw the passage of many trains until its closing in 1974. Beautifully restored in 1996, it now serves as a trailhead for users of the Prairie Spirit Rail Trail. The depot visitor center provides tourism information and has exhibits of railroad memorabilia on display, along with a wildflower garden. Free. (785) 448-5496.

where to eat

Maloan's. Fourth Avenue and Oak Street. Housed in an 1883 building that was once a bank, the restaurant offers a fine-dining experience in a lovely setting that features high ceilings and oak furniture. Flavorful prime rib, steaks, and shrimp are favorites. Open Monday through Friday from 11:00 a.m. to 1:30 p.m. and Wednesday through Saturday evenings from 5:00 to 9:00 p.m. Sunday brunch is served from 10:00 a.m. to 1:00 p.m. $$. (785) 448-2616.

chanute, ks

Close your eyes. Imagine, if you will, that you are in the middle of deepest Africa. All around you is the sound of jungle drums and pounding hooves of thousands of zebras and wildebeests. Well, open your eyes, get in your car, and head for Chanute, home of the Martin and Osa Johnson Safari Museum. Exhibits here showcase the life of two of the most extraordinary explorers, naturalists, and photographers of the twentieth century.

For other tourist information, contact the Chanute Chamber of Commerce: 21 North Lincoln, Chanute, KS 66720; (877) 431-3350 or (620) 431-3350; www.chanutechamber.com.

where to go

Chanute Art Gallery. 17 North Lincoln. The gallery provides a showcase for local area artists and Kansas Prairie Printmakers, such as Birger Sandzen and Charles Capps. Recent acquisitions include etchings by Luigi Kasimir. Unique for a small town, the gallery has more than 1,000 square feet of exhibit space and includes a gift shop featuring handcrafted items and original art. Special exhibits change monthly. Closed Sunday. (620) 431-7807.

Chanute Historical Society Museum. 101 South Lincoln Street. Sports fans will enjoy the exhibits on former KU and NBA star Ralph Miller and on Paul Lindblad, who played for the Texas Rangers, Oakland Athletics, and New York Yankees. Both are from Chanute. Other exhibits focus on the railroad history of the area. The museum is located in the historic Flat-Iron Building, constructed in 1907. The unique wedge-shaped building has been home to the Western Union Telegraph, a drugstore, a tavern, and a confectionery. The museum is also the only outlet outside of retail stores to carry American Eagle Outfitter's new line of "Martin & Osa" clothing, inspired by the intrepid husband-and-wife explorer team. Open weekends or by appointment. (620) 431-0081 or (620) 431-1814.

The Martin and Osa Johnson Safari Museum. 111 North Lincoln Street. The number-one museum in Kansas, this repository of rare artifacts and memorabilia offers a look at Africa in the early part of the twentieth century, when it was still a mysterious, dark continent. At that time Africa was confined to the machinations of movie moguls, who plied the public with yarns about Tarzan the Apeman and mega-monkeys like King Kong. Yet deep in the heart of Kansas, in the little town of Chanute, there is the ultimate documentation of wilderness and cultures that have long since vanished from the earth.

At one time the cannibals of Borneo and game-choked savannas of Africa represented an overwhelming diversity of life on this planet. The early work of Martin and Osa Johnson captured the first photographic records of remote and little-known regions of the world in the early decades of the twentieth century. The intrepid Kansas couple were explorers in the same mold as Sir Richard Burton and Stanley and Livingstone. Their revealing photography, field journals, detailed expedition reports, and extensive correspondence—spanning fifty years—are showcased inside displays at the Martin and Osa Johnson Safari Museum.

The tangled forests of Borneo, the Congo, and the Solomons are displayed in a treasure trove of wildlife motion pictures, thousands of still photos, and an assortment of artifacts brought back from the primitive regions they described in their best-selling books and articles. The couple made two expeditions to the South Seas, in 1917 and 1919, and later ventured to Borneo. Barely managing to escape with their lives, they filmed the exploits of a cannibal chief and his band of merry men, who were much more interested in sampling the tasty specimens from Kansas than posing for the camera.

The Johnsons' extended voyages to Africa, coupled with their South Seas films, brought them global fame, during which time the Johnsons made *safari* and *simba* household words. To understand the couple's enormous popularity in the 1920s and 1930s, one has only to look at their friends: Charlie Chaplin gave them a one-reel film to show to the South Seas cannibals, and the great Harry Houdini held a going-away party in the couple's honor. George Eastman, founder of Eastman Kodak, traveled with the Johnsons on occasion, financially supporting one of their trips and making sure the Johnsons were adequately supplied with Kodak products. Supported by private membership (famed naturalist George Schaller and his wife are Honorary Life Members), the museum is getting national attention.

The Martin and Osa Johnson exhibit is located inside the restored Santa Fe Train Depot, where it shares space with a magnificent collection of masks and artifacts touted by *African Arts Magazine* as "the finest West African collection between Chicago and California."

Dioramas portray African art and artifacts from Mali, horned crocodile headdresses and wood carvings from Nigeria, carved masks from Guinea, 14-foot-high Sirige masks held in place by mouthpieces worn by warriors, and much more, plus a 10,000-volume natural history library and research facility that is open to the public to enjoy.

Educational programs on Africa, including special shows for groups of handicapped or visually impaired visitors, are also available. Do not miss the museum's extraordinary gift shop, which is filled with imported art and handcrafted items that you won't see elsewhere, unless you plan to travel to Africa sometime. Open daily. Fee. (620) 431-2730; www.safarimuseum.com.

Walking/Driving Tours of Historic Chanute. c/o The Chanute Office Of Tourism, 21 North Lincoln Street. There are twenty-four homes on the drive-by tour, and some are spectacular. The Greystone Estate (209 South Highland Street) was built in 1910 in the Italian Renaissance style. It features a red tile roof with dormers, redbrick walls, beveled and leaded glass in the main entrance, a carriage house, a garden house, reflecting pools, and a gazebo. Other homes in the area feature everything from Spanish-Mediterranean and art deco architecture to Queen Anne–Gothic Revival structures and "Painted Ladies." A second self-guided tour takes you through the history of twelve downtown businesses. (877) 431-3350 or (620) 431-3350; www.chanutechamber.com.

where to go

Cardinal Drug Store. 103 East Main Street. This old-fashioned drugstore is owned by Jim Chappell, who bought it in 1972. At the time, the soda fountain had been torn out to make more sales space. Chappell spent a lot of time looking for soda-fountain furniture and found an impressive array of furnishings that included a 1914 solid oak back bar complete with stained glass and enormous mirror, plus a 1937 marble fountain and equipment. Four high-seated chairs with arms and a 1908 solid brass cash register complete the illusion that you've just entered another era. Coca-Cola is made the old-fashioned way, using syrup and carbonated water. You can also get everything from sodas and sundaes to limeades and phosphates. The soda fountain is flanked by cabinets displaying old patent medicines, such as Lydia Pinkham's Blood Medicine, still in the original box. Dr. Miles' Heart Tonic and Regulator and a bottle of Scarless Liniment dating back to 1910 are among the curiosities. Closed Sunday. $. (620) 431-9150.

where to eat and stay

Tioga Suites Hotel and Safari Grill & Brewing Company. 12 East Main Street. This historic hotel that dates to 1926 has been lovingly restored by local businessman Todd Johnson, who also has a passion for home-brewed beer. Upper floors are still being remodeled but at press time twenty-one suites were complete. Suites are individually decorated, each named for a legendary Kansas figure—among them Wyatt Earp, Amelia Earhart, Dwight Eisenhower, and William Allen White. The decor of each suite is inspired by the figure for whom it is named. The second floor has a large deck/patio area, which is popular for murder mystery weekends and other special events.

But downstairs in the Safari Grill, Johnson's passion comes through in twelve original home brews and a selection of burgers, pastas, and other munchies to accompany the ales. Open Monday through Saturday, 11:00 a.m. to midnight, Sunday, 11:00 a.m. to 2:00 p.m. $. (620) 431-3343; www.tiogasuites.com.

The Red Pepper Restaurant. 116 West Main Street. Local ethnic cuisine of Chanute is provided by the Navarez family. Aunts, uncles, nieces, and nephews are involved in making corn tortillas and other original Mexican dishes. Try the chimichangas! Open for lunch and dinner, but closed for a few hours in mid-afternoon for siesta. Closed on Sunday. $. (620) 431-4380.

day trip 03

southwest

front porch to the flint hills:
ottawa, ks; williamsburg, ks;
lebo, ks; emporia, ks

This interesting day trip is one that hard-core foodies will like. It takes you to a truck stop, a barbecue joint, and an old-fashioned soda fountain where you can actually get a decent limeade.

Don't worry if you can't find the actual town of Lebo. You're basically looking for a big plateful of chicken-fried steak, and it can be found at a sprawling truckers' paradise called Beto Junction—which is designated as being in Lebo but is actually off U.S. Highway 75 at exit 155.

There's nothing much to do in Williamsburg but eat spicy pork ribs, play pool, and listen to the jukebox at Guy and Mae's Tavern. Ottawa, on the other hand, has great soda fountains, historic homes and buildings, lovely nature trails, and more.

ottawa, ks

For this excursion head south on I-35 to Ottawa (see Southwest from Kansas City, Day Trip 2).

williamsburg, ks

South of Ottawa, on I-35, is the dot-on-the-map town of Williamsburg. Its sole claim to fame is Guy and Mae's Tavern, which is worth a trip if you like hearty ribs and tasty sandwiches of beef and ham.

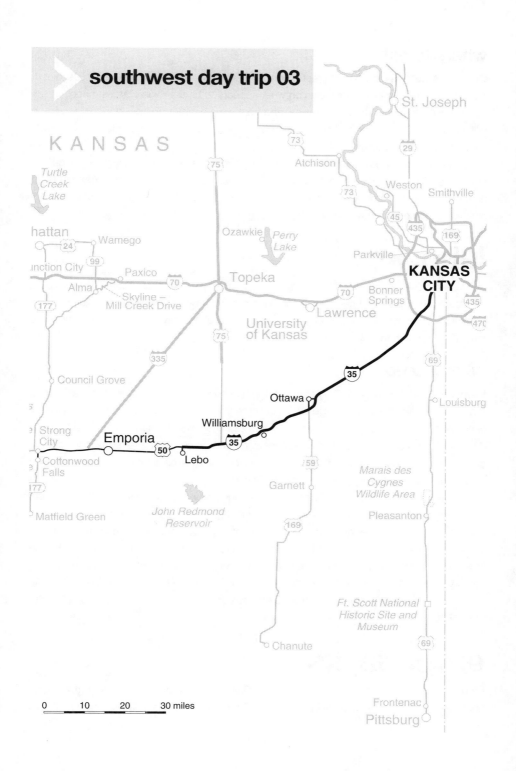

southwest day trip 03

KANSAS

Turtle
Creek
Lake

St. Joseph

73

29

Atchison

Weston   Smithville

73

45

435

169

Parkville

KANSAS
CITY

435

470

hattan

24

Wamego

99

nction City

Paxico

Alma

Skyline –
Mill Creek Drive

177

70

Topeka

Ozawkie   Perry
Lake

75

70

Bonner
Springs

Lawrence

University
of Kansas

69

Council Grove

335

75

35

Ottawa   Louisburg

Strong
City

Emporia

50

Lebo

Williamsburg

35

Cottonwood
Falls

59

177

Garnett

Marais des
Cygnes
Wildlife Area

Matfield Green

John Redmond
Reservoir

169

Pleasanton

Chanute

Ft. Scott National
Historic Site and
Museum

69

0   10   20   30 miles

Frontenac

Pittsburg

where to eat

Guy and Mae's Tavern. Main Street. There is no address for this unusual barbecue joint. It sits among some timeworn buildings on what appears to be the town's largest street. Inside you'll find thick sandwiches of lean beef and ham, plus hearty slabs of pork ribs served on butcher paper. The sweet and spicy sauce is served on the side; other side dishes include baked beans, coleslaw, and potato salad.

Written up in regional and national magazines, the place offers an unusual ambience that features a jukebox, a pool table, and good food served at yesterday's prices. You can fill up here or pack some to go and keep heading south to Beto Junction for the rest of your movable feast. Closed Sunday and Monday. $–$$; (no cards). (785) 746-8830.

lebo, ks

Fearless foodies will not shudder at the thought of downing enough cholesterol to plug a pipeline. You've had ribs, beef, and ham in Williamsburg; now head south on I-35 to Lebo and Beto Junction, where you can fill up on "truck stop cuisine" and have an oil change at the same time. (For your car, that is.)

where to go

Beto Junction. I-35 and US 75, Lebo. From Williamsburg keep heading south to US 75 and exit 155. This sprawling truck stop takes its name from the first letters of four nearby cities: Burlington, Emporia, Topeka, and Ottawa. Food fans may want to make the trip just to chow down on trailblazer breakfasts that feature eggs with such meaty items as pork chops, chopped sirloin steak, ham, and Polish sausage. You can even have Beto Junction's fabulous chicken-fried steak with eggs, or order it for dinner.

Indeed, it is worth the drive just to savor the huge portions of this spectacular tenderized steak—dipped in a light, flaky batter and fried just right—nestled atop buttery, made-from-scratch mashed potatoes and crowned with country gravy. More than a meal, this is an all-you-can-eat experience. Catering to anybody on two wheels or more, the entire facility also includes a travel store that is great fun to browse through. If you're looking for a combination hair dryer/vacuum, you'll find it here, along with a wide range of Kansas gifts, greeting cards, and more. There's also a lube bay that specializes in vehicle repairs. Open daily. $$. (620) 256-6311.

emporia, ks

Emporia touts itself as the "Front Porch to the Flint Hills," an area that makes up the largest unbroken tract of tallgrass prairie in the county. Certainly Emporia is a gateway that connects several highways leading to and from the Flint Hills region. Nine recreational lakes are located in and around Emporia, including John Redmond Reservoir and Melvern Lake. You can reach this historic town by following I-35 southwest from Lebo or by connecting with Emporia on U.S. Highway 50 from Cottonwood Falls (see West from Kansas City, Day Trip 5). You can also make a Flint Hills loop, taking Emporia north to Manhattan, Kansas (see West from Kansas City, Day Trips 4 and 5).

Founded in 1857, Emporia has made a name for itself by being the home of the National Teachers Hall of Fame and birthplace of Pulitzer Prize–winning journalist William Allen White. White died in 1944, having achieved success and fame. President Franklin Delano Roosevelt eulogized him, saying that he "ennobled the profession of journalism." White's birthplace in Emporia is now a state historic site.

For a complete rundown of many other things to see and do in Emporia, plus self-guided-tour brochures of the Flint Hills, contact the Emporia County Convention and Visitors Bureau, 719 Commercial Street, P.O. Box 703, Emporia, KS 66801; (800) 279-3730 or (620) 342-1803; www.emporiakschamber.org.

where to go

All Veterans Memorial Park. 933 South Commercial Street. In a continuing effort to pay tribute to military veterans and Emporia's heritage of recognizing the service of veterans, this park, dedicated in 1991, features a World War II–era Sherman tank and a Vietnam-era Huey helicopter. The Kansas Purple Heart Monument is here, as is a monument to a local Medal of Honor recipient who gave his life for his country. The easily accessible park is located on the banks of the Cottonwood River, where lovely walking trails offer an opportunity for reflection. Open daily, dawn to dusk. (620) 342-1803.

David Traylor Zoo of Emporia. 75 Soden Road. This is one of the five smallest accredited zoos in the country at just eight acres. The mountain lion and Nelson's elk are among the more popular exhibits. The zoo also has a nice assortment of birds, mammals, and reptiles housed in natural habitats. The zoo also features exceptional botanical displays and spectacular holiday lights. Open daily, with extended hours in the summer. Free. (620) 342-6558; www.emporiazoo.org.

Emporia State University. 1200 Commercial Street. Founded in 1863, the university was the state's first school for training teachers. Located on 200 acres, the campus offers special attractions of interest to tourists, such as the William Allen White Library. Manuscripts, correspondence, photographs, and other materials about the life and times of William Allen White can be found here. The student union has a Veteran's Wall of Honor that pays tribute to students and alumni who served in the armed forces. The Johnston Geology Museum and the Peterson Planetarium are worthy of your time. Free admission to all campus-related exhibits. ♿.(620) 341-5037; www.emporia.edu.

Flint Hills National Wildlife Refuge. Fifteen miles southeast of Emporia, near Hartford. (Contact the refuge manager at 530 West Maple Street, P.O. Box 128, Hartford, KS 66854.) One of a system of 400 refuges administered by the U.S. Fish and Wildlife Service, the area is dedicated to the preservation and conservation of wildlife, primarily migratory waterfowl and bald eagles. Hiking, photography, boating, picnicking, camping, fishing, wild-food gathering, and hunting are allowed. Open daily. Free. (620) 392-5553; www.flinthills.fws.gov/.

Lyon County Historical Museum. 118 East Sixth Avenue. Located in the 1904 Carnegie Library Building, this is one of many sites in Emporia listed on the National Register of Historic Places. The building still contains its original leaded-glass windows, an ornate water fountain, beautiful oak woodwork, and other unique features. It houses artifacts and exhibits on a rotating schedule that help illustrate and interpret various phases of Kansas's Lyon County history and heritage. A great gift gallery specializes in items made by Kansas artisans. Closed Sunday and Monday. Free. (620) 340-6310; www.lyoncountymuseum.org.

Mr. K's Bicycle Museum. 1929 Road 175 (exit 138 north to Road 175, then east 1.3 miles). John and Carolyn Kuhn operated a bicycle store for more than thirty-five years and today have about sixty-five unusual bicycles and accessories on display. Their museum includes other collectibles, such as school items, cars, and toys. There's no admission, but a donation is welcome. Make a reservation in advance to make sure Mr. and Mrs. K are there, or take a chance on the museum being open. (620) 342-5136.

National Teachers Hall of Fame. 1320 C of E Drive. One of the city's premier attractions, the hall of fame nationally recognizes five teachers annually who have demonstrated a commitment to educating children from prekindergarten through high school. The walls hold tributes to some of the best teachers in America, and there are galleries with cultural and artistic exhibits of general interest. Closed Sunday. Free. (800) 96-TEACH or (620) 341-5660; www .nthf.org.

Prairie Passage. Lyon County Fairgrounds, West US 50 and Industrial Road. Eight massive limestone sculptures celebrating Emporia's origins and history were designed by artist Richard Stauffer and produced by the 1992 Kansas Sculptors Association. The sculptures present a variety of images about the land, its forces, and its people. Open daily. Free. (800) 279-3730 or (620) 342-1803.

William Allen White State Historic Site. 927 Exchange Street. William Allen White, born in Emporia in 1868, is the man for whom the University of Kansas School of Journalism is named. A prolific journalist who shaped public discussion on political and social matters nationwide for more than half a century, White won a Pulitzer Prize for editorials in his paper, the *Emporia Gazette,* and came to be respected around the world. His home is one of many sites in Emporia that explore the wit and wisdom that is studied today by journalists and educators around the world. Open Wednesday through Saturday, March through November; weekends only December through February. Fee. (620) 342-2800; www.kshs.org/places/white.

honoring our nation's veterans

For a generation of Americans, November 11 was first known as Armistice Day—the eleventh day of the eleventh month where at eleven minutes after 11:00 a.m., tribute was paid to those who had fought and died in World War I.

It was to have been the war to end all wars, but as Americans lost their lives in World War II and then in Korea, Alvin King of Emporia realized that wars would keep coming and that there was an ongoing need to recognize the veterans who fought in them.

In 1953 King approached his Congressional representative, Ed Rees of Emporia, and suggested the day be changed to Veteran's Day to honor veterans of all military conflicts. Rees took King's proposal to Washington and to President Dwight Eisenhower, another Kansan and veteran of World War II.

The first nationwide observance of Veteran's Day was on November 11, 1954. And each year, Emporia continues its recognition of veterans with a weeklong tribute that includes reenactments, lectures, parades, and other opportunities to learn about the contributions of military veterans. An All Veterans Park, at the intersection of Commercial Street and Soden's Road, is a must-see while visiting Emporia.

Many other parks and memorials around the community honor the contributions of veterans, including an exhibit at Emporia Service Area on the Kansas Turnpike honoring veteran Ken Bradstreet, who coordinated the work of many memorials and programs to Emporian veterans.

where to stay

White Rose Inn. 901 Merchant Street. This elegant Victorian bed-and-breakfast features four private suites with sitting rooms, Jacuzzis, and kitchen privileges. Guests arrive for afternoon tea and sumptuous treats and wake up the next day to the aroma of fresh-baked biscuits, coffee cakes, and muffins—or breakfast in bed for a special romantic treat. $$. (620) 343-6336; www.whiteroseinnemporia.com.

west

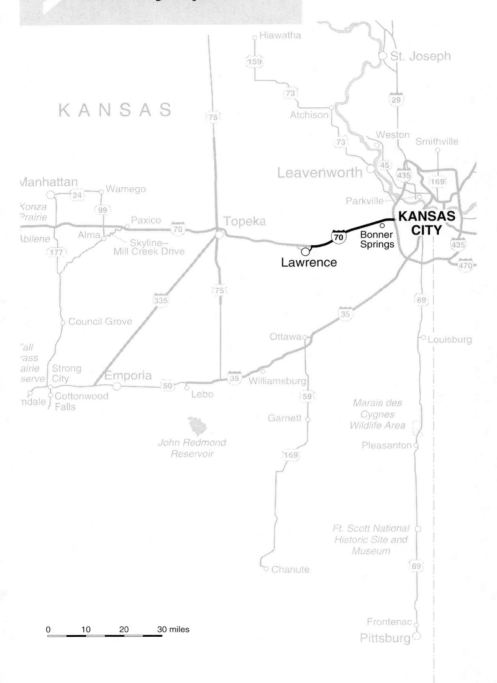

day trip 01

west

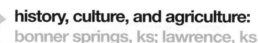

history, culture, and agriculture:
bonner springs, ks; lawrence, ks

bonner springs, ks

Bonner Springs is a short drive west from Kansas City on Interstate 70. It is home to Verizon Wireless Amphitheatre and the renowned Renaissance Festival held here in fall. For information: Bonner Springs/Edwardsville Chamber of Commerce, 205 East Second Street, P.O. Box 38, Bonner Springs, KS 66012; (913) 422-5044; www.wherelifeisbetter.org.

where to go

Grinter House. 1429 South Seventy-eighth Street (Seventy-eighth Street and Kansas Highway 32), Kansas City. Located 8 miles east of Bonner Springs, this house stands on the site of the first ferry across the Kansas River. The two-story brick structure was built by Moses R. Grinter in 1857. Today it is a historic site and museum open to tour. Closed December through February, and on Mondays the remainder of the year. Fee. (913) 299-0373; www.kshs.org/places/grinter/index.htm.

Holy-Field Vineyard & Winery. 18807 158th Street, Basehor. This family-owned winery currently produces about fifteen varieties of wine from a twelve-acre vineyard, which is open for tour. The tasting room is also the site of such fun events as murder mysteries, jazz concerts, and holiday celebrations. Check out the gift shop for the wine-filled chocolates. (913) 724-9463; www.holyfieldwinery.com.

The National Agricultural Center and Hall of Fame. 630 Hall of Fame Drive (North 126th Street, northeast of I-70 at K–7). Visitors can view 30,000 historic agricultural museum exhibits at The National Farmers Memorials located on the premises. There are a turn-of-the-twentieth-century home and farm implements, a century-old railroad depot, a blacksmith shop, a one-room schoolhouse, and a mile-long nature trail with eighty-nine marked and identified specimens. A mini-train ride is fun for the kids in warm weather months. Tour guides are available. Open daily March through November. Fee. (913) 721-1075; www.aghalloffame.com.

Verizon Wireless Amphitheatre. I-70 at the Bonner Springs exit; mailing address for special ticket arrangements: c/o 2310 West Seventy-fifth Street, Prairie Village, Kansas 66208. Verizon Wireless Amphitheatre is one of the Midwest's premier outdoor entertainment facilities. It offers a state-of-the-art sound system that caters to the biggest names in the music industry. Summer concerts feature everything from comedy and rock-and-roll to country and pop music. For special seating arrangements call (913) 721-3400; www.verizonwireless amphitheatre.com.

Wyandotte County Bonner Springs Park. 3488 West Drive (office), Bonner Springs. This 640-acre park is adjacent to The National Agricultural Center and Hall of Fame and features ball fields, tennis courts, shelter houses, a radio-controlled airplane flying field (permit required), and the Wyandotte County Museum. Open daily. Free. (913) 299-0550.

The Wyandotte County Historical Society and Museum. 631 North 126th Street, Wyandotte County Bonner Springs Park, Bonner Springs. The museum tells the history of Wyandotte County through exhibits that cover 350 million years of development, spanning a period from the Stone Age to today. Displays document the immigrant cultures who settled Kansas, from the native Kanza Indians to the pioneers who came from around the world to live and work in the area. A scale model keelboat as used by the Lewis and Clark Expedition introduces an exhibit on the Corps of Discovery's experiences in Kansas. Photographs and artifacts relating to Wyandotte County's industrial heritage and multicultural background can be found throughout the exhibit gallery and archives. Newspapers, county records, books, maps, and other materials offer a wealth of information for those interested in the early settlement of the state. Closed Monday. Free. 🏕. (913) 721-1078.

where to go, eat, and stay

Back N Thyme Guest House and Herb Garden. 1100 South 130th Street. This charming Victorian retreat features a hearty breakfast buffet in a sunny room overlooking the kitchen herb garden. The bed-and-breakfast offers four guest rooms, all with spacious private baths and one with a Jacuzzi and double vanity. Rates also include evening hors d'oeuvres and dessert. Young children can be accommodated if families wish to reserve the entire second floor. $$–$$$. (913) 422-5207; www.backnthyme.com.

lawrence, ks

In 1863, when William Quantrill and his raiders burned Lawrence to the ground in the name of pro-slavery, who could know that the town would bounce back and become the foodie hangout and cultural mecca that it is today?

With a long tradition of supporting the arts, the University of Kansas, or KU for short, offers one of the finest art museums in the Midwest, a theater that features twelve productions annually, and a School of Fine Arts that produces more than 400 events each year.

The university's diverse student mix has brought innovation and energy to the unusually stable local economy. On a hill where pioneers once paused along the Oregon Trail, KU's limestone buildings play host to scholars who come to study and learn on the beautiful, user-friendly campus.

Lawrence today offers plenty of attractions and a downtown filled with boutiques, galleries, and gourmet restaurants, yet it also has a history behind it worth learning.

It's hard to forget that Lawrence was Indian country for more than fifty years after the 1803 Louisiana Purchase. Kansas itself was a territory opened for settlement in 1854. During this time, the issue of slavery in the soon-to-be-state dominated all aspects of life. A bitter struggle ensued for territorial control. Lawrence had Yankee blood, and pro-slavery neighbors in Missouri found that hard to bear. When the town became a center for free-state activity, trouble soon brewed between the abolitionists and the pro-slavers. Quantrill's morning raid on August 21, 1863, left Lawrence a shambles, with hundreds reported dead or missing and homes and businesses destroyed.

And as much as officials at the University of Kansas and University of Missouri would like the term "border wars" to disappear from local parlance, each time the two rival sports teams meet in competition, the days of the Civil War in this region are remembered in a healthy sporting event.

When the Civil War ended, Lawrence's economy grew. The Kansas Pacific Railroad reached Lawrence in 1864, bringing new businesses and industry. In 1866 KU held its first session; Haskell Indian Nations University, now a registered National Historic Landmark, opened in 1884.

Today Lawrence, with its nineteenth-century Victorian homes and ornate downtown landmarks, has an identity all its own. A visitor center is open seven days a week at 402 North Second Street in a restored Union Pacific depot. In addition to all sorts of information about the area, you can watch a film on Quantrill's Raid, view exhibits of Lawrence history, or simply watch the dozens of trains that still travel these tracks every day. (785) 865-4411. Contact the Lawrence Convention and Visitors Bureau, 734 Vermont Street, Suite 101, Box 586, Lawrence, KS 66044; (888) LAW-KANS or (785) 865-4499; www.visitlawrence.com.

where to go

Clinton Lake. U.S. Army Corps of Engineers, 872 North 1402nd Road. Located 3 miles southwest of Lawrence, off Clinton Parkway (West Twenty-third Street), the lake provides 7,000 surface acres for boating, fishing, and swimming. Excellent opportunities for bicycling and for viewing wildlife abound. There are more than 70 miles of hiking trails, plus camping and picnicking areas. The Clinton Lake Museum is open weekends during the summer and houses artifacts and exhibits on local history. Free. (785) 842-8562; www.kdwp.state.ks.us.

Haskell Indian Nations University. 155 Indian Avenue. This is one of the oldest educational institutions for Native Americans and Alaska Natives supported by the federal government. Founded in 1884, Haskell has evolved from an elementary school to a university offering a baccalaureate in elementary teacher education. Open only to members of federally recognized Indian nations, enrollment averages 1,000 students a semester.

The Haskell Cultural Center and Museum, houses exhibits on the history of the university and the Native American experience in Kansas. Cultural performances are held at the adjacent outdoor amphitheater. The grounds include a memorial to Native Americans who have served in the United States military. Walking-tour brochures that explain the history and significance of buildings on campus are available at the center. The museum is closed on Saturday.

In the fall Haskell hosts an outdoor Indian Art Market in conjunction with Lawrence's annual Indian Arts Show. In the spring an outdoor powwow attracts hundreds of Native American and Alaska Native dancers and singers from across the United States. (785) 749-8404; www .haskell.edu.

Lawrence Arts Center. 940 New Hampshire. Although it opened its doors to the public in 1975, the Lawrence Arts Center is now housed in a modern facility that opened in April 2002 and is designed specifically for art education. Two visual arts galleries showcase area artists' works, and a gallery gift shop offers additional items for sale. Performing arts presentations are scheduled regularly in the theater. Open seven days a week. Free. (785) 843-2787; www .lawrenceartscenter.com.

Old West Lawrence Historic District. From Sixth to Ninth Streets between Tennessee and Illinois Streets. The impressive nineteenth-century architecture here is listed on the National Register of Historic Places. Drive by the Plymouth Congregational Church, 925 Vermont Street, for a vision of spires, buttresses, and stained glass. (785) 865-4499; www.visitlawrence.com.

University of Kansas. Mount Oread Campus. The university is the only one in the nation with a Jayhawk mascot, a familiar image seen all over the campus and the city. The 1,000-acre campus is one of the prettiest in the country and features a pond called Potter Lake at the bottom of a grassy wooded knoll between the Campanile and Memorial Stadium. From the stop sign at the west end of Memorial Drive, you can turn left onto West Campus Road, where there are some sorority and fraternity houses. This leads to the Chi Omega Fountain. At the south side of the intersection is a large rock marking the site of many Oregon Trail campfires. If you go around the fountain, you'll wind up making a left turn onto Jayhawk Boulevard, the main drag of the campus. If school is in session, you'll need to stop and get a visitor's pass at the booth. Jayhawk Boulevard has some wonderful old buildings, including Strong Hall, Watson Library, and others. Detailed information and a map of the campus can be found at www.ku.edu. Some stops on your itinerary might include these:

Helen Foresman Spencer Museum of Art. Behind the Kansas Union on the KU campus, at 1301 Mississippi Street. This gem of a place houses one of the finest university art museums in the country. The facility is never boring; you can return each time and see something new. Eleven galleries offer changing exhibitions and art from the museum's collections that represent more than 4,000 years of world art history and include wonderful European and American paintings, sculpture, and photography. Japanese Edo-period painting and twentieth-century Chinese painting are of particular interest. The Spencer also affords art lovers a chance to experience touring exhibitions of remarkable works not found elsewhere in the area. Closed Monday. Free. (785) 864-4710; www.spencerart.ku.edu/.

KU Natural History Museum. Dyche Hall, KU, Fourteenth Street and Jayhawk Boulevard. Listed on the National Register of Historic Places, the museum holds exhibits of Kansas and Great Plains animals and offers a historic panorama of North American plants and animals. On display are live bees, fish, snakes, and minerals. Open daily. Donations suggested. (785) 864-4450; www.nhm.ku.edu.

The Lied Center. Fifteenth and Iowa Streets, on the campus. Located on the highest ridge on campus, this is the home for KU's Concert, Chamber Music, Broadway, and New Directions series. The lobbies here offer a magnificent view of the rolling hills and the Wakarusa Valley. The Lied Center provides a state-of-the-art setting for music, dance, theater, lectures, films, and convocations. Visitors are welcome to view the building during business hours Monday through Friday. Tickets to events can be purchased at the box office. (785) 864-ARTS; www.lied.ku.edu.

The Robert J. Dole Institute of Public Policy. 2350 Petefish Drive. Adjacent to the Lied Center is the newest addition to the University of Kansas campus honoring the public service of Kansas senator Bob Dole. The interactive exhibits here chronicle the life of the senator who served Kansas for forty-six years and ran three times for president of the United States. The state-of-the-art presentations on this history of Kansas, the soaring stained-glass windows, and the Memory Wall honoring World War II veterans make the center worthy of a visit, no matter what your politics. The center hosts political presentations and historic discussions throughout the year. Open daily. Free. (785) 864-4900; www.dole institute.org.

where to shop

Lawrence offers an exciting array of galleries, specialty and outlet shops, museums, and artists' studios. We can mention only a few in the space of this book. For a complete list, contact the Lawrence Convention and Visitors Bureau, 734 Vermont Street, Suite 101, Box 586, Lawrence, KS 66044; (888) LAW-KANS or (785) 865-4499.

The Bay Leaf. 725 Massachusetts Street. This interesting shop features the unusual and the essential in kitchen accessories and gifts for the home. It also offers a large variety of fresh-roasted gourmet coffees and teas from around the world. Open daily, and late on Thursday. (785) 842-4544.

Community Mercantile. 901 Iowa Street. "The Merc" has been serving the Lawrence community since 1974. It is cooperatively owned and offers a full selection of organic and local produce in season. It has an extensive bulk department, with an excellent selection of coffees and

mustard madness

March is always a frenzied time in Lawrence thanks to March Madness—that hysterical time of year when college basketball fans overdose on their favorite sport via televised tournaments across the country night and day. The pack of sixty-five NCAA teams becomes the Sweet Sixteen, which is then pared to the Final Four. And more times than not, the Jayhawks are in that final number.

At the Free State Brewery, which is always packed with red and blue Jayhawk fans on game day, March Madness is not so much about basketball as it is mustard. You have to know Free State Brewery proprietor Chuck Magerl to truly understand the connection between basketball and mustard, and even then, it doesn't make much sense. After seeing a program on public television about the Mustard Museum in Mount Horeb, Wisconsin, Chuck decided to combine mustard tastings at his restaurant with the tournament brackets for basketball, allowing guests to sample sixty-five flavors, then sixteen, then select a Final Four of mustards.

(Note: Mount Horeb, Wisconsin, is about 20 miles west/southwest of Madison. The Mustard Museum tells the exciting story of this condiment and displays more than 4,000 containers of historic, thought-provoking mustard. The museum gift shop and catalog carry 400 varieties for sale.)

Each February the phone calls and e-mails fly fast and furious between Lawrence and Mount Horeb, scientifically identifying the precise varieties of mustards that will fill in the tournament brackets. All told, about 200 containers of Wisconsin mustard make their way to the Free State Brewery, a little more or a little less, based on how well the Jayhawks perform.

teas, herbs, dairy products, and more. There are books and housewares, plus a meat department that features locally raised beef and poultry. Freshly baked goods, crafts by area artists, and a deli department round out the fare. Member benefits include special discounts and a monthly newsletter. Open daily. (785) 843-8544.

Farmers Market. 1000 block of Vermont Street. This is the largest and oldest farmers' market in the state. Local growers and farm producers offer products and produce ranging from fresh fruits and veggies to baked goods, herbs, and homemade condiments. Open Saturday morning and Tuesday and Thursday afternoon, May to November. (785) 865-4499.

Phoenix Gallery. 919 Massachusetts Street. Works by local and regional artisans are represented here and include pottery, blown glass, jewelry, weaving, paintings, prints, and textiles. Open daily. (785) 843-0080; www.phoenixgallery.biz.

The Raven Bookstore. 8 East Seventh Street. This bookstore specializes primarily in mysteries and hosts two mystery reading groups a month for customers. It also offers a British-import mystery section for many titles that are hard to find in this country. Fiction, history and regional studies, travel, nature, and other works of literature also fill the shelves. Open daily. (785) 749-3300.

Silver Works & More. 715 Massachusetts Street. This gallery sells gold and silver jewelry by local metalsmith Jim Connelly. It also offers crafts, claywork, textiles, handmade paper, studio glass, and designer-craftsman furniture. Closed Sunday and Monday. (785) 842-1460.

Waxman Candles. 609 Massachusetts Street. Situated at the northern end of Historic Downtown Lawrence, this unique shop produces handmade candles, including the one-of-a-kind "Silhouette," which has a backlit effect as it burns and is quite a showstopper. Three tons of candles wait to be sold here, including clean-burning beeswax and soy candles. A product catalog is also available. Open daily. (785) 843-8593.

where to eat

Free State Brewing Co. 636 Massachusetts Street. This is the first brewery to operate in Kansas since the state passed a prohibition law more than a century ago. Located inside a renovated trolley barn, this combination brewery-restaurant produces a small variety of high-quality beer, using fresh, natural ingredients. The restaurant offers an interesting menu that includes everything from stir-fried veggies to fresh fish and steak. Brewery tours are offered Saturday at 2:00 p.m. Open daily. $–$$. (785) 843-4555; www.freestatebrewing.com.

Pachamama's. 800 New Hampshire Street. This restaurant features an international menu that changes monthly. The uniquely inspired cuisine features everything from fish to wild-game entrees. Come for the wine tastings on Friday evenings. Open daily at 5:00 p.m. $$–$$$. (785) 841-0990.

Paisano's II. 2112 West Twenty-fifth Street. Like its sister restaurant in Topeka, Kansas, this bistro serves excellent Italian-inspired food. Entrees range from veal and chicken dishes to pasta dishes redolent with delectable sauces. The portions are large and the prices reasonable. Open daily for lunch and dinner. $$. (785) 838-3500.

Plum Tree. 2620 Iowa Street. Make the drive to Lawrence just to dine at this restaurant. Here authentic Chinese cuisine is showcased in an extensive menu featuring more than eighty different dishes from all the provinces of China. There are Peking duck, Hunan shrimp, and many other old and new favorites. A complete American menu is also available. Banquet facilities are offered for up to one hundred people. Closed Tuesday. $$. (785) 841-6222.

Stone Creek Pizza. 3801 West Sixth Street. The water landscaping, outdoor bar, and rotating menu of pasta specialties in this old warehouse building create a wonderful environment for family outings or big gatherings with friends. $. (785) 830-8500.

Sylas and Maddy's Homemade Ice Cream. 1014 Massachusetts Street. This is the place to come for banana splits, sundaes, malts, milk shakes, sodas, and homemade waffle cones filled to the brim with fantastically rich and creamy ice cream made on the premises. Choose from 130 rotating flavors that include Da Bomb (Oreos, chocolate chips, and cookie dough), prairie pumpkin nut, and pineapple cheesecake, or try the chocolate chip and peanut butter chocolate chip made with superior chunks of chocolate. Take a cooler so that you can pack a pint or a quart to go. Yum! Open daily. $. (785) 832-8323.

Teller's Restaurant. 746 Massachusetts Street. Located in a historic 1877 bank building, Teller's features Italian cuisine, including pasta, chicken, lamb, and wood-fired brick-oven pizza, all of which should be enjoyed with a selection from Teller's award-winning wine list. A contemporary blend of works by Kansas artists Stan Herd and Jon Havener complements original bank fixtures, such as the 20,000-pound safe door securing the restrooms. Open daily. $$. (785) 843-4111; www.746mass.com.

Wheatfield's Bakery and Cafe. 904 Vermont Street. This delightful place features fresh-baked breads made with Kansas wheat. Everything from traditional favorites like sourdough and raisin breads to cookies and truffles are made on the premises, along with soups, sandwiches, and stuffed pastries. Open daily for lunch and dinner; a full breakfast is served until 2:00 p.m. on Sunday and until 11:00 a.m. on weekdays. $–$$. (785) 841-5553.

where to stay

Circle S Guest Ranch & Country Inn. 3325 Circle S Lane. This charming retreat has been continuously owned and operated through five generations since the late 1800s. The ranch spans more than 1,200 acres and includes more than 400 head of cattle. More than twenty ponds dot the surroundings and there is abundant wildlife. The inn itself was built to resemble a Kansas barn. Twelve spacious guest rooms offer private baths and views. Some feature claw-foot or whirlpool baths and fireplaces. Breakfast is included in the price of the room. Dinner is available on Saturday night by request. Call for directions. $$$. (785) 843-4124 or (800) 625-2839; www.circlesranch.com.

The Eldridge Hotel. 701 Massachusetts Street. This downtown hotel is the only hotel in Lawrence listed as an official Historic Hotel of America. Completely destroyed during Quantrill's Raid in 1863, the structure was promptly rebuilt and named the Hotel Eldridge. After a period of decline in the mid-twentieth century, the hotel was renovated and reopened in 1986. All forty-eight rooms are suites, and the hotel restaurant serves a great Sunday brunch. $$. (785) 749-5011 or (800) 527-0909; www.eldridgehotel.com.

Halcyon House Bed and Breakfast. 1000 Ohio Street. A century-old restored home, Halcyon House offers a living room, two patios, and a lovely glass-enclosed kitchen. Nine uniquely styled and furnished bedrooms include a master suite with a king-size bed and private bath and a suite with two double beds, private bath, and fireplace. A complete breakfast is served daily and features homemade muffins, omelets, fresh fruit, and coffee. $$. (785) 841-0314; www.thehalcyonhouse.com.

day trip 02

west

state capital:
topeka, ks

topeka, ks

Heading west on I-70, you'll reach Topeka, one of the largest cities on the historic Oregon Trail. The capital of Kansas, Topeka lies on rich, sandy river-bottom land where Indians lived for many years using the Kansas (Kaw) River for navigation. Each year Topeka celebrates its Native American heritage with the Shawnee Country Allied Tribes All Nations Powwow, held Labor Day weekend.

The Kaw River also drew to it three French Canadian brothers who started a ferry service across the river in 1842. They married three Kanza (Kansas) Indian sisters whose tribe had lived in the area for many years. Thus marked the beginnings of Topeka as a stopping point on the Oregon Trail. Years later one of the couples celebrated the election of their grandson, Charles Curtis, as vice president of the United States—the only U.S. vice president of Native American descent.

Topeka has a rich abundance of attractions, including one of the most extensive rose gardens in the country, a tropical rain forest, an international raceway offering topflight motor sports events, and several interesting museums. With a host of citywide festivals, area attractions, and historic sites, Topeka is enjoying newfound popularity as a great place to live and visit. For more information, contact the Topeka Convention and Visitors Bureau, 1275 Southwest Topeka Boulevard, Topeka, KS 66612; (800) 235-1030 or (785) 234-1030; www.topeka cvb.org.

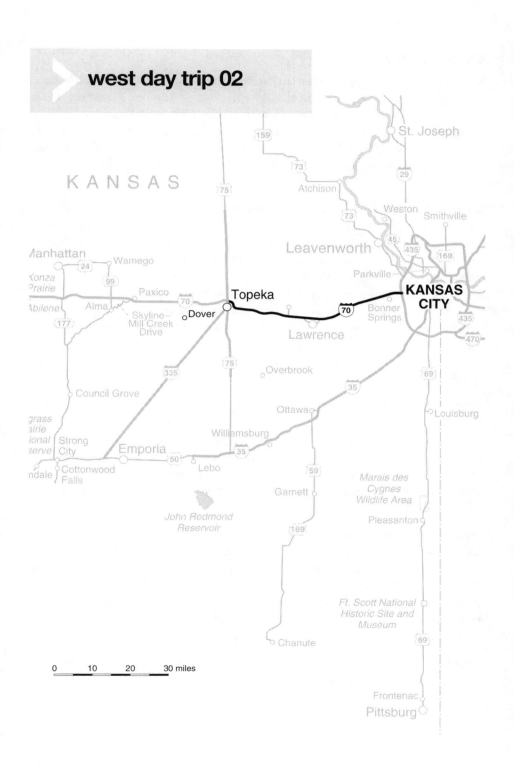

west day trip 02

where to go

Binkley Gardens. c/o Topeka Beautification Association, 4536 Southwest Elevation Lane. Every April visitors can see more than 35,000 tulips and 12,000 daffodils in this three-and-a-half-acre private garden, which features formal flower beds, informal gardens, woods, a formal pond, and a meandering stream. The garden has many flowering trees and more than twenty-five varieties of shrubs, along with hundreds of perennials. Exotic birds in aviaries also add to the colorful surroundings. Call for annual dates and times. Fee. (800) 235-1030 or (785) 478-4624.

***Brown v. Board of Education* National Historic Site.** 1515 Southeast Monroe Street. Located in the former Monroe School, one of four African-American schools in the Topeka School District prior to 1954, this site represents the segregation of publicly funded schools, the Civil Rights movement of the time, and the landmark Supreme Court ruling on May 17, 1954, that ended segregation. Oliver Brown, a Topeka minister, was the first of thirteen parents in Topeka to file suit on behalf of twenty children; thus, the name Brown on the case. However, the case represents similar lawsuits filed in five states at that time on behalf of more than 150 children. Today the building has been restored to its condition of the early 1950s. Numerous interactive exhibits encourage visitors to explore the concept of racial segregation and record their feelings at the conclusion of the tour. Free. (785) 354-4273; www.nps .gov/brvb.

Cedar Crest. Located off I-70 and Fairlawn Road. The home has been the official residence of the Kansas governor since 1962. Built in 1928, this twelve-room French Norman–style home overlooks the Kansas River Valley. It was designed by W. D. Wight of Kansas City and was named for the numerous cedar trees on the property. The home is nestled on 244 acres that include hiking trails, fishing ponds, and nature areas open to the public. Public tours are offered on Monday between 1:00 and 4:00 p.m. Groups of eight or more require reservations. Free. (785) 296-3636.

Combat Air Museum. Head west on I-70 and stay on the turnpike until you reach exit 177 (southbound Topeka Boulevard). Watch for signs leading to the main entrance of Forbes Field and Hangar 602. Dedicated to restoring, preserving, and displaying aircraft and artifacts, this museum is the only one in the world to display operational aircraft from every armed conflict utilizing powered aircraft. Housed here are surveillance aircraft fighters, missiles, and other military pieces dating to 1917. Visitors can walk through one of the early 1950 radar planes and browse through the many exhibits. Open daily. Fee. (785) 862-3303.

Gage Park. 635 Southwest Gage Boulevard. Topeka's 160-acre Gage Park features many attractions, including the following:

Carousel in the Park. The antique carousel was built around 1908 by New York's Herschell-Spillman Company. It was purchased by the city of Topeka in 1986 and totally restored for the public to enjoy and ride. Open daily in warm weather. Fee. (785) 368-3838.

Reinisch Rose Garden. This is one of the most extensive rose gardens in the country, with more than 350 varieties and 7,000 bushes. It is one of twenty-three test gardens in the nation for hybridizers and has one of the most complete displays of All-American Winners selected since 1940 on public view. Internationally famous for its beauty, the Reinisch Rose Garden was founded in 1931 and named after Topeka's first park superintendent. Today the roses grow in a lovely setting of rock gardens and pools. The red Topeka Rose stands majestically in the center of the garden. Blooming season normally is June through October; peak time, early June and mid-September. Open daily. Free. (785) 272-6150.

Topeka Zoological Park. Exhibits include the Tropical Rain Forest (see below) and "Gorilla Encounter," which allows visitors to view the creatures in an open environment from a glass-enclosed area. African lions, Japanese macaques, and Chinese muntjac deer are part of the displays. Warm weather makes the Water Bird Lagoon a pleasant place for bird-watching. There are many attractions to visit, including the Children's Zoo; it features a traditional red barn and a series of wooden corrals that create a farmlike setting for visitor-friendly animals. Another nice attraction is Black Bear Woods. Opened in 1996, this is the first of several natural exhibits devoted to Kansas animals. A large wood ramp and deck provide viewing areas of the bears' home. There are a pool, tall trees for them to climb, natural berries to eat, and a large area for playing, sleeping, and just being bears. Open daily. Fee. (785) 368-9180; www.topeka.org/zoo.

The Tropical Rain Forest. Located inside Topeka Zoological Park, this re-creation of a South American ecosystem sprouted from the plains in 1974 and continues to flourish. On cold-weather days there's nothing like a warm and toasty rain forest to keep you warm. The damp, pungent smell mingles with the sweet odor of rare flowers and plants; coupled with the cries of exotic birds, the rain forest is a rare experience to savor. Housed in a 30-foot-high geodesic dome, 100 feet in diameter, the Tropical Rain Forest supports some of the rarest and most exotic plant and animal life in the world. This is a bird lover's paradise. The feathered creatures here are so lavishly colored that they look as though they have been dipped in richly textured paints. Many of the other inhabitants are so well camouflaged that most visitors miss them. Many are nocturnal and quite a few move freely about the dome, so be careful not to step on anybody's toes! Exhibits are open daily. Fee. (785) 272-5821.

Great Overland Station. 701 North Kansas Avenue. Topeka's proximity to the Oregon and Santa Fe Trails and the railroads played a key role in the city's development. The museum is housed in a former Union Pacific depot and helps tell the story of life on the rails and how those rails brought Topeka to life. Check the Web site for special exhibits. Closed Monday. Fee. (785) 232-5533; www.greatoverlandstation.com.

Heartland Park Topeka. 1805 Southwest Seventy-first Street. Hailed as one of the finest motor-sports facilities in North America, Heartland Park Topeka opened in 1989 as the only major, multimillion-dollar, multiuse motor-sports complex to be built in this country in thirty years. The fastest quarter-mile elapsed time in the history of drag racing was set at the facility in 1990, when the late Gary Ormsby hurtled his Top Fuel dragster down the Heartland strip at an incredible 296 miles per hour.

All the state-of-the-art elements found here are designed with the spectator in mind, from the 2.5-mile road-race course to the 0.25-mile drag strip—one of the fastest in the world. The viewing berms afford spectators an excellent view of the Grand Prix road-race course, while the modern grandstands offer onlookers a look at the pit-stop action. Open for seasonal events. Fee. (800) 43-RACES or (785) 862-4781; www.hpt.com.

Kansas Museum of History. 6425 Southwest Sixth Street. Located on the historic Oregon Trail, the museum holds one of the country's largest prairie collections of memorabilia and historic objects. In the permanent gallery, "Voices from the Heartland: A Kansas Legacy" tells the story of Kansas, from its first inhabitants to modern-day culture. The past comes alive through interactive video displays and exhibits that feature an 1866 log house; a Southern Cheyenne buffalo-hide tepee; a locomotive with coal, dining, and sleeping cars attached; and more. You can catch the pioneer spirit as you browse through special areas, such as a children's Discovery Place, where hands-on discovery is encouraged. Open daily. Free. (785) 272-8681; www.kshs.org.

Kansas State Capitol Building. Tenth and Jackson Streets. A multi-year renovation of the capitol building, completed in the spring of 2008, makes visiting the capitol a more enlightening experience than ever before. Original construction of the building began in 1861 but wasn't completed until 1903. The grounds surrounding the building contain monuments of interest, including a statue of Abraham Lincoln located southeast of the capitol. In 1915 Robert Merrell Gage was just out of school and living with his parents when he completed the figure of Lincoln in the barn adjacent to his parents' home.

Southwest of the capitol is another monument by Gage, dedicated to the pioneer women of Kansas. A bronze replica of the Statue of Liberty, at the northwest section of Capitol Square, and a replica of the Liberty Bell, at the east side of Capitol Square, complete the grouping.

Inside the building, murals by John Steuart Curry and David Overmyer tell an unusual pioneer story. Check out the huge panel of a furious John Brown on the second floor. The dome has a great view, but you've got to climb 296 steps to get there. The Governor's Office and both houses of the Kansas Legislature are worth noting. There are guided tours Tuesday through Saturday. Free. (785) 296-3966; www.kshs.org.

Mulvane Art Museum. Washburn University, Seventeenth and Jewell Streets. Built in 1922, this is the oldest visual-arts museum in the state. It offers changing exhibits from its permanent collection and focuses on contemporary art from the Mountain-Plains region. The exterior courtyard features sculptures and fountains, along with native wildflowers. Closed Mondays. Free. (785) 231-1124; www.washburn.edu.

Old Prairie Town. 124 Northwest Fillmore Street. Old-fashioned fun can be had at this unusual city park. It features five and a half acres of living history that includes a restored 1870 Victorian mansion, a log cabin, a train depot, a one-room schoolhouse, a stone barn, a drugstore, and botanical gardens.

The Potwin Drug Store is worth seeing. A 1920s-style building was designed to house fixtures that were once part of Edelblute's Drug Store in Potwin, Kansas. There is a superb back bar and marble counter perfect for sipping sodas. On the second floor of the Potwin Drug Store, professional, medical, and dental offices appear as they would have a century ago. Also on the park premises is the Mulvane General Store, featuring yesteryear decor and gift items for sale.

Staffed by volunteers, the park offers special meals for groups and organizations. One of the most popular and original dinners is served at fireside tables in the Ward Cabin. The hearthside-cooked food includes ham or smoked turkey, sweet potatoes, Irish potatoes, spiced fruit, baked biscuits, and cookies; homemade ice cream is served as well. The family-style fare is offered from October 15 through March 15. Reservations are required. Old Prairie Town also features an elegant Victorian dinner, served buffet-style in the dining room of the mansion. You get a choice of entree, salad, and vegetable, plus homemade scones and ice cream for dessert. A minimum of twenty-five persons is required, as are reservations. Fee. Open daily. (785) 368-3888.

where to eat

Topeka is filled with family restaurants and fast-food places. The official visitor's guide has a complete list. Contact the Topeka Convention and Visitors Bureau, 1275 Southwest Topeka Boulevard, Topeka, KS 66612; (800) 235-1030 or (785) 234-1030. In the meantime, here are some recommendations:

Annie's Place. Gage Shopping Center, 4014 Gage Center Drive. This family-owned restaurant bakes its buns fresh daily, along with dinner rolls, cinnamon rolls, and desserts. The baker is visible through a "showroom" in the restaurant. Annie's also grinds prime beef to make its famous gourmet burgers. Don't forget to try the renowned "hot air fries," cooked without grease. Ask for a side order of chicken gravy, which is served with chunks of white-meat chicken. $$. (785) 273-0848.

Paisano's Ristorante. Fleming Place, 4043 Southwest Tenth Street. Like its Lawrence, Kansas, counterpart, Paisano's serves superior Italian food. Appetizers include tasty mushroom caps stuffed with sausage and baked in white wine cream sauce. Entrees include veal and chicken dishes, Pesce al Vino Bianco (lobster, shrimp, scallops, crab, and whitefish in a sage and garlic cream sauce), and penne primavera (penne pasta sautéed in extra-virgin olive oil, garlic, and fresh basil sauce, then tossed with vegetables and topped with crumbled Gorgonzola cheese). The portions are large and the prices reasonable. Early-bird lunch special: Entrees are half-price before 11:30 a.m. Open daily for lunch and dinner. $$. (785) 273-0100.

The Plantation Steak House. 6646 North Topeka Boulevard. In business for more than thirty years, the restaurant puts out a good steak at a reasonable price. $$. Open for dinner only. Closed Sunday. (785) 246-9797.

where to stay

The official visitor's guide to Topeka lists everything from good motel chains to bed-and-breakfasts. For information contact the Topeka Convention and Visitors Bureau, 1275 Southwest Topeka Boulevard, Topeka, KS 66612; (800) 235-1030 or (785) 234-1030; www.topeka cvb.org.

Brickyard Barn Inn. 4020 Northwest Twenty-fifth Street. This 1927 dairy barn has been converted into an elegant country inn with an inviting pool and hot tub. The three guest rooms are furnished with antiques and have private baths. A good choice for business travel and romantic getaways, the Brickyard Barn Inn features a full or continental breakfast served in relaxing surroundings. As a "private party facility," it is also available for corporate entertaining, weddings, luncheons, cocktail parties, and dinners. $$. (785) 235-0057; www.brickyardbarn inn.com.

1878 Sage Inn and Stagecoach Stop. 13553 Southwest K–4 Highway, Dover. History surrounds you at this historic stagecoach stop that shows exterior scars from numerous gunfights and attacks by Indians more than 125 years ago when this was the wild, wild West. As you climb the narrow, original stairs to the second floor, it's easy to imagine the weary travelers who made this climb before. However, the surroundings provided to you by owners Ken and Joan Benjamin are certainly more comfortable than those of the late 1800s. Joan's stuffed French toast for breakfast will fill you up for the rest of the day. A gift shop on the property also carries a few antiques. $$. (785) 256-6050 or (800) 466-6736.

Senate Luxury Suites. 900 Southwest Tyler Street. As intimate as a bed-and-breakfast and as grand as a first-class hotel, the Senate Luxury Suites was originally built in the 1920s as an elegant apartment building. Today, the location appeals to business and leisure travelers alike, with fifty-two elegantly furnished suites, some with kitchenettes, some with hot tubs and fireplaces. Guests are treated to a complimentary breakfast. $$–$$$. (800) 488-3188 or (785) 233-5050; www.senatesuites.com.

day trip 03

west

scenic drive into the past:
skyline–mill creek drive, ks;
wamego, ks

skyline–mill creek drive, ks

Drive west on I-70 to Paxico. From Paxico head south to Alma along Skyline–Mill Creek Drive, which you can pick up outside of town. Look for signs or ask for directions. The scene is miles of rolling hills and prairie under a sweeping sky. Native bluestem prairie grass follows vast stretches of virgin land in a seemingly endless vista. At times the expanse is so immense that one can see the curve of the earth. Sky and land merge as one. It takes the breath away.

Where is this? Surely not Kansas. It's supposed to be flat. It shouldn't look like New Mexico or Montana. But it does along Skyline–Mill Creek Drive. The drive is clearly marked, and the byway takes you past land covered with stone fences. A historical marker tells you that the 1867 law abolishing open range provided payment to landowners for building and maintaining the venerable stone fences that still stand today. The only sound is your car as it hums along the road, and if you stop along the way and sit quietly, you can almost feel the 1800s surround you: the buffalo, the Indians, the pioneers—they were here, and it's hard to tell where the past stops and the present begins.

wamego, ks

Head north on Kansas Highway 99 to Wamego. A small community of 4,000, the town is located on the Vermillion River, where Louis Vieux, a Potawatomie Indian, operated the first ferry along

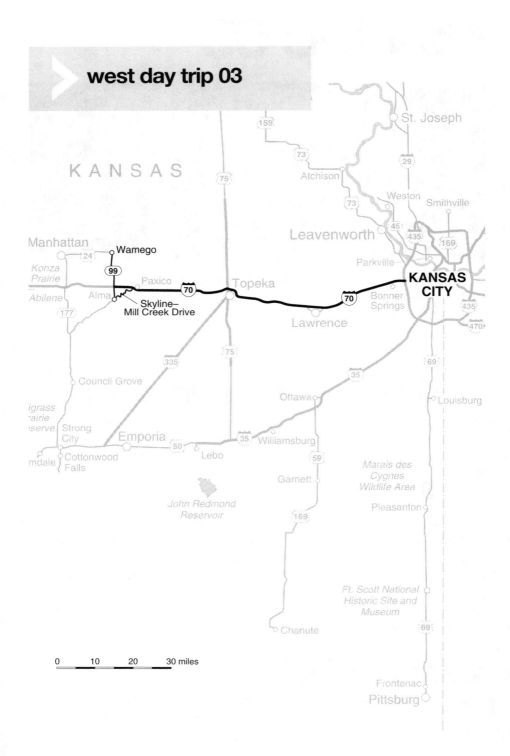

KANSAS

St. Joseph

Manhattan

Wamego

Konza
Prairie

99

Paxico

Topeka

KANSAS
CITY

Abilene

Alma

Skyline–
Mill Creek Drive

70

70

Bonner
Springs

Lawrence

Atchison

Weston

Smithville

Leavenworth

Parkville

Council Grove

Ottawa

Louisburg

grass
rairie
serve

Strong
City

Emporia

50

Lebo

35

Williamsburg

59

Garnett

Marais des
Cygnes
Wildlife Area

Pleasanton

mdale

Cottonwood
Falls

John Redmond
Reservoir

169

Ft. Scott National
Historic Site and
Museum

Chanute

0   10   20   30 miles

Frontenac

Pittsburg

the Oregon Trail. Wamego is also the birthplace of Walter P. Chrysler, who built the car named after him. The annual Tulip Festival, held in April at the city park, offers a beautiful floral display, along with entertainment and food. For information: Wamego Area Chamber of Commerce, 529 Lincoln Street, Wamego, KS 66547; (785) 456-7849; www.wamegochamber.com.

where to go

The Columbian Theatre Museum and Art Center. 521 Lincoln Avenue. In 1994 a $1.8-million renovation restored the luster and elegance to this century-old theater. Rare 1893 murals, the only remaining set of decorative art from the 1893 Chicago World's Fair, grace the walls of the 250-seat theater, which features a guest-artist series, musical concerts, drama and dance productions, educational programs, and regional art exhibits. Docent-guided tours are by appointment. A performing arts schedule is available. Fee (for events). (800) 899-1893 or (785) 456-2029; www.columbiantheatre.com.

Dutch Mill. Wamego Area Chamber of Commerce, P.O. Box 34, Wamego, KS 66547. This is Kansas's only authentic operating stone Dutch mill. Built in 1879 and listed on the National Register of Historic Places, the mill overlooks the beautiful city park—a perfect place for picnicking. The mill grinds wheat to flour while you watch, and you can purchase products to take back home. An adjacent museum contains historical and American Indian artifacts. (785) 456-2040 or 456-9119.

The Marvelous Land of Oz Museum. 511 Lincoln Avenue. A Wamego native began collecting *Wizard of Oz* items as a child and has now donated more than 2,000 pieces to this magical museum. As you enter, you find yourself in the Gale barnyard looking at the weathered farmhouse Dorothy flew in over the rainbow. The museum progresses chronologically through both the movie and the books by L. Frank Baum, taking visitors through Munchkinland, the Haunted Forest, and Emerald City. An in-house theater runs original black-and-white silent *Wizard of Oz* movies. A gift shop should satisfy any cravings you have for *Wizard of Oz* memorabilia. If not, an *Oz* festival in October brings remaining actors from the movie to sign autographs. Fee. Open daily. (866) 458-TOTO; www.ozmuseum.com.

where to eat

Friendship House. 507 Ash Street. The bakery items sold here use stone-ground flour from the Dutch Mill and are made from scratch each day along with tasty sandwiches, homemade soups, breads, and pastries that include cookies, muffins, and sweet rolls. Weekly menu items include bread pudding, fresh-baked pie (Friday), and honey wheat *bierocks,* unique hamburger and cabbage pocket sandwiches. Work by local artists and crafters is also on display and for sale. Open for lunch Tuesday through Saturday. $. (785) 456-9616.

day trip 04

west

>>> the "little apple":
manhattan, ks

manhattan, ks

Touting itself as the "Little Apple," Manhattan is located in the heart of the scenic Flint Hills—the last large preserve of native tallgrass prairie in America. From Wamego, Manhattan is only a short drive west on U.S. Highway 24. This thriving college town isn't a destination for tourists looking for whopper-size attractions—and that is part of its charm. Like the prairie itself, Manhattan has a lot to offer, but you have to look for it.

Kansas State University and the K-State Wildcat football team are located here, and home games are held on "Wildcat Weekends," drawing thousands of fans who converge on the city wearing purple to participate in numerous events and activities that are part of the fun.

The university also boasts scientific research that is on the cutting edge of agricultural technology. Thanks to new techniques instituted here, K-State has produced great-tasting hormone- and antibiotic-free beef, poultry, pork, bread, pasta, pastry, milk, eggs, and ice cream.

Manhattan is a pretty place to visit. The streets are filled with lovely homes and venerable shade trees that offer respite on a hot Kansas day. Just a short drive from here is the Konza Prairie, a Nature Conservancy Preserve that features a pristine and beautiful landscape with a hiking trail open to the public. Manhattan is also the starting point for one of the most gorgeous scenic drives in America, according to *National Geographic's Guide to Scenic Highways and Byways*.

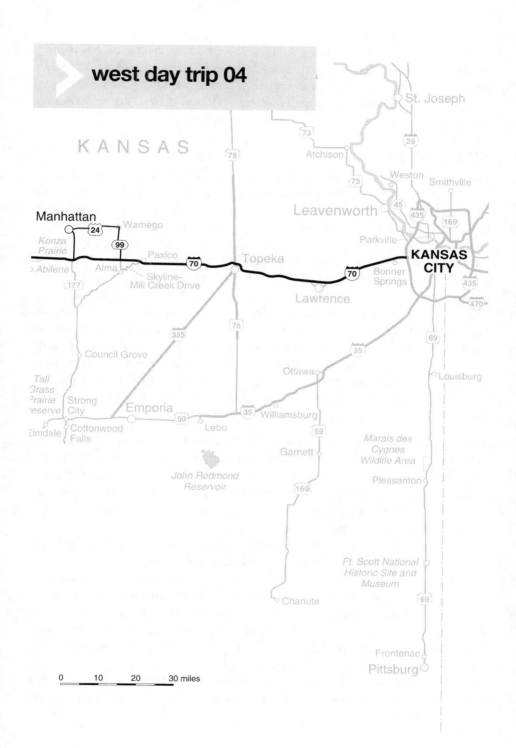

You'll want to spend more than a day here, so it's fortunate that the city has plenty of good restaurants, shops, and places to stay. For more information on what to see and do in the area, call the Manhattan Visitor Information Line at (800) 528-4748. For a free *Manhattan Visitors Guide,* contact the Manhattan Convention and Visitors Bureau, 501 Poyntz Avenue, Manhattan, KS 66502; (785) 776-8829; www.manhattan.org.

where to go

Fort Riley. Located 10 miles west of Manhattan, the grounds of historic Fort Riley hold colorful exhibits that showcase the history of the Great Plains. The beautifully restored Custer House stands as the only set of surviving officers' quarters from the fort's early history. Built in 1855 of native limestone, the quarters are nearly identical to the house that George Armstrong Custer and his wife occupied while residing at the fort. The Custer House also depicts military and family life on the western frontier during the Indian wars.

The U.S. Cavalry and First Infantry Division Museums are housed in separate buildings on the Main Post. The U.S. Cavalry Museum, located in Building 205 on Custer Avenue, houses displays that chronicle the years of the American mounted horse soldier from the Revolutionary War to 1950. Adjacent to the U.S. Cavalry Museum, the First Infantry Division Museum offers the history of this decorated division in life-size dioramas that portray the trenches and battlefields of both World War I and World War II, as well as the jungles of Vietnam and the sands of Desert Storm. Buffalo are still kept in a nearby corral as a further reminder of the history of America before fast-food franchises and tract housing bulldozed away much of the tallgrass prairie. Open daily. Free. (785) 239-2737; www.riley.army.mil.

Kansas State University. The 668-acre campus is located throughout Manhattan. Founded in 1863, K-State has a number of internationally recognized programs that attract teachers and students from around the globe. Its College of Agriculture offers the only worldwide programs in grain, milling, baking, and feed science and management. Its College of Architecture, Planning, and Design, where all programs are professionally accredited, is one of only five public, comprehensive design schools in the nation.

The College of Veterinary Medicine is internationally recognized as a center for the study of livestock diseases. It has a top-notch veterinary medicine program and hospital—complete with emergency rooms for both large and small animals—that is considered to be one of the finest in the country. (It's not unusual to find a trio of doctors simultaneously performing eye surgery on a cat, leg surgery on a llama, and something you don't want to know about on a cow.) Ongoing cancer research and numerous projects with NASA have enhanced its educational reputation. In addition, the university is drawing attention for its excellent hotel and restaurant management business programs.

As far as cutting-edge research goes, the Department of Animal Sciences and Industry has invented a new steam process to kill those nasty bacteria that thrive on uncooked meat and has also created a way to produce hormone- and antibiotic-free dairy products. (785) 532-6011; www.k-state.edu.

K-State's campus holds several attractions, including the following:

Aggieville. Located on the southeast edge of the K-State campus. This full-service shopping area is a center for student activity and is the oldest shopping center of its kind in Kansas (see also Where to Shop).

Call Hall. Dairy and Poultry Science Building, Claflin and Mid-Campus Road, across from the Bob Dole Center on campus (see Where to Eat).

Marianna Kistler Beach Museum of Art. 701 Beach Lane, K-State Campus. A 17,000-square foot-expansion in 2007 added two galleries, bringing the museum's capacity to six galleries. The museum promotes appreciation of the fine arts through exhibitions of works by popular regional artists and through various educational and outreach programs. It also offers displays held in conjunction with other museums of art around the country. As a Lending Affiliate for the National Gallery of Art in Washington, D.C., the museum enables teachers to borrow educational resource materials developed by the National Gallery. Closed Monday. Free. (785) 532-7718.

Milford Lake. Four miles northwest of Junction City, c/o Milford State Park, 8811 State Park Road, Milford. Kansas's largest reservoir is one of the state's most productive for anglers. Walleye, crappie, smallmouth bass, and wiper—a hybrid between white and striped bass—abound in the lake waters. Weighing six to eight pounds, they join up with white bass and cruise together in the early summer to the main part of Milford to search for their favorite food of shad. According to experts, that's the time the wipers and white bass are easy to catch. With more than 16,000 surface acres and 163 miles of shoreline, there are plenty of fish around for the eating. Milford Lake and its surrounding 21,000 acres make up one of Kansas's prime outdoor habitats, and the body of water is one of the more scenic lakes in the area.

The Milford Nature Center/Fish Hatchery is located at the base of Milford Dam and offers displays and exhibits that explore the surrounding natural area. Free. (785) 238-3014; www.kdwp.state.ks.us/milford.

Strecker-Nelson Gallery. 406½ Poyntz Avenue. This upstairs gallery highlights the work of about forty local artists whose media include ceramics, silk, and oil. If you enjoy the beauty of the Flint Hills, you will find many of those images reflected in the work here. Closed Sunday. (785) 537-2099; www.strecker-nelsongallery.com.

Sunset Zoo. 2333 Oak Street. From I-70 take exit 303 into Manhattan to Fort Riley Boulevard; take this east to Westwood and turn north onto Westwood and then left onto Oak Street. This fifty-six-acre zoo may be small, but it is one of the most romantic zoos in the Midwest. That's because love is always in bloom here and lots of animals grow up healthy thanks to the zoo's excellent breeding program. There are thirteen endangered species in the zoo, including snow leopards and red pandas that have managed to thrive in captivity.

Other zoos, including the famed San Diego Zoo, send their animals here for breeding purposes because of the zoo's spectacular success rate at producing healthy zoo babies. The medical care for animals is unique. With K-State's renowned veterinary medical school and exotic medicine program available at all times, two K-State vets are employed by the zoo to monitor and care for the animals and their offspring. Most of the keepers and docents are pre-veterinary-med students, a factor that also helps to maintain the high standard of animal care and exhibition. Sunset Zoo has the only traveling Zoomobile program in the state and offers a lineup of special events annually, including festivals on both Memorial Day weekend and Labor Day. Open daily. Fee. (785) 587-APES; www.sunsetzoo.com.

Tuttle Creek Lake. Kansas Department of Wildlife and Parks, Tuttle Creek, 5020–B Tuttle Creek Boulevard. Fifteen miles north of I-70 on Kansas Highway 177 and framed by the Flint Hills, the reservoir is one of the region's largest. The 14,000-acre lake is surrounded by 104 miles of irregular, wooded shoreline, and its wildlife, water, and climate make it a good spot for outdoor recreation. White bass, crappie, channel catfish, and spawn fishing draw anglers, who come in spring and summer to drop a line in any of the numerous sites around the lake that are available for fishing. Other activities include boating, waterskiing, swimming, hunting, picnicking, camping, and other outdoor sports. Pontoon and fishing boat rentals, fishing supplies, fuel, boat-slip rentals, and concessions are available at the marina. Dinner cruises aboard a houseboat are offered for small groups. Free (user fees and permits charged in certain areas). (785) 539-7941; www.kdwp.state.ks.us.

University Gardens, Butterfly Conservatory, and Insect Zoo. Located at Denison Avenue, north of Claflin Road, the University Gardens is a work-in-progress that, when completed, will be nineteen acres of hardscape and tested ornamental plant material in different aesthetic settings. Included in the garden is a visitor information center with computers and other resource materials for public use. Located in an old dairy barn is the Butterfly Conservatory, which houses about fifty species of tropical plants that are home to dozens of species of butterflies. The best time to see butterflies in action is between 10:00 a.m. and noon. Maybe not as beautiful, but certainly as interesting, is the Insect Zoo, where you'll see many exhibits of live insects and their relatives, as well as displays featuring preserved specimens of exotic butterflies, moths, beetles, and other arthropods. The Butterfly Conservancy is open seven days a week. The Insect Zoo is open Monday, Wednesday, Friday, and Saturday. Free. (785) 532-2122; www.k-state.edu/butterfly.

where to shop

Aggieville. Southeast of the K-State campus, Manhattan. The first shopping center in Kansas is named for the former K-State Aggies. Today it is a pre- and postgame host to Wildcat sporting events. Aggieville offers more than one hundred businesses that feature shopping, dining, dancing, and nightlife, all within walking distance of K-State and concentrated in a little over 4 blocks. Everything from barbecue to women's clothing can be found here. Part of the fun is trying out the food, which ranges from cappuccino and croissants to Cajun jambalaya and gumbo. (785) 776-8050; www.aggieville.org.

Manhattan Town Center. 100 Manhattan Town Center. This regional mall in the heart of downtown Manhattan offers an assortment of fine stores, specialty shops, restaurants, and services. Anchored by Dillard's, Sears, and JCPenney, it offers one-stop shopping if you're in a hurry to find what you're looking for. Open daily. (785) 539-9207; www.manhattantowncenter.com.

where to eat

Call Hall. Dairy and Poultry Science Building, Claflin and Mid-Campus Road, across from the Bob Dole Center on the K-State campus, Manhattan. Although the locals know about it, newcomers seldom realize that a place like this could actually exist outside a health food store. Thanks to the scientific laboratories in the Dairy and Poultry Science Building, all the superb-tasting milk, butter, cheese, and ice cream comes straight from the cow to your mouth, hormone-free with no antibiotics. The pure and natural ice cream is made fresh weekly and contains 12 percent butterfat (the special vanilla ice cream has 16 percent butterfat—which is to swoon over). There are forty flavors of ice cream that change daily, and each one is better than the one before it. You could spend an entire day snarfing down sundaes, sodas, malts, and shakes, but then you would be waddling rather than walking back to your car. You might want to bring a cooler and plenty of ice to take back some of the terrific cheese and butter sold here. Closed Sunday. $; (no cards). (785) 532-1292.

Harry's Uptown Supper Club. 418 Poyntz. Turn-of-the-twentieth-century elegance, complete with wingback chairs, crystal chandeliers, and cloth-covered tables, highlights the ambience at this establishment. The wine list is extensive, and the menu features hand-cut Kansas choice beef, fresh seafood, chicken, and pasta. The raspberry cheesecake is delightful and so is the apple pie. Closed Sunday. $$–$$$. (785) 537-1300.

Hibachi Hut. 608 North Twelfth Street. The Cajun-inspired menu offers everything from *boudin* (rice and pork Cajun sausage), red beans and rice, jambalaya, and bayou catfish served with jambalaya on the side. The Cajun Feast includes gumbo to red beans and rice, and choice of blackened catfish fillet or top sirloin, served with cornbread, plus homemade bread pudding with whiskey sauce. $–$$. (785) 539-9393.

Little Apple Brewing Company. 1110 Westloop Shopping Center, Manhattan. Five refreshing handcrafted brews and certified Angus beef steaks are the claim to fame at this friendly restaurant and pub that caters to football lovers. $–$$. (785) 539-5500.

where to stay

Guest Haus Bed-and-Breakfast. 1724 Sheffield Circle. A Flint Hills view, a fishpond, and a cedar-lined walking path are part of the amenities here. Two antiques-filled guest rooms share a bath in the upstairs loft area. A continental breakfast is offered with your choice of room. $$ (no cards). (785) 776-6543; www.guesthaus.com.

Morning Star. 617 Houston Street. Within just blocks of the K-State campus, Morning Star features large windows and an expansive front porch for watching the comings and goings around town or spending some quality time with Ginger and Lucy, the two resident Boston terriers. Each of the five guest rooms is a corner room with private bath and in-room whirlpool. Are you familiar with Greek omelets? If not, you'll be delighted when breakfast is served. No children. $$. (785) 587-9703; www.morningstaronthepark.com.

day trip 05

west

national geographic scenic byway:
konza prairie research natural area; council
grove, ks; tallgrass prairie national preserve
(strong city, ks); cottonwood falls, ks; emporia, ks

national geographic
scenic byway

If you're feeling stressed out, burned-out, or just plain bummed out, then get in your car and head west on I-70 in the direction of the National Geographic Scenic Byway (Kansas Highway 177) and the Kansas Flint Hills. K–177 runs for 84 miles meandering from Manhattan to Cassoday, through a region of rounded limestone hills covered with bluestem prairie. Along the way you'll reach the eastern segment of the Konza Prairie Research Natural Area, and from there you can visit the Tallgrass Prairie National Preserve, Kansas's first national park. Keep traveling south and you'll come to the bed-and-breakfast country of Council Grove and Cottonwood Falls. For more information on all eight Kansas scenic byways, visit www.ksby ways.org. Or for information on other fun things happening in the Kansas Flint Hills, visit www.kansasflinthills.travel.

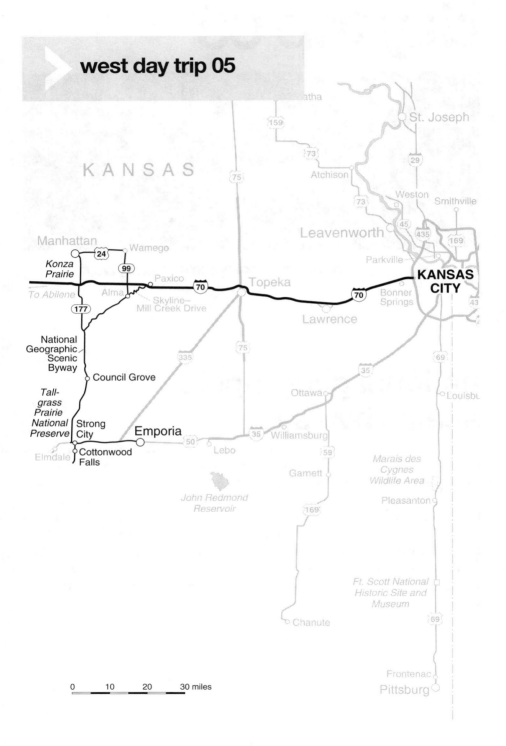

KANSAS

St. Joseph

atha

159

73

29

Atchison

Weston   Smithville

73

45

Leavenworth

435

169

Manhattan   Wamego

24

Parkville

**KANSAS
CITY**

Konza
Prairie

99

Paxico

Topeka

70

Bonner
Springs

70

43

To Abilene   Alma

Skyline—
Mill Creek Drive

177

Lawrence

National
Geographic
Scenic
Byway

335

75

69

Council Grove

35

Tall-
grass
Prairie
National
Preserve

Ottawa

Louisbu

Strong
City

Emporia

Elmdale   Cottonwood
Falls

50   Lebo

35   Williamsburg

59

Marais des
Cygnes
Wildlife Area

Garnett

Pleasanton

John Redmond
Reservoir

169

Ft. Scott National
Historic Site and
Museum

59

Chanute

Frontenac

Pittsburg

0   10   20   30 miles

konza prairie research natural area

Just south of Manhattan, the Konza Prairie Research Natural Area is easily viewed from adjacent highways. K–177 parallels the eastern segment of the preserve, and I-70 runs along most of its southern border. To reach the Konza Prairie entrance from K–177, drive to the east end of the Kansas River Bridge and turn onto McDowell Creek Road (County Road 901S). The entrance is about 6 miles down the road on the left. (From I-70 take exit 307 and drive northeast on McDowell Creek Road. The entrance is approximately 5 miles on your right.)

Owned by the Nature Conservancy and managed by Kansas State University for the purpose of scientific study of this natural ecosystem, the Konza Prairie is the most intensively studied grassland on earth. This scenic area, named for the Kanza Indians who once roamed here, covers more than 8,600 acres of unplowed, uncultivated land filled with seventy species of dominant grasses and more than 500 species of wildflowers, shrubs, and trees.

The bison herd that lives here is part of a scientific effort to study the effect of these native grazers upon the grasslands. Fire, along with innumerable animals who grazed here, shaped the landscape, and it is here at Konza that the effects of both are being investigated.

Most of the Konza Prairie Research Natural Area is closed to the public. However, a self-guided nature trail is open daily and trail maps are available at the front gate.

The Fall Visitors Day, offered every other year on even-numbered years, is filled with special tours and presentations. Tour guides are available with advance reservations. Pack your binoculars, since deer and hawk sightings are a common occurrence. Open from dawn to dusk year-round. Free. (785) 587-0441; www.konza.k-state.edu.

council grove, ks

Council Grove can be reached by heading south from Manhattan on scenic K–177 or by taking the equally pretty Skyline–Mill Creek Drive from Alma to K–177 and going south from there. By now your eyes must be used to the gentle, undulating countryside around you, so it should come as no surprise that Council Grove is smack in the middle of Kansas's native grassland, known as the Flint Hills.

The historic town of Council Grove got its name from a negotiated treaty between U.S. commissioners and the Osage Indian chiefs in 1825, an agreement that granted whites safe passage along the Santa Fe Trail.

A camping and meeting place for explorers, soldiers, traders, and Native Americans, Council Grove offered ample water, grass, and abundant wood, making it a rendezvous point for wagon trains heading west.

John Fremont's expedition of 1845 and Colonel A. W. Doniphan's troops bound for Mexico in 1846 camped on this site. In 1849 the Overland Mail was established with the supply headquarters at Council Grove, followed the next year by monthly coach service.

Council Grove today offers a quaint shopping district, restaurants, and lodging. The third weekend in June, it hosts Wah-Shun-Gah Days, a major festival with a parade, Indian pow-wow, rafting, and arts-and-crafts fair.

The historic town offers an informative self-guided walking-tour brochure, filled with historic things to see that include the wheel ruts left by the wagon trains heading west; the Custer Elm, where George Armstrong Custer camped prior to his Little Big Horn encounter; and the Council Oak, named for the treaty signed beneath the tree by the Osage Indians and the U.S. commissioners.

For group tours contact the Council Grove/Morris County Visitors Bureau, 207 West Main Street, Council Grove, KS 66846; (800) 732-9211 or (620) 767-5882; www.councilgrove.com.

where to go

Flint Hills Tours. c/o Council Grove Convention and Visitors Bureau, 212 West Main Street. This four-county consortium promotes travel throughout the region and offers tours to Council Grove, Emporia, Cottonwood Falls, and other places of interest. All excursions travel through the Flint Hills—the largest unbroken tract of tallgrass prairie left in North America. Draped in bluestem grasses and colorful wildflowers during warm weather, the Flint Hills are an ancient reminder of our planet's ecological history. The surface of the Flint Hills is composed of limestone sediment and thin layers of *chert* (commonly known as flint) that were deposited by inland seas more than 200 million years ago.

Centuries of erosion formed the rugged, high escarpments found in Chase County and the gently rolling landforms around Council Grove. Woodland Indians once roamed the area, and archaeological digs at Eldorado and Council Grove have unearthed many prehistoric campsites.

The early settlers in the area found that a combination of farming and ranching was not only possible in this region but often necessary for survival. Today's successful farmer-stockman must also use the rich bottomland soil for growing crops such as wheat, soybeans, corn, milo, and alfalfa, while employing the upland prairie, with its wonderful native grasses, for grazing cattle.

Kansas has produced nine world-champion rodeo cowboys, and six of them have lived in the region. The Flint Hills Rodeo, the oldest consecutively held rodeo in Kansas, occurs annually the first weekend in June in Strong City. The event is included in tour packages offered by Flint Hills Tours, Inc., which also features a "Santa Fe Trail" excursion that travels from Emporia to Council Grove, the main rendezvous on the trail. From here the trip heads to Cottonwood Falls and Strong City, traversing miles of grazing land, where prairie grasses and wildflowers thrive.

Cottonwood Falls offers attractions such as the Chase County Courthouse, the oldest courthouse still in use west of the Mississippi. It was completed in 1873. Entered on the National Register of Historic Places in 1971, the 113-foot structure is constructed of hand-cut native limestone and was built in the Louis XIII French Renaissance architectural style.

Visitors can tour the Chase County Historical Museum, which holds a collection of artifacts that interpret the history of the county. The museum also has interesting memorabilia relating to the 1931 Knute Rockne plane crash that occurred 10 miles south of Cottonwood Falls and claimed the life of the famed Notre Dame football coach.

The Flint Hills Tours through German-Mennonite country is another experience to savor. The German-speaking Mennonites who settled the region in the 1870s have left a rich legacy behind. Stops include a private farm on the Gnadenau Trail, where the wheel ruts left by the immigrant wagons en route to Hillsboro and Goessel can still be seen. (800) 732-9211 or (620) 767-5882.

where to shop

The Apothecary Shops. 115–119 West Main Street. The Canopy, Aldrich Apothecary, and Santa Fe T-Shirt Shop constitute a grouping of stores that feature a pharmacy, a boutique, and one of the last remaining soda fountains in Kansas. The soda fountain was installed in the 1920s and is marked by distinctive tile that adorns the fountain front, an original back bar, and a brass foot rail. In addition to cherry phosphates, sodas, sundaes, and shakes, you can order a cup of gourmet coffee or some frozen yogurt to go.

The adjacent full-line pharmacy opened in 1892 and has been refurbished with a nostalgic charm highlighted by a restored pressed-tin ceiling and antique fixtures. The soda fountain and pharmacy are connected with the Santa Fe T-shirt shop, which specializes in T-shirts, gifts, and collectibles. (800) 499-9747 or (620) 767-6731.

Trowbridge Classics. 113 West Main Street. You aren't likely to find another person wearing the same dress you've bought at this unusual women's clothing boutique that offers accessories, purses, and jewelry to go with your one-of-a-kind find. (620) 767-6992.

where to eat

Hays House 1857 Restaurant and Tavern. 112 West Main Street. This National Historic Landmark was built in 1857 by Seth Hays, great-grandson of Daniel Boone and cousin of Kit Carson. As the oldest continuously operated restaurant west of the Mississippi, the tavern is an attraction on the Santa Fe National Historic Trail tour. In its early days it was host to theatricals, court proceedings, mail distribution, and church services, as well as serving good food to all.

Now a comfortable stop for modern-day travelers, the Hays House offers delicious foods served in a relaxed atmosphere. Specialties include aged Kansas beef, homemade breads, and desserts. The Victorian-inspired second floor houses the Hays Tavern, which offers a fully stocked bar in the evening. The restaurant also features several private dining rooms. Open seven days a week. $$. (620) 767-5911.

where to stay

The Cottage House Hotel/Motel. 25 North Neosho Street. This restored Victorian hotel is on the National Register of Historic Places and has been serving travelers for more than a century. It features modern comforts in nostalgic surroundings and offers a relaxing atmosphere, with gazebo-style porches, a sauna, and period furnishings. Each of the twenty-six rooms in the main hotel has a distinctive style. Stained glass and a brass-and-iron bed are featured in the bridal chamber. A continental breakfast is served each morning. $$. (800) 727-7903 or (620) 767-6828; www.cottagehousehotel.com.

tallgrass prairie national preserve (strong city, ks)

This unique cooperative between the National Park Trust and the National Park Service is 2 miles north of Strong City (on Route 1) and contains 10,894 acres of tallgrass prairie, which is leased to the National Park Service. Expansive rolling hills and wide-open vistas greet you as you experience the beauty of this quiet land. From April 10 through October 31, a 7-mile bus tour is available to take you through the area. The natural prairie cycle of climate, fire, and animal grazing has sustained this beautiful land, where nearly 400 species of plants, 150 kinds of birds, 31 species of mammals, and assorted reptiles and amphibians reside.

Also at the preserve is the Z-Bar/Spring Hill Ranch, home of the original owner, Stephen F. Jones. The eleven-room structure, built with hand-cut native limestone, is characteristic of the Second Empire style of nineteenth-century architecture. Also on the premises is a massive three-story barn and Lower Fox Creek School, a one-room schoolhouse located on a nearby hilltop. Brochures are available for self-guided tours. Docent tours are given hourly between April 10 and October 31. Fee. For information: Tallgrass Prairie National Preserve, c/o National Park Trust, Route 1, Box 14, Strong City, KS 66869. (620) 273-8494; www.nps.gov/tapr.

where to stay

Clover Cliff Ranch. Rural Route 1, Box 30–1, Elmdale. Bring your own horse along to ride the trail that runs along this 4,000-acre working cattle ranch located east of Strong City, off U.S. Highway 50. Hiking, fishing, and general all-purpose relaxing are other amenities found at the ranch, which is listed on the National Register of Historic Places. The main house offers four guest rooms, two with private baths. There are also adjacent guest houses that are truly "homes away from home." The larger one features two bedrooms, a loft area with twin beds, a sitting room, two baths, kitchen facilities, a fireplace, and a television. The smaller guest house has two bedrooms, a sleeper sofa, one bath, kitchen facilities, a fireplace, and a television. Breakfast is served in the main house. Meetings, receptions, luncheons, or a tour and tea can also be scheduled. $$–$$$; (no cards). (800) 457-7406 or (620) 273-6698; www.clovercliff.com.

cottonwood falls, ks

The oldest settlement in Chase County, the tiny hamlet of Cottonwood Falls is located in the center of the picturesque Flint Hills. The best time to visit the area is spring, fall, or early summer, rather than during a hot summer scorcher. Don't be fooled by appearances; there are plenty of things to see and do around the town, provided you know where to go. Cottonwood Falls also boasts a renowned country inn that is definitely worth the drive. For information on Cottonwood Falls: Chase County Chamber of Commerce, 318 Broadway, Cottonwood Falls, KS 66845; (800) 431-6344; www.chasecountyks.org.

where to go

Chase County Courthouse. Broadway and Pearl Streets. Built in 1872 of native limestone, the courthouse is an impressive structure. Listed on the National Register of Historic Places, it remains the oldest courthouse in continual use in Kansas. Each year more than 6,000 visitors from around the country visit the structure, marveling at the architectural design, stonework, and spiral staircase. Guided tours of the courthouse can be arranged in advance. Fee. For information: Chase County Chamber of Commerce, 318 Broadway, Cottonwood Falls, KS 66845; (800) 431-6344.

Chase County Historical Society Museum. 301 Broadway. The museum holds historic memorabilia and artifacts of the area, including information about the demise of Knute Rockne, the famous Notre Dame coach who was killed when his airplane crashed in heavy fog near here in 1931. Donation requested. Closed Sunday and Monday. (620) 273-8500.

where to shop

Fiber Factory. 209 Broadway. Watch century-old looms in operation. Customers can make their own rope on an original old-time rope machine. You can purchase handwoven rugs, placemats, blankets, and scarves to take home. There's also an unexpected, yet interesting, display of old camera equipment and other items used by the Kansas Bureau of Investigation in solving crimes in this area years ago. Open daily. (620) 273-8686.

Flint Hills and Tallgrass Gallery. 321 Broadway. The gallery features the paintings of Chase County artists, along with custom-made spurs, knives, belt buckles, and hat racks. The shop also sells jewelry, Indian baskets, drums, and stained glass. Closed Sunday. (620) 273-6454.

Jim Bell & Son. 322 Broadway. If you're looking for a unique shopping experience, try this place. The restored building was opened in 1927 as a retail store for real cowboys. It still supplies any piece of custom-made tack the working cowboy needs, plus there's a boot and saddle repair shop located in the store's basement in case you decide to gallop into town on your horse. Even nonworking cowboys and cowgirls can find the latest styles in western and casual wear for the entire family, from boots and hats to outdoor wear, hunting apparel, and more. Open daily. (620) 273-6381.

where to eat

Emma Chase Cafe. 317 Broadway. The restaurant serves delightful sandwiches, entrees, ice cream, and desserts in a laid-back setting. If you choose to fly early into Cottonwood Falls the fourth Sunday of the month, owner Sue Smith will pick you up at the airport for breakfast. Call before you go. Visit on the first Friday of the month for catfish and music by local performers. $; (no cards). (620) 273-6020.

Grand Central Hotel and Grill. 215 Broadway. Looking for a little espresso, Asti Spumante, champagne, or Carmel Valley sauvignon blanc to perk up your day? What better place to find it than smack in the middle of a vast midwestern plain.

Located in the center of the Flint Hills, along the one and only main thoroughfare of town, this restaurant specializes in Sterling Silver, a line of Certified Premium USDA Choice steaks so terrific that you'll think you've died and gone to Kansas.

Entrees are served with salad, choice of potato or vegetable, and fresh bread and butter. Dessert can be Grand Central cheesecake topped with cherries or almond amaretto or homemade bread pudding with New Orleans bourbon sauce. The full-service restaurant offers lunch and dinner to the public and an elegant continental breakfast daily to hotel guests. Closed Sunday. $$–$$$. (800) 951-6763.

where to stay

Grand Central Hotel. 215 Broadway. Definitely not your little roadside prairie motel, the Grand Central Hotel is a must-stop on your way through Kansas. The AAA four-diamond hotel and restaurant opened in 1884 and reopened in 1995; the hotel has been restored beyond its original elegance. Located 2 miles from the Tallgrass Prairie National Preserve and 1 block west of scenic K–177, the Grand Central offers ten beautifully appointed rooms, all designed with a western flair. Its full-service restaurant offers lunch and dinner to the public and an elegant continental breakfast daily to hotel guests.

For starters, there are queen- and king-size beds draped with Egyptian cotton duvets and sheets purchased in Paris. Plush VIP robes, Jacuzzi showers, full concierge service, complimentary continental breakfast, and meeting rooms for private dining and corporate retreats are offered. A very nice wheelchair-accessible room on the first floor has its own outdoor porch.

Symphony on the Prairie

The best seat in the house for this performance is a hay bale, facing west.

In the most unlikely, but undeniably natural and appropriate setting, the Kansas City Symphony has found a new audience in the annual Symphony on the Prairie. Begun in 2006 as a tenth anniversary tribute to the Tall Grass National Prairie, the Symphony has become an immediate and sold-out hit.

The Symphony on the Prairie is held the second weekend in June, while the nights are still cool. Eighty-five musicians from the Kansas City Symphony perform under the stars, accompanied by singing cicadas and crickets, as the sun sets dramatically beyond the Flint Hills. Before the performance, visitors can take part in guided nature walks through the prairie, horse-drawn wagon rides, and a musical-instrument petting zoo. The location moves each year, but note that tickets go on sale in March and sell out quickly. (620) 273-8955; www.symphonyintheflinthills.org.

The hotel is happy to provide guests with a variety of outdoor experiences that include nature hiking, horseback riding, and fishing.

Another unusual offering is the "Prairie Drifter"—the hotel's 1958 wheat truck takes you on a 16-mile trip through the prairie, a trek ending with a sunset that stretches over the horizon with no man-made obstructions to mar the view. $$$. (800) 951-6763 or (620) 273-8381; www.grandcentralhotel.com.

emporia, ks

From Cottonwood Falls take US 50 back to Emporia (see Southwest From Kansas City, Day Trip 3).

day trip 06

west

presidential town:
abilene, ks
worth more time: salina, ks

abilene, ks

The name *Abilene* immediately conjures up images of the wild, wild West, with cowboys, cattle herds, and Main Street shoot-outs at the end of the Chisholm Trail. Although that image was certainly true in the mid-1800s, Abilene is now a quiet town that gave birth to one of the United States' most decorated military officers and beloved presidents.

Abilene comes from a Bible scripture that means "city of the plains," and although "city" may be a stretch, it is certainly a pleasant community on plains worthy of exploration. Too often, Kansas Citians blow through Abilene on I-70 on their way to more glamorous destinations at the other end of the interstate. However, those who stop for just a few moments or a few days will find a town void of many chain restaurants and commercial establishments, but with a vibrant downtown, lovely neighborhoods of historic homes, and a gentler pace of life.

Founded in a small dug-out homestead and stagecoach stop in 1857, Abilene had grown only slightly when the railroads began to reach across the Plains after the Civil War. The railroads meant a way to move cattle to market on the East Coast, and the Chisholm Trail brought cattle and cowboys from southern Texas by the millions beginning in 1867. For the next five years, more than three million cattle arrived in Abilene before being shipped east by rail. Some days as many as 5,000 cowboys received their pay for moving the cattle along the trail, so undoubtedly, things got a little rowdy downtown.

Today you can learn much of the history of Abilene via a trolley ride that departs from the restored train depot. The influx of wealth at the end of the nineteenth century resulted

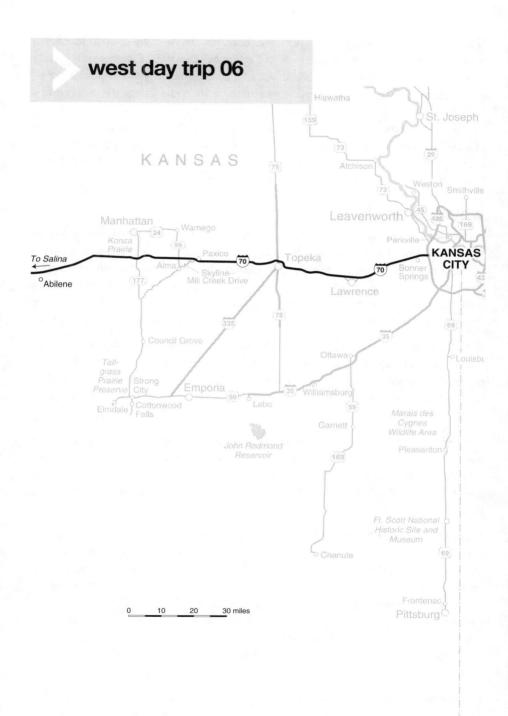

west day trip 06

Hiawatha

St. Joseph

KANSAS

159

73

29

Atchison

Weston

Smithville

73

45

435

169

Manhattan

Wamego

Leavenworth

24

Konza
Prairie

99

Parkville

To Salina ←

Paxico

70

Topeka

70

Bonner
Springs

**KANSAS
CITY**

Alma

Skyline—
Mill Creek Drive

43

Abilene

177

Lawrence

335

75

75

Council Grove

35

69

Ottawa

Louisbu

Tall-
grass
Prairie
Preserve

Strong
City

Emporia

50

35

Williamsburg

Elmdale

Cottonwood
Falls

Lebo

59

Garnett

Marais des
Cygnes
Wildlife Area

John Redmond
Reservoir

Pleasanton

169

Ft. Scott National
Historic Site and
Museum

Chanute

69

Frontenac

Pittsburg

0   10   20   30 miles

in several elegant homes, two of which have been restored and are open to tour today. However, Abilene is perhaps best known as the home of Dwight D. Eisenhower, the leader of Allied Forces in Europe during World War II, who became the thirty-fourth president of the United States. He and his five brothers were raised here, and a tour of the presidential library and grounds is a must for anyone visiting the community.

Several other museums, restaurants, and a professional theater company provide plenty of activity for a few hours or a few days. For more information about the history and interesting things to do in Abilene: Abilene Convention and Visitors Bureau, 201 Northwest Second Street, Abilene, KS 67410; (800) 569-5915; www.abilenekansas.org.

where to go

Abilene Smoke Valley Excursion Train. Depot located on Southeast Fifth Street, adjacent to the Greyhound Hall of Fame. Enjoy the Kansas countryside as you ride in a century-old dining car or open-air gondola car, or, for a special fare, you can ride in the caboose or the engine. The train is powered by a 1945 ALCO S–1 engine originally designed for World War II submarines. A gift shop in the depot carries all sorts of train memorabilia. Closed November through April. Call for fares and schedules. (785) 263-1077 or (888) 426-6687; www.asvrr.org.

American Indian Art Center. 206 South Buckeye. This unassuming facility showcases the artwork of nearly one hundred American Indian artisans, representing thirty tribes from the region. American Indian history books, music, and weaponry are also for sale, but the good-natured humor from owner Patt Murphy, a member of the Ioway-Sauk Tribe, is free. Closed Wednesday. Free. (785) 263-0090.

Bow Studio and Gallery. 921 South Buckeye. Take a piece of native Kansas home with you after a visit to the studio of Inga and Bob Bow. The wildflower garden that fills their property is for more than show. This is where Inga gathers ideas and materials for her work. You'll find leaves, flowers, wheat, and other designs of nature pressed and painted into original clay designs and fired on site. Open daily. (785) 263-7166; www.bowsart.com.

Dickinson County Historical Museum. 412 South Campbell. Here's where you can learn about the wicked history of Abilene in the days when it was known as one of the wickedest towns in the West. From jail records to antique guns confiscated from rowdy cowboys, the artifacts here tell the story of the conflicts between American Indians, white settlers, the military, and cattle herders more than a century ago. Within the museum is the Museum of Independent Telephony, which chronicles the early days of telephone service in small, rural towns like Abilene. In a separate building behind the museum is an operating C. W. Parker Carousel, one of the original hand-carved track-operated machines created by the Abilene-based entertainment company in the early 1900s. Open daily. Fee. (785) 263-2681.

Eisenhower Center. 200 Southeast Fourth Street. This complex tells the life story of native son Dwight D. Eisenhower, one of America's most honored military leaders and the thirty-fourth president of the United States. Historians of all genres and generations will appreciate the details presented from World War II and the D-day invasion led by then-General Eisenhower, as well as the global conflicts that followed WWII. Plan on spending several hours here touring the Eisenhower home, library, museum, and memorial chapel, where the former President and First Lady are buried. Fee for those sixteen and older for the museum only. Open daily. (785) 263-4751 or (877) RING-IKE; www.eisenhower.archives.gov.

Greyhound Hall of Fame. 407 South Buckeye. Sharon and Chig, two retired racing dogs, will greet you before you begin a self-guided tour, which showcases the "Sport of Queens." You may pet greyhounds and learn about the history of the world's fastest dogs all the way back to prehistoric times. Races and auctions of these animals are held here each April and October. Fee. Open daily. (800) 932-7881 or (785) 263-3000; www.greyhoundhalloffame.com.

Lebold Mansion. 106 North Vine Street. Built in 1880 by a wealthy banker, this twenty-three-room mansion is on the exact location of Abilene's first homestead, which still exists. The hand-painted ceilings, elaborate draperies, and French-style music room have been meticulously restored by owners Gary Yuschalk and Larkin Mayo, who are known internationally for their authentic Victorian decorating skills. The home housed telephone operators in the 1920s and became an orphanage in the 1930s. A bag of toys from that period was found hidden under the floorboards in the attic during renovation. The home is filled with period antiques. Three tours daily Tuesday through Sunday. Fee. (785) 263-4356.

Seelye Mansion. 1105 North Buckeye. Step back in time as you are guided through this 1905 Georgian-style mansion built by Dr. and Mrs. A. B. Seelye, the name that for years was associated with rural medical care and patent medicines. Stroll through the gardens and learn about the patent medicine manufacturing business located in Abilene that once rivaled the names of Bayer and Eli Lilly. Built in the early years of the twentieth century, the home contains many items and fixtures purchased at the 1904 World's Fair in St. Louis. Thomas Edison worked with the architect to bring lighting and other modern conveniences to the home. A basement-level bowling alley and a third-level ballroom speak to the opulence found on the Great Plains during this period. Christmas is an especially beautiful time to visit the Seelye Mansion to see the forty decorated Christmas trees and more than 200 poinsettias throughout the home. Open for tours daily. Fee. (785) 263-1084.

where to eat

Brookville Hotel. 105 East Lafayette. If you like fried chicken, you're in luck here because fried chicken is the only item on the menu. Since the 1870s, the Brookville Hotel, once located in the little town of Brookville, has been famous for its family-style fried-chicken dinners. Now the fourth generation of the Martin family continues the tradition in a replica of the original hotel from Brookville built in Abilene in 1999. Many of the furnishings are original to the old hotel. This Kansas institution received a 2007 James Beard Foundation America's Classics Award. Closed Monday. $$. (785) 263-2244; www.brookvillehotel.com.

The Kirby House. 205 Northeast Third Street. This elegantly restored home-turned-restaurant was built in 1885 by Thomas Kirby, a banker in early Abilene. Coconut walnut bread or a chilled strawberry soup are signature items here, but a little hardier fare is available with country-fried steak or a half-pound hamburger on sesame-seed bun. A Kirby House cookbook for sale on the premises has these recipes and other regional favorites. For special occasions, ask about dining in the cupola. Closed Sunday. $. (785) 263-7336; www.kirby-house.com.

Mr. K's Farmhouse. 407 South Van Buren. This rambling old farmhouse was a favorite of Dwight and Mamie Eisenhower when they lived in or returned to Abilene, and it's still popular today for homemade pies, roast beef, and huge pork chops. You may want to keep it quiet if you eat here on your birthday. You might just receive a paddling from one of the many wooden paddles hanging from the ceiling, a tradition that was begun when Dwight Eisenhower dined here on his seventy-fifth birthday. Closed Monday. $–$$. (785) 263-7995; www.mrksfarm house.com.

where to stay

Abilene's Victorian Bed and Breakfast Inn. 820 Northwest Third Street. This home dates to 1900 and today has six spacious guest rooms across the street from Eisenhower Park and within walking distance of downtown. Homemade cookies await your check-in, as well as board games, a video library, and a spacious porch for relaxing. A full breakfast is served each morning. $–$$. (785) 263-7774; www.abilenesvictorianinn.com.

worth more time: salina, ks

salina, ks

As long as you are in Abilene, drive just another 25 miles west on I-70 to Salina. Or, on your next trip to Colorado, plan an overnight stop in Salina. Either way, make sure you're wearing your Lee jeans when you come to town. This is where Henry David Lee founded a mercantile company in the late 1800s that eventually became Lee Jeans, now based in Merriam, KS.

The Historic Lee District in downtown Salina is now a pedestrian-friendly shopping district with more than 300 businesses. A number of festivals and special events take place here throughout the year.

Salina is also home to the Smoky Hill Vineyards and Winery, a fabulous wildlife center, and NJCAA Women's Basketball Tournament each March that makes the hoops-lovers in Lawrence pause to take notice.

For more information, contact the Salina Chamber of Commerce, 120 West Ash Street, Salina, KS 67402; (785) 827-9301; www.salinakansas.org.

northwest

day trip 01

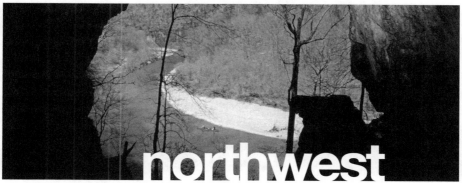

northwest

military memorabilia, mansions, museums, and memorials:
leavenworth, ks; atchison, ks; hiawatha, ks

leavenworth, ks

Located off U.S. Highway 73, Leavenworth contains an amazing amount of memorabilia and history. As the "First City of Kansas," Leavenworth was at the forefront of the transportation revolution. From boat to wagon to railroad, the town led the way in opening the vast resources of America. The new transportation-themed Leavenworth Landing Park, located adjacent to the Missouri River, features exhibits that portray the town's part in forging a path through the American West.

All along the Overland Trails, U.S. Cavalry fortifications such as Fort Leavenworth sprang up to defend western settlement. Between 1838 and 1845 a military road was constructed through the Indian Territory to connect Fort Leavenworth in Kansas and Fort Gibson in Oklahoma. Throughout the years the road was traveled by soldiers, immigrants, Indians, outlaws, and traders.

Today the old military road no longer exists, but modern U.S. Highway 69 and other connecting pathways located near its original route have been designated the Frontier Military Scenic Byway. Fort Leavenworth and Fort Scott, two of the remaining historic Kansas forts lying along that route, are open to tour today.

Established by Colonel Henry Leavenworth in 1827, Fort Leavenworth was a cantonment to protect wagon trains headed west and to help maintain peace with the Native Americans. Leavenworth was also the starting point for exploration parties. When travel to California began in the 1840s, thousands of prairie schooners passed through the posts. Supplies to support the wagons flowed upriver in great quantities. The freight firm of Russell, Majors, and Waddell supplied 4,000 ox teams that hauled sixteen million pounds of freight annually by wagon train.

By 1857 Leavenworth, with a population of nearly 5,000, had survived a disastrous fire to greet Abraham Lincoln as he gave his fifth address in the territory on December 3, 1859.

During the pre–Civil War strife, Leavenworth suffered, but unlike other towns that were ruined by the war, Leavenworth curiously experienced growth. The railroads grew, as did schools and businesses. Like Weston and St. Joseph, Leavenworth also saw steamboat and river traffic, and by 1883 it was well on its way to becoming the leading city in the West.

But expansion came too rapidly for the town, and eventually the bubble burst. Leavenworth did not become the capital of Kansas as everyone had predicted. Instead, it has remained the seat of Leavenworth County.

Yet Leavenworth has had its share of the famous and infamous. In 1895 the Fort Leavenworth Military Prison was transferred to the Department of Justice, and Congress authorized 1,000 acres of military reservation for a penitentiary.

The U.S. Penitentiary at Leavenworth was completed in 1906 and has housed infamous criminals within its walls, including Al Capone, "Machine Gun" Kelly, and Robert Stroud, the "Birdman of Alcatraz."

Leavenworth has a long list of good guys, too. Civil War General William T. Sherman practiced law here, and restaurateur Fred Harvey built his magnificent home on one of the tree-shaded streets. William F. "Buffalo Bill" Cody, army scout and showman, came to Leavenworth in 1853 when he was ten years old. Working for J. B. "Wild Bill" Hickok, he helped outfit trains with supplies for the Overland Stage Company. Cody married a Missouri bride and settled down in Leavenworth, employed as a scout for the Kansas Cavalry.

Leavenworth's U.S. Army Command and General Staff College, on the post, educated such famous students as Douglas MacArthur, George Marshall, Black Jack Pershing, Dwight Eisenhower, and Colin Powell.

To learn more about Leavenworth's history, you can visit its museums and monuments. A drive on scenic US 73 past St. Mary's College, established in 1858, will take you there. Or if you are coming from Weston, it's a short drive south down Kansas Highway 45 and a jog west on Kansas Highway 92 into town.

The Leavenworth Area Convention and Visitors Bureau, 518 Shawnee Street, P.O. Box 44, Leavenworth, KS 66048, can supply you with brochures, self-guided-tour booklets, and other information on the city. (913) 682-4113; www.lvarea.com.

where to go

Carroll Mansion. 1128 Fifth Avenue. More than a museum, this elegant 1882 Victorian home is a masterpiece of elaborately carved woodwork and stained-glass windows. You can feel the style and spirit of the age as you travel through this sixteen-room mansion. The parlor contains fine Sevres, Dresden, and Early American porcelain; Steuben glass; and lovely furniture. Elsewhere in the museum you'll see antiques from Leavenworth homes, some of them brought up the river by steamer in the past.

In the kitchen, along with the pitcher pump and woodstove, is a copper sink, a refinement of the period. The bathroom contains a lead tub that supplied both hot and cold water and a shower-bath, newfangled oddities that were probably among the first in the West. Old quilts and hand-loomed coverlets are displayed in the bedrooms, and a child's room contains a collection of antique toys. The museum is maintained by the Leavenworth County Historical Society and is a must for nostalgia lovers. Closed on Sunday and Monday, and in January and February. Fee. Group tours can be arranged by calling (913) 682-7759.

Chapel of the Veterans. Dwight D. Eisenhower VA Medical Center, US 73. The stained glass here will take your breath away, as will the Gothic architecture of the building. Constructed in 1893, the Chapel of Veterans was included in 1921's *Ripley's Believe It or Not,* which stated that this was the only chapel in the world where Catholic and Protestant services could be held simultaneously under one roof. The Catholic chapel is on the lower level, with the Protestant chapel above it. Open Monday through Friday 9:00 a.m. to 4:00 p.m.

Combined Arms Center & Fort Leavenworth. Seventh and Metropolitan Streets, Fort Leavenworth. Established in 1827, this is the oldest military installation in continuous service west of the Mississippi River. In the early part of the nineteenth century, it played an important role for settlers and wagon trains heading west. Generals George Custer, William Sherman, Robert E. Lee, Douglas MacArthur, Dwight D. Eisenhower, George S. Patton, Omar Bradley, "Stormin' Norman" Schwarzkopf, and Colin Powell were stationed here. Today it is home to the Combined Arms Center, the Command and General Staff College, and the U.S. Disciplinary Barracks. A self-guided-tour booklet is available in the Frontier Army Museum Gift Shop on the premises. Visitors are welcome to drive through the fort year-round, but be prepared to present photo identification and have your vehicle searched upon entering the gates. (913) 684-5604; www.leavenworth.army.mil. The following on-site places are of note:

Berlin Wall Monument. Three sections of the destroyed Berlin Wall were donated to Fort Leavenworth because of the worldwide influence of the U.S. Army Command and General Staff College. The design of the memorial expresses three themes: a "falling position," representing the crumbling of the wall; a horizontal position, depicting the wall's destruction; and a vertical position, symbolizing democracy. Open daily. Free. (800) 844-4114

Buffalo Soldier Monument. Grant Avenue and the south bank of Smith Lake, Fort Leavenworth. This monument, dedicated July 25, 1992, honors the African-American soldiers who served in the Ninth and Tenth Cavalry Regiments from 1866 until the armed services were integrated following World War II. Open daily. &. Free. (913) 684-5604.

The Frontier Army Museum. Off Reynolds Avenue, Fort Leavenworth. The museum blends the history of Fort Leavenworth with that of the Frontier Army from 1817 to 1917. The outstanding exhibits graphically relate the history of the U.S. Army and its role in western expansion beginning with the Lewis and Clark Expedition of 1804–1806. The carriage used by Abraham Lincoln on his visit to Kansas in December 1859 is displayed here. A special story hour about pioneer life is offered to elementary school children by appointment. Open daily. 🏠 . Free. (913) 651-7440.

Fort Leavenworth National Cemetery. More than 20,000 veterans representing every war since 1812 are buried here. The large monument near the flagpole marks the grave of Colonel Henry Leavenworth, for whom the fort and the city of Leavenworth are named. Captain Thomas West Custer, brother of General George A. Custer, is buried here beside other officers of the Seventh Cavalry who died at Little Bighorn. Open daily. Free. (913) 684-5604.

Rookery. 12–14 Sumner Place, Fort Leavenworth. This was the temporary home of the first territorial governor of Kansas and is the oldest continuously occupied house in the state, built in 1834. A National Historic Landmark, it once housed First Lieutenant Douglas MacArthur, who lived here as a bachelor officer. The Rookery is not open to tour. (913) 684-5604.

C. W. Parker Carousel Museum. Esplanade and Choctaw Streets. The C. W. Parker Amusement Company, which began in Abilene in 1896, later moved to Leavenworth, where it operated successfully until the start of the Great Depression. The museum to this amusement company houses a carousel from 1913 that is considered unique because of its two hand-carved rabbits used as a focal point. The carousel also has twenty-four hand-carved horses, three ponies, and a lover's cup to ride in. A flying horse carousel from the 1850s also makes its home here. Open Thursday through Saturday. Donations accepted. (913) 682-1866; www.firstcitymuseum.org.

First City Museum. 734 Delaware Street. Here you can find a collection of early frontier memorabilia and artifacts, including buggies and cutters that were manufactured in Leavenworth. Donations. (800) 844-4114 or (913) 682-1866.

Heimhof Winery. 25168 Tonganoxie Road, Leavenworth. If you like German wines, this is the place to visit for eight varieties of locally produced wines. There's a great pavilion for large group events. Or you can come just to explore the gift shop, which has an impressive collection of stained-glass art and handcrafted products to accent any wine-tasting event. Closed Monday. (913) 351-3467; www.heimhofwines.com.

Leavenworth Landing Park. Missouri River and Esplanade. This transportation-themed park is decorated with sculptures depicting different modes of transportation throughout Leavenworth's history. The Paddle Wheel Plaza is reminiscent of the actual riverboat landing located in this same area. The Roundhouse Plaza uses inlaid paving stones depicting the railroad roundhouse that was located at the eastern end of the downtown area. Another unique feature is a raised four-state map constructed of terrazzo and brass; it locates the rivers, trails, and railroads that were an important part of Kansas's history. A diorama explains the scientific value of plant specimens gathered during the Lewis and Clark Expedition. Open daily. ♿ , 🏠 . Free. (913) 651-2132.

National Fred Harvey Museum. 624 Olive Street, Leavenworth. In the early days of rail-roading, passengers on the Santa Fe stopped at Fred Harvey restaurants for good food. The Harvey waitresses were the subject of a 1946 movie (*The Harvey Girls*). Fred Harvey, founder of the chain, made a fortune on his restaurants. He lived in the house that later became this museum in the nineteenth century until his death in 1901. The home is filled with artifacts of the Harvey House chain. (800) 844-4114 or (913) 682-4113.

Performing Arts Center. 500 Delaware Street. This 1938 theater is an interesting example of American art deco architecture. Now on the National Register of Historic Places, the struc-ture was donated to the city by Durwood, Inc., and today hosts live performances by Leaven-worth's River City Community Players. Call for a schedule of upcoming performances. (913) 682-4113 or (800) 844-4114.

Riverfront Community and Convention Center. 123 South Esplanade. The totally reno-vated and expanded 1888 Union Pacific Train Depot, now called the Riverfront Convention and Community Center, is located on the banks of the picturesque Missouri River in the heart of historic downtown Leavenworth. The multipurpose complex provides attractive, well-equipped meeting rooms, with on-site recreational opportunities and banquet service by the Harvey Girls upon request. Open daily. ♿ . Tours are free (fee charged to use the facility). (800) 844-4114 or (913) 651-2132.

where to eat

The Corner Pharmacy. Fifth and Delaware Streets. The pharmacy has been around since 1871, and its old-fashioned soda fountain and lunch counter are a throwback to the days when you could get good food and medicine all in one trip. Breakfast and lunch are served at the Victorian-style soda fountain, which comes complete with mahogany bentwood swivel stools and a mirrored back bar. The shakes, malts, and sodas are served in glass containers with the cans from the mixer alongside. The Corner also features homemade chili and an assortment of sandwiches, plus terrific fresh-squeezed limeades and homemade lemonades. Closed Sunday. $. (913) 682-1602.

High Noon Saloon. 206 Choctaw Street. Housed in the old 1858 Great Western Manufac-turing Company Building, the restaurant features good barbecue and the Frontier Prairie Brew-ing Company. Daily specials include meatloaf and mashed potatoes and roast beef sandwiches. The Leavenworth Players Group, a local acting company, stages monthly mur-der mystery dinners at the High Noon. Find the schedule on the Web site. $$. (913) 682-4876; www.thehighnoon.com.

Mama Mia's. 402 South Twentieth Street. During the summer months, enjoy the lovely land-scaped backyard with a garden pool while you wait for your table. The menu features Italian dishes and hand-cut steaks. Open Tuesday through Friday for lunch and Tuesday through Saturday for dinner. $$. (913) 682-2131.

where to stay

The Prairie Queen Bed and Breakfast. 221 Arch Street. Named in honor of a Missouri riverboat that stopped in Leavenworth, this 1868 home has been restored to elegance. It features three bedrooms with king-size beds and private baths, and a full breakfast, afternoon tea, and evening snack of your choice. $$; (913) 758-1959; www.prairiequeen.com.

atchison, ks

A picturesque drive north on US 73 from Leavenworth takes you past green rolling hills and valleys that lead to Atchison. It was here on July 4, 1804, that Lewis and Clark and the Corps of Discovery camped and celebrated the twenty-eighth birthday of the United States by firing their cannon. Independence Creek, the waterway that runs through Atchison into the Missouri River where Lewis and Clark camped, received its name that day. During the mid-nineteenth century, Atchison was an important center of overland freighting. In 1859 the Atchison, Topeka, Santa Fe Railway Company was founded here. A renovated 1880s-era freight depot now houses the Santa Fe Depot Visitors Center, historical museum, and gift shop.

Atchison is filled with history, museums, antiques and specialty shops, and magnificent nineteenth-century mansions, many of which are located on the beautiful Missouri River bluffs. A walking-and-driving-tour brochure is available from the Atchison Chamber of Commerce, Santa Fe Depot Visitors Center, 200 South Tenth Street, P.O. Box 126, Atchison, KS 66002. Guided tours for groups of fifteen or more are available with advance notice. 🔺. (800) 234-1854 or (913) 367-2427; www.atchisonkansas.net.

where to go

Amelia Earhart Birthplace Museum. 223 North Terrace Street. This historic home, where Amelia Earhart was born in 1897, is listed on the National Register of Historic Places. Interpretive displays, newspaper and magazine clippings, and family belongings tell the story of the leg-endary aviatrix. Open daily February through mid-December, afternoons and by appointment from mid-December through February. Fee. (913) 367-4217; www.ameliaearhartmuseum.org.

Amelia Earhart Earthwork. This one-acre portrait of Amelia Earhart is on a hillside near Warnock Lake. It comprises live plantings, stone, and other natural materials. It is the first perpetual crop artwork created by famed Kansas artist Stan Herd and was designed to com-memorate Earhart's one-hundredth birthday. A nearby viewing deck offers a good look at the

glaciers and guitars

The latest addition to the Kansas Scenic Byway Program is located along Kansas Highway 7 from Leavenworth, and north through Atchison, all the way to the Nebraska border. Also called the Glacial Hills Scenic Byway because of the region's glacier-created rolling hills and valleys, this part of Kansas looks more like "Little Switzerland" than it does flatland.

In downtown Leavenworth, K–7 is also known as Fourth Street, and it's where you'll find two guitar-shaped signs proclaiming Leavenworth to be the hometown of Melissa Etheridge. The Grammy award–winning singer was born here in 1961, graduated from Leavenworth High School in 1979, and returns often for benefit concerts and other events to support the community.

earthwork and photographic displays that illustrate how the artist created his unusual portrait. Free. (800) 234-1854 or (913) 367-2427.

Atchison County Historical Society. 200 South Tenth Street. Located in a restored Santa Fe Depot, this museum hosts some interesting exhibits on Amelia Earhart, Lewis and Clark, and other events, large and small, in the area. It is also home to the Unofficial David Rice Atchison Presidential Library. (Atchison served as president for a twenty-four-hour period in March 1849.) Open daily. (913) 367-6238; www.atchisonhistory.org.

Atchison Trolley. 200 South Tenth Street. The trolley offers hour-long tours of the city and its historic sites and attractions. Special themed tours are offered for fall, Halloween, and Christmas. Open May, June, July, and August. Dates vary. Fee. (913) 367-2427.

Benedictine College. 1020 North Second Street. Founded more than 145 years ago by the joint Catholic communities of Mount St. Scholastica and St. Benedict's Abbey, the entire Second Street complex is listed on the National Register of Historic Places. Visitors can tour the campus, which is located above a river bluff affording a breathtaking autumn view. Tours are given through prior arrangement and are free. (913) 367-5340; www.benedictine.edu.

International Forest of Friendship. South of Atchison on K–7 near Warnock Lake. Trees from all fifty states and from thirty countries grow here. Spend a pleasant afternoon walking along a path engraved with the names of famous aviators, and spend a minute or two reflecting at a memorial for the astronauts who died aboard the space shuttle *Challenger*. There's no charge here, but donations are welcome. (913) 367-2427.

Muchnic Art Gallery. 704 North Fourth Street. Monthly displays by regional artists are exhibited amid the elegant furnishings of one of Atchison's most spectacular Victorian mansions.

The interior features rich woodwork, fine hand-tooled leather, brilliant stained-glass windows, and elaborate fireplaces. Open Saturday and Sunday afternoon and 10:00 a.m. to 5:00 p.m. on Wednesday. Closed January through March. Free (fee for tour groups). (913) 367-4278; www.atchison-art.org.

where to shop

Ball Brothers Gift Shop. 504 Commercial Street. An old-fashioned lunch counter with a soda fountain is the centerpiece on the main floor of this always-busy drugstore. Downstairs is a gift shop specializing in housewares, Atchison souvenirs, and Department 56 collectibles. Closed Sunday. (913) 367-0332.

Nell Hill's. 501 Commercial Street. This large, upscale store specializes in furniture, prints, pictures, and home accessories. Closed Sunday. (913) 367-1086; www.nellhills.com.

Room to Breathe. 507 Commercial Street. Just around the corner from Nell Hill's, this garden shop features practical and whimsical items for your home and garden. From candles and stepping-stones to wind chimes and doormats, sisters Erin and Ryanne O'Reilly have created a delightful collection of indoor and outdoor art. Closed Sunday. (913) 367-6171.

where to eat

Marigold Bakery and Cafe. 715 Commercial Street. This European-style cafe serves fresh-baked breads and breakfast goods. Lunches feature specialty sandwiches, soups, and salads, along with homemade pies, cakes, and cookies. Come Friday night for gourmet pizza. Closed Sunday. $. (913) 367-3858.

The River House Restaurant. 101 Commercial Street. American fare is served in an open, airy atmosphere amid the charm of a restored 1870 building that was the former headquarters and business hotel of the Atchison & Nebraska Railroad. You may choose to dine on the outdoor patio during warm weather and enjoy a nice view of the Amelia Earhart Bridge, which spans the Missouri River. Open daily. $$. (913) 367-3330.

where to stay

Glick Mansion Bed and Breakfast. 503 North Second Street. Listed on the National Register of Historic Places, the mansion was built in 1873 and named after its owner, Governor George Washington Glick. In 1913 the home underwent renovation by Kansas City's most innovative architect, Louis Curtiss, who converted it from a Victorian-style structure to a Tudor-Revival manor. Guest rooms feature private baths and queen-size beds. A full breakfast is served in the spacious dining room. Ask about the ghosts that haunt the neighborhood around Glick Mansion. $$–$$$. (913) 367-9110; www.glickmansion.com.

St. Martin's Bed and Breakfast. 324 Santa Fe Street. Built in 1948, this yellow two-story B&B's five individually decorated rooms have canopied beds, claw-foot tubs, and antiques.

It's a great getaway for adults but not for kids under age ten. $$. (913) 367-4964; www.st martinsbandb.com.

hiawatha, ks

A "grave situation" awaits you in the tiny town of Hiawatha, Kansas. It's a *Ripley's Believe It or Not* kind of thing, and if you want to know more, head north on US 73 from Atchison to U.S. Highway 159 and on to Hiawatha, or if you're coming from St. Joseph, take U.S. Highway 36 West to one of the most unusual monuments to love you'll ever see.

where to go

The Davis Memorial. Mount Hope Cemetery, Hiawatha. From Horton take US 159/73 north to Hiawatha. Or if you're coming from St. Joseph, take US 36 West. It's worth the drive to see one of the most unusual monuments ever built. Each year thousands of people come to see the tomb and sign their names on the guest register mounted at the site of this strange rendering of love and loss.

When Sarah Davis of Hiawatha died in 1930, her husband, John M. Davis, perpetuated her memory by building a memorial that contains eleven life-size figures depicting the couple at various stages of their married life.

Davis spent a whopping sum of $500,000 to have the imported marble and granite figures carved by Italian craftsmen. He died penniless in a county home for the aged in 1947. A statue of Sarah, complete with angel wings, was positioned over the vault in which his coffin was placed, and her body rests in the crypt next to his. Atop that stone slab is a kneeling statue of Davis.

Although Davis's death and funeral were written up in *Life* magazine, few people attended the service. Only one man, Horace England, the tombstone salesman, seemed genuinely concerned by Davis's passing. Open daily. Free. No phone.

Native American Heritage Museum. 1737 Elgin Road, Highland. Located one mile north of US 36, this state historic site was once a Presbyterian Mission built in 1845. You'll find beautiful examples of the baskets and other handiwork of the Sac and Fox tribes of this area and learn more about the people who made this area home. Closed Monday and Tuesday. Fee. (785) 442-3304; www.kshs.org/places/nativeamerican/index.htm.

where to eat

Gus's Restaurant. 604 Oregon Street. Here you'll find a basic country-style interior and an open kitchen area, so you'll have the opportunity to talk with Gus or the other cooks as they prepare hot beef sandwiches or pork tenderloin with a Greek flair, courtesy of Gus. $; (no cards). (785) 742-4533.

day trip 02

northwest

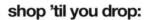

shop 'til you drop:
parkville, mo; weston, mo

parkville, mo

The land for the town of Parkville was purchased in 1840 by Colonel George S. Park, a veteran of Sam Houston's cavalry who recognized the value of riverfront land for steamboat trade. As trade and commerce grew along the river, so did Parkville.

Despite floods, tornadoes, and train derailments, the town of Parkville is not only alive and well, it's thriving. There isn't a single vacancy in its downtown shops, which combine specialty items with antiques, crafts, clothing, home furnishings, and art.

Park University, formerly Park College, was founded in 1875 and sits high on a bluff overlooking the town. It has always been an integral part of city activities, frequently opening its facilities to the community.

Getting to Parkville from Kansas City is easy. It's northwest of the city on Missouri Highway 45 and is also accessible by Interstates 435, 70, and 635. The town's amenities include English Landing Park, a short block from downtown. It offers a walking trail by the river, picnic facilities, basketball goals, a volleyball court, and the unique Waddell A-Frame Bridge, listed on the National Register of Historic Places. Parkville also boasts an unusual nature sanctuary that makes for a pleasant retreat, as well as a popular farmers market on Wednesday afternoons and Saturday mornings.

The city has a festival atmosphere year-round. There's a Parkville Jazz and Fine Arts River Jam in June and Christmas on the River in December. Information on Parkville, as well as a

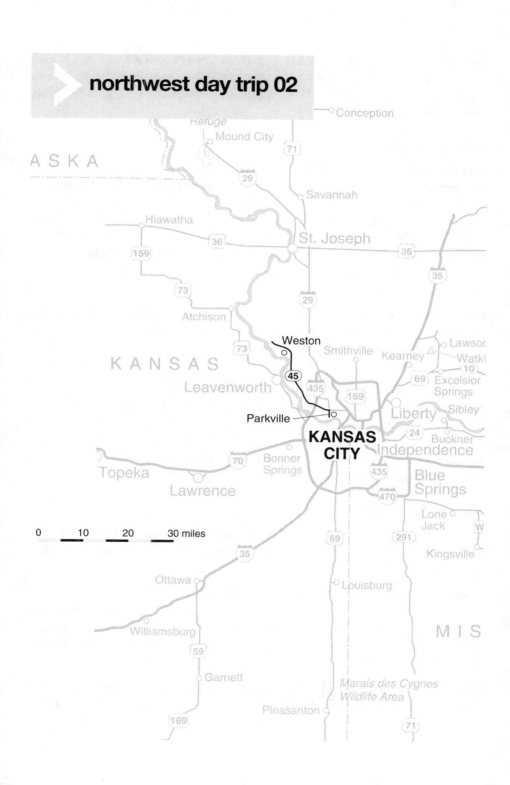

northwest day trip 02

Conception

Refuge

Mound City

71

ASKA

29

Savannah

Hiawatha

36

St. Joseph

36

159

35

73

29

Atchison

73

Weston

Smithville

Kearney

Lawson

Watki

10

KANSAS

45

435

169

69

Excelsior
Springs

Leavenworth

Parkville

Liberty

Sibley

KANSAS
CITY

24

Buckner

Independence

70

Bonner
Springs

Topeka

435

Blue
Springs

Lawrence

470

Lone
Jack

W

0   10   20   30 miles

69

291

Kingsville

35

Ottawa

Louisburg

Williamsburg

MIS

59

Garnett

Marais des Cygnes
Wildlife Area

Pleasanton

169

71

walking-tour brochure, can be obtained from the Main Street Parkville Association, 207 Main Street, Suite B, Parkville, MO 64152, (816) 505-2227, www.parkvillemo.net; or the Parkville Chamber of Commerce, 8701 NW River Park Drive, Parkville, MO, 64152, (816) 587-2700, www.parkvillechamber.com.

where to go

Park University. 8700 Northwest River Park Drive. The university has a unique and contrasting campus that boasts buildings listed on the National Register of Historic Places. A variety of educational offerings is available to the public. Free tours are given Monday through Friday. Be sure to visit the underground library and the Campanella Gallery, which highlights the work of students, faculty, and some community members. The Jenkin and Barbara David Theatre hosts six impressive performances each year, and the Graham Tyler Memorial Chapel is home to musical performances by the Parkville Community Band and other community groups. (816) 741-2000, ext. 6211; www.park.edu.

Parkville Mini Golf. 7 Mill Street. This challenging eighteen-hole miniature golf course is great for families with children. There is room for private parties and birthday groups. Located on the bluff overlooking downtown Parkville, the course offers an unbeatable view of the town below and a clubhouse that houses a full-service snack bar and video game entertainment. Hours change seasonally. Fee. (816) 505-9555; www.parkvilleminigolf.com.

Parkville Nature Sanctuary. Main entrance behind Platte County Health Department, 1201 East Street. Featuring more than 110 acres of natural fields, woodlands, ponds, and small waterfalls, the sanctuary makes a wonderful getaway from the stress of the city. The volunteer staff offers guided nature hikes and special events. Open daily. Free. &. (816) 741-7676; www.parkvillemo.com.

where to shop

Angela & Company. 112 Main Street. This interesting shop offers a wide variety of items, including safari-inspired pillows, trunks, animals, and other home accessories. Closed Monday. (816) 741-9675.

H.M.S. Beagle. 180 English Landing Drive. Part museum, part retail center, this fun science store is owned by the family of an archeologist who is often away on assignment, digging for fossils and such around the world. Check out the remains of Polly, a 125-million-year-old dinosaur. Anything the aspiring astronomer or archeologist could want can be found here. (816) 587-9998; www.hms-beagle.com.

Home Embellishments. 102 Main Street. This shop provides contemporary local art for your home, from knobs and pulls to whimsical yard accessories. Closed Monday. (816) 505-1022.

9 Lives. 103 Main Street. "Reincarnated" furniture is given another life here. It's cleaned, repaired, and sold good as new. Also featured are unusual furnishings from the '30s through the '70s. Closed Monday. (816) 741-4448.

Northland Exposure Artists Cooperative Gallery. 104 North Main Street. If you're looking for one-of-a-kind finds, check out this artists' cooperative and gallery. The Northland Exposure Gallery is owned and operated by fifty regional artists from a two-state area. Inside you'll find exceptional silver and glass jewelry designs and exciting works in watercolor, acrylic, oil, mixed media, pottery, and handcrafted paper. Closed Monday. (816) 746-6300.

River's Bend Gallery. 201 Main Street. This spacious gallery represents the work of about one hundred artists from around the country and is known for high-end glass art. But owner Rick McKibben also carries a nice selection of wooden bowls, jewelry, and some hand-woven scarves. Closed Monday. (816) 587-8070.

where to eat

Cafe des Amis. 112½ Main Street. Fine French cuisine is available in the upper level of a building built in 1844. The restaurant is building a reputation for delicious crepes, but daily specials run the gamut of everything delectable from the French. $$. (816) 587-3844.

Piropos Argentinean Restaurant. The original location at 1 West First Street in Parkville, with magnificent views of the Missouri River valley, is still available for private parties, such as wedding receptions or corporate events. However, couples looking for a romantic dinner will need to drive just a few miles east on Missouri Highway 9 to Briarcliff Village, where the second Piropos opened in November 2006 (4141 Mulberry Drive). Offering a magnificent view of the downtown skyline, Piropos continues to include an expansive selection of South American and European wines with a lunch and dinner menu that highlights empanadas, Milanesa de Tilapia, and Argentinean beef. $$–$$$. (816) 741-3600; www.piroposkc.com.

Stone Canyon Pizza Co. 15 Main Street. Appetizers, pizza, pasta, salads, and sandwiches are served at this popular Parkville establishment. Clowns and magicians entertain kids on Friday night. Open for lunch and dinner. This is Parkville's only nonsmoking restaurant. $. (816) 746-8686.

where to stay

Main Street Inn. 504 Main Street. Fans of Piropos Argentinean Restaurant will love a night at this historic inn, owned by the same Parkville couple who developed Piropos. This 1886 home, built from bricks kilned by Park College students in the 1880s, has three warm and cheery guest rooms named after various blends of wine, highlighted with intriguing stained glass and tastefully furnished with antiques and modern amenities. The Chardonnay Room overlooks Main Street, the Pinot Noir Room has a private entrance, and the Merlot Room has the easiest access to the centrally located coffee and refreshment bar. Your room rate also includes a bottle of the house wine served at Piropos and a $15 gift certificate toward dinner at the romantic restaurant. Innkeeper Becky Fritz offers a gourmet breakfast that may include ham strada or sticky bun French toast. $$–$$$. (816) 741-9800; www.main-street-inn.com.

Porch Swing Inn. 702 East Street. Built in the 1890s for a Park College professor, this three-story home overlooks the Park University soccer fields today and is two blocks from downtown shops. Each room is named for and themed around western characters, such as Jesse James and Calamity Jane. $$. (816) 587-6282; www.theporchswinginn.com.

weston, mo

Taking Highway 45 out of Parkville leads you to Weston in a matter of minutes. Weston is one of the oldest and most picturesque river towns in Missouri. Founded in 1837, Weston still preserves its antebellum homes, which rest peacefully on hillsides and bluffs that once overlooked the Missouri River. It seems that the Missouri, mighty fickle lady that she is, decided to change her course after the flood of 1884. This left Weston drained of its bustling potential as a river town, with the river diverted to a channel 2 miles away. Long before that, the Lewis and Clark Expedition camped at what is now the foot of Main Street during the summer of 1804. A marker identifies the significance of the explorers' presence in Platte County.

Weston's many antiques shops contain a treasure trove of goodies. Everything from country primitives, antique dolls, and Depression glass to European furniture and country crafts can be found along Main Street. A brochure listing many of the places to visit is available from the Weston Development Company, 502 Main Street, P.O. Box 53, Historic Weston, MO 64098; (816) 640-2909; www.westonmo.com. Call ahead; many businesses are closed on Monday. Weston telephone numbers listed with a 640 exchange are toll-free from Kansas City. 🛖 .

where to go

National Silk Art Museum. 616 Thomas Street. This unusual museum houses a collection of 150 silk tapestries dating to 1872. It's the largest private collection of such works in the world and is the result of John Pottie's fascination with the intricate art form. Open Thursday through Sunday. Free. (816) 640-2608.

Pirtle's Winery. 502 Spring Street. Housed in a former church, this winery has vineyards in northern Platte County. Wine and cheese tastings are available for groups. Mead (honey wine) is a specialty here. On the premises is a wine garden where you can sip wine and enjoy sausage, cheese, Tuscan loaves, and fruit. Open daily. (816) 640-5728; www.pirtlewinery.com.

Red Barn Farm. 163000 Wilkerson Road. Get the kids and yourself into life on a real working farm. Turkeys, geese, and chickens roam the property along with goats, pigs, and cows in pens. Take a hayride through corn and soybean fields, or pick apples and pumpkins during the autumn months. Pick strawberries in May and June. There's a small gift shop in the big red barn. The farm is open daily April through December or by appointment. Fee. (816) 386-5437.

Riverwood Winery. 22200 Highway 45 North. Located in an old school house, Riverwood offers nine varieties of dry and sweet wines. There's always has something going on—from programs highlighting regional foods and cheeses, to book signings, to musical events. Open weekends from noon to 5:00 p.m. (816) 579-9797; www.riverwoodwinery.com.

Snow Creek, Inc. Snow Creek Drive. Five miles north of Weston on Highway 45, Kansas City's own downhill ski area includes intermediate trails, chairlifts, and beginner areas with rope tows. A day lodge features a cafeteria-style restaurant, a lounge, ski rentals, a ski school, and ticket sales. Open daily and at night from mid-December through March, depending on the weather. Fee. (816) 640-2200; www.peakresorts.com; Snow Report Line: (816) 589-SNOW (toll-free from Kansas City).

Weston Historical Museum. 601 Main Street. Founded in 1960, the museum offers displays depicting life in Platte County from prehistoric days through World War II. Exhibits include household items, tools, glassware, china, furniture, historic documents, and other items. Mini tours can be arranged by reservation. Open afternoons; closed Monday and mid-December through mid-March. Free. (816) 386-2977 or (816) 640-2650.

where to shop

McCormick Distilling Company Country Store. 420 Main Street. Founded in 1856, McCormick Distilling Company is best known for being the oldest continuously active distillery still operating on its original site. The store sells McCormick products and other Weston memorabilia. Closed Monday. (816) 640-3149.

Missouri Bluffs Boutique. 512 Main Street. Clothes hounds looking for something nobody else has will love this place. You'll find a variety of styles here, from Native American, Asian, and African to vintage-inspired, contemporary, and locally made natural fiber garments. Like most other customers, you may wind up spending a lot of time trying on various ensembles and playing with the unusual baubles, so tell your significant other to bring along reading material while you shop. (816) 640-2770; www.missouribluffs.com.

The Youngblood Gallery. 415 Main Street. This gallery offers a wide variety of accessories for the home, including antique reproduction furniture, willow furniture, brass and pewter, home fragrances, and an interesting art collection by artists from across North America. Closed Monday. (816) 640-2996.

where to eat

America Bowman Restaurant. Short and Welt Streets. This is the place to find a fine home-cooked lunch and dinner, served in a pre–Civil War setting. Inside this restaurant is Pat O'Malley's Pub. It was patterned after Granary Tavern in Limerick, Ireland. Closed Monday. $$. (816) 640-5235.

Avalon Cafe. The restaurant is located inside an 1847 antebellum home and features Continental cuisine prepared by French-trained chefs and co-owners. Choose from beef tenderloin in Missouri bourbon sauce to American lamb chops in burgundy butter. Desserts are excellent. Closed Monday. $$. (816) 640-2835.

The Vineyards. 505 Spring Street. Local wines are served up in this 1845 antebellum structure, together with lamb, duck, beef tenderloin, and other house specialties. Closed Monday. $$–$$$. (816) 640-5588.

where to stay

Benner House Bed-and-Breakfast. 645 Main Street. This beautiful Victorian home, overlooking downtown Weston, offers four guest rooms with two private baths. A main parlor, a sitting room, and a wraparound front porch are available for relaxing. $$. (816) 640-2616; www.bennerhouse.com.

The Hatchery House. 618 Short Street. This 1845 antebellum bed-and-breakfast has four guest rooms with queen-size beds, gas-burning fireplaces, and private baths. A large outside garden is available for teas and weddings. Ask innkeepers Anne and Bill Lane where the name "The Hatchery House" comes from. You might be surprised. $$–$$$. (816) 640-5700.

The Inn at Weston Landing. 526 Welt Street. Located at the end of a block lined with pre–Civil War homes, the inn offers deluxe accommodations with the ambience of a mid-nineteenth-century Irish cottage. A high-pitched roof, low-set dormers, and gables define Celtic and rural British Isles influences. A full authentic Celtic breakfast features rashers, kippers, trifle cakes, and bramble jelly. An 1842 Irish pub is a favorite for private parties. $$. (816) 640-5788.

Laurel Brooke Farm. 22520 Highway M. Stay out in the country surrounded by apple trees, ponds, and the sweet sounds of birds calling on this acreage owned by Warren and Debra Keith. The couple renovated a historic barn for this bed-and-breakfast and filled it with antiques they purchased from estate sales around northwest Missouri. You'll enjoy an in-ground swimming pool in warm weather and freshly baked treats by Warren, the family chef. $$. (816) 640-2525; www.laurelbrookefarm.com.

The Lemon Tree Bed and Breakfast. 407 Washington Street. Guests stay in an antebellum-era cottage with three guest rooms that feature adjoining private baths. Breakfast is held in the adjacent three-story Victorian home, separated from the cottage by multilevel decks, a koi pond, a swimming pool, and a spa. Guests are free to use all amenities. Fresh coffee and homemade muffins are delivered to your room in the morning, followed by a sumptuous breakfast served in the dining room or poolside. Guests only on Friday and Saturday. $$–$$$. (816) 386-5367.

day trip 03

northwest

the start of "snail mail":
st. joseph, mo; savannah, mo;
conception, mo

st. joseph, mo

Located north on Interstate 29, St. Joseph has the look and feel of a town that played a key role in American history. When the Lewis and Clark Expedition camped here in 1804 and 1806, they named the area St. Michael's Prairie. You can pick up pieces of the past by strolling down streets lined with elegant mansions and restored buildings that were built at a time when raising hemp and selling supplies to wagon trains made fortunes.

Founded in 1826 by Joseph Robidoux as a fur-trading post located in the Blacksnake Hills along the Missouri River, the town later became the starting point for settlers heading west over the Oregon Trail. In 1843 the community was named St. Joseph in honor of Robidoux's patron saint. Five years later gold was discovered in California, and in 1849 more than 20,000 forty-niners migrated through St. Joseph, buying food and supplies to sustain them on their journey.

Steamboats made this an important river town, but with the coming of the railroad in 1859, St. Joseph became the farthest point west to be reached by rail. Trains eventually eclipsed steamboats as the prevailing mode of transportation, but still a fast mail service was needed to the West Coast. Thousands of people turned out to watch the first run of the Pony Express on April 3, 1860. But the effort was too expensive and was abandoned, leaving the mail to the rails.

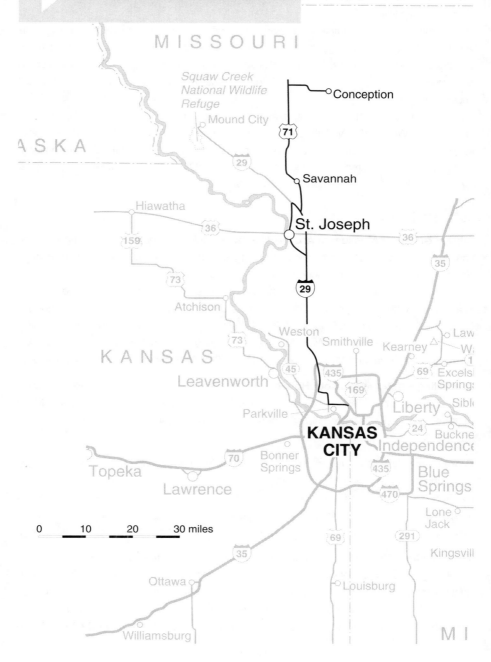

St. Joseph's Golden Age began in 1875, after the Civil War. During this time many commanding buildings were erected. The Victorian years made fortunes for many that would last several generations. Many of the luxurious dwellings still stand and are on the National Register of Historic Places.

But for some history buffs, St. Joseph will forever be associated with the infamous outlaw Jesse James, who was gunned down here by a member of his own gang in April 1882. The 2007 release of *The Assassination of Jesse James by the Coward Robert Ford,* starring Missouri native Brad Pitt, further fueled interest in the sites associated with Missouri's best known bad guy.

Several annual events in St. Joseph remain quite popular. These include the Pony Express–Jesse James Weekend in April, the Apple Blossom Parade and Festival in May, and Trails West in mid-August. For more information on events and attractions, contact the St. Joseph Convention and Visitors Bureau, 109 South Fourth Street, P.O. Box 445, St. Joseph, MO 64502. . (800) 785-0360 or (816) 233-6688; www.stjomo.com.

where to go

Albrecht-Kemper Museum of Art. 2818 Frederick Boulevard. The museum holds one of the finest and most comprehensive collections of eighteenth-, nineteenth-, and twentieth-century American art in the Midwest. Included here are works by Thomas Hart Benton, Albert Bierstadt, George Caleb Bingham, George Catlin, and others. Since 1966 the museum has been housed in a 1935 Georgian-style mansion designed by architects Edward Buehler Delk and Eugene Meyer for William Albrecht, founder of the Western Tablet Company. For guided tours call in advance. Lunch is served on Wednesday and Thursday. Wine tastings are held on the third Thursday of each month. Closed Monday. Fee. (816) 233-7003; www.albrecht-kemper.org.

Creverling's Antique and Tour House. 1125 Charles Street. This thirty-room Romanesque mansion was built in 1880 and contains beautiful woodwork and antique furnishings. Many of the collectibles on display inside the home are for sale. Open by appointment. Fee. (816) 232-9298.

Glore Psychiatric Museum. 3406 Frederick Street. The permanent display covers 400 years of psychiatric history and includes exhibits such as the Bath of Surprise, O'Halloran's Swing, the Tranquilizer Chair, and the Hollow Wheel. There are also displays from St. Joseph State Hospital's history. However interesting this museum is, it is not necessarily for children or those easily upset by the human condition. Open daily. Free. (816) 364-1209; www.gloremuseum.org.

The Hall Street Historic District. North on Sixth Street to Hall Street. Built during St. Joseph's Golden Age, the Hall Street mansions are on the National Register of Historic Places. The elegant homes display the fine designs inherent in nineteenth-century architecture. Stained-glass windows, towers, turrets, and trim make the area a showplace. For more information on self-guided walking tours, contact the St. Joseph Convention and Visitors Bureau, 109 South Fourth

Street, P.O. Box 445, St. Joseph, MO 64502; (800) 785-0360 or (816) 233-6688; www.stjomo
.com.

Jesse James Home Museum. Twelfth and Penn Streets. The outlaw Jesse James was only
thirty-four when he was killed by Bob Ford, a member of the former James Gang. James was
living in the house with his wife and two children, under the assumed name of Tom Howard.
Ford shot him from behind while James stood on a chair to straighten a picture. The bullet
passed through his head and entered the wall. Visitors today can still see the bullet hole. Exhibits
include artifacts obtained from the outlaw's grave when he was exhumed in 1995 for DNA
tests, which showed a 99.7 percent certainty that it was Jesse James who was killed in his
home on April 3, 1882. Open daily. Fee. (816) 232-8206.

Patee House Museum National Historic Landmark. Twelfth and Penn Streets. Opened
in 1858 by John Patee, this was a luxurious hotel built at a cost of $180,000, a substantial sum
for that era. It contained 140 guest rooms. Later it served as headquarters for the Pony Express.
Exhibits feature a restored 1860 Pony Express headquarters, a replica of the first railway mail
car invented for the Pony Express, and other Pony Express memorabilia. Railroad displays
include an 1860 Hannibal and St. Joseph locomotive.

The 1854 Buffalo Saloon on the premises serves soft drinks and ice cream. Kids will also
enjoy a ride on the Wild Things Carousel, a vintage 1941 merry-go-round. Open daily. Fee. (816)
232-8206.

Pony Express Museum. 914 Penn Street. On April 3, 1860, a lone rider on horseback left
from this stable to begin his historic ride. Now on the National Register of Historic Places, the
Pony Express National Memorial features state-of-the-art exhibits that tell the dramatic story
of the creation and operation of the Pony Express. Visitors can take a walk along the 70-foot
diorama of the Pony Express Trail. Among the many hands-on displays is the mochila (mail-
bag), which can be changed from one saddle to another. Visitors can also pump water from
the original stable well. Open daily; closed holidays. Fee. (816) 279-5059 or (800) 530-5930;
www.ponyexpress.org.

Society of Memories Doll Museum. 1115 South Twelfth Street. Doll collectors will find happi-
ness in this collection of more than 600 dolls, ranging from 1840s "covered wagon dolls" to
Barbies and Cabbage Patch Kids. Tours are available. Open Tuesday through Sunday or by
appointment. Closed November through May. Fee. (816) 233-1420.

St. Joseph Museum. 1100 Charles Street. This 1879 Gothic-style mansion turned museum
was copied after a castle on the Rhine and decorated later by the famed Tiffany Company of
New York. The 5,000-piece Native American ethnographic collection is the largest in Missouri
and represents more than 300 North American tribes. Items in the collection range from Pomo
feather baskets to Haida copper masks. There are also local and natural history exhibits of
interest. Open daily. Fee. (816) 232-8471 or (800) 530-8866; www.stjosephmuseum.org.

where to shop

Penn Street Square. Twelfth and Penn Streets. Located in the heart of the city's historic museum area, Penn Street Square offers more than 20,000 square feet of antiques and collectibles. (816) 232-4626.

Stetson Factory Outlet Store. 3601 South Leonard Road. Abraham Lincoln was the nation's president when John B. Stetson made his first western fur-felt hat. The St. Joseph-based company still makes a wide selection of world-famous western felt, straw, and dress hats at direct-from-the-manufacturer prices. This is the nation's only Stetson outlet store. Closed Sunday. (816) 233-3286.

where to eat

Barbosa's Castillo. 906 Sylvanie Street. Located inside a family-owned 1891 mansion, Barbosa's offers authentic home-style Mexican food and good service in a pleasant atmosphere. Open for lunch and dinner daily. $. (816) 233-4970.

The Old Hoof and Horn Steakhouse. 429 Illinois Street. Located in the heart of the Stockyards, this venerable restaurant has been serving good prime rib, steaks, and seafood for more than a century. $$. (816) 238-0742.

where to stay

River Towne Resort. 4012 River Road. Located on the Missouri River, these beautifully decorated and furnished riverfront cottages feature kitchenettes, spacious living areas, and patio areas with tables and chairs. Some cabins have Jacuzzi tubs and fireplaces. The resort is located on an official Lewis and Clark campsite. $$–$$$. 🔔 . (816) 364-6500.

savannah, mo

From St. Joseph, head north on I-29 to U.S. Highway 71 and Savannah. There's not much to do in town; the real reason to come here, if you are an animal lover, is to see how hundreds of injured or unwanted birds and raptors, dogs, cats, cougars, and other creatures are being saved and cared for by the owners of M'shoogy's. Who knows? Maybe you'll even find a nice, healthy neutered pet to take home.

where to go

M'shoogy's Famous Emergency Animal Rescue World Headquarters. 11519 State Route C. You don't have to be crazy to be "M'shoogy's," but you do have to love animals. Nestled on twenty-two acres of hilly country, M'shoogy's is a little over an hour from downtown Kansas City and is north of St. Joseph, on US 71. More than 750 dogs, cats, and other assorted creatures are kept at this roadside haven, which is the largest no-kill animal shelter in the country. M'shoogy's compassionate owners, Gary and Lisa Silverglat, group all of the dogs by temperament in well-maintained outdoor runs. Each animal gets its turn to play in a large fenced area that surrounds a pond. About 3,000 of M'shoogy's residents are adopted out each year, which evens the odds that they're going to live much happier lives. M'shoogy's is also a Federal Migratory Rehabilitation Center and is now trying to restore injured birds to the wild.

To get there from St. Joseph, take US 71 toward Savannah. Once you're in town, take a right at the Texaco station (Highway E). Take a left on Highway C and go down to the bottom of the hill. It's best to call for exact directions. Open Saturday for adoptions. (816) 324-5824; www.critterconnections.com.

conception, mo

Conception can be reached from Kansas City by taking I-29 north to US 71, or from Savannah by going north on US 71 toward Maryville. Just before you reach Maryville, turn east on Highway M. You'll see a sign for Conception Abbey. Drive on for 7 miles until you see the sign for Highway AH. Go left here and follow the road for 6 miles. Take a right on Highway VV and drive up two small hills to the abbey. Park in front of the church and walk to the guest entrance to the right. You can always call for further directions before you go. (660) 944-3100.

where to go

Conception Abbey. P.O. Box 501, Conception, MO 64433. Individual and group retreats are offered at this Benedictine monastery, founded in 1873. Located just south of Maryville off US 71, the monastery is an architectural masterpiece designed in the Romanesque style. Also on the premises is Conception Seminary College, a four-year seminary established in 1886.

Conception Abbey was dedicated in 1891 and was designated a Minor Basilica on its fiftieth anniversary by Pope Pius XII, becoming the fifth Minor Basilica in the country. The Basilica of the Immaculate Conception is breathtaking in design and, for those of any faith, represents a place to sit and contemplate.

The abbey has continued for years to open its doors to the public, inviting people in from the cold and often stressful environment around them. Many come here on weekend retreats to sit or walk the grounds in quiet meditation. The basilica is open each day to "pilgrims" for prayer and meditation and serves as a house of prayer for people of all faiths who enter its impressive wooden doors. It is open to the public during prayer services, including the evening vesper services, when the joyful and spirited harmony of the monks' voices becomes a welcome respite from the cacophony of the world.

Since hospitality is one of the defining characteristics of the Benedictine order, you can drop by any day for lunch at the abbey. The modestly priced, wholesome, and simple meal is served promptly at 12:35 p.m. and includes a salad, two main dishes, vegetable, dessert, and home-baked bread. Sunday dinner is also served here, at 11:30 a.m.

Lodging rates are also inexpensive. The abbey is not a resort, so don't expect fancy rooms and amenities. Do expect shared baths, long walks, beautiful sunsets, and plenty of fresh air.

If you have time, you might want to visit the gift shop, where you can buy unique cards and gifts from the abbey's Printery House. You can also write for the monastery's holiday catalogs, which feature everything from religious art and Terra Sancta gifts to El Salvador folk art and icons. Art from the Holy Land, carved by artists from around the city of Bethlehem; porcelain and hand-carved nativity scenes; and limited offerings of gold-plated and polished bronze jewelry are also offered. Open daily. Fee for overnight accommodations and meals. (660) 944-3100; www.conceptionabbey.org.

day trip 04

northwest

bird heaven and haven:
squaw creek national wildlife
refuge (mound city, mo)

squaw creek national wildlife refuge (mound city, mo)

Squaw Creek National Wildlife Refuge is part of the National Wildlife Refuge System, administered by the U.S. Fish and Wildlife Service. Established in 1935, it provides more than 7,000 acres of man-made marshes where waterfowl and other creatures can find food, water, and shelter. The refuge is located 5 miles south of Mound City, a town that gets its name from the loess mounds that bound Squaw Creek to the east. The loess bluffs are a rare geologic formation of wind-deposited soil from the past glacial period. The stuff is crumbly and falls apart in your fingers.

You can reach the refuge by taking I-29 North to exit 79, then onto US 159. Follow US 159 West for 2.5 miles and it will take you in front of the refuge headquarters. The drive is about 90 miles and takes around two hours.

Birding is good year-round, although fall and spring are the most spectacular times. White pelicans are present during September and April. In November and December the refuge offers visitors a special treat when bald eagles migrate to the area. During winter Squaw Creek is said to have one of the highest concentrations of eagles in the United States, and eagle counts on the refuge have soared beyond 300 in the past.

IOWA

MISSOURI

Squaw Creek National Wildlife Refuge

Conception

Mound City

71

Bigelow

29

ASKA

Savannah

Hiawatha

36

St. Joseph

36

159

35

73

29

Atchison

Weston

Law

73

Smithville

Kearney

W

69

Excels

Spring

KANSAS

45

435

Leavenworth

169

Liberty

Sibl

Parkville

24

Buckne

KANSAS CITY

Independence

Topeka

70

Bonner Springs

435

Blue Springs

Lawrence

470

Lone Jack

0   10   20   30 miles

69

291

Kingsvill

35

Ottawa

Louisburg

The refuge holds an annual Eagle Days the first full weekend in December, from 9:00 a.m. to 4:00 p.m. The event includes a live eagle program, special viewing sites, an auto tour, handouts, and various other programs—every hour on the hour. Open-house weekends are held in spring and fall and center on the bird migrations.

If you are making your first visit to Squaw Creek, you may want to ask some questions at the refuge headquarters, where you'll also find brochures about area wildlife. The refuge itself is open year-round from sunrise to sunset. Poaching has forced stricter adherence to the refuge's opening and closing hours. If you're found on the refuge after closing time, you risk receiving a stiff fine for trespassing.

After leaving the headquarters, take the bridge directly in front of it to the first observation tower you see, then turn left. An auto-tour route completes a 10-mile loop going through a variety of habitats. Follow the road around to Eagle Overlook, which is clearly marked on a sign. This is a split of land that extends into Eagle Pool, where you can mingle with the birds firsthand.

In warm weather look for red-tailed hawks, ring-necked pheasants, sandpipers, ring-billed gulls, terns, and owls. Fall and spring migrations often bring close to 200,000 snow geese, 150,000 ducks, and millions of blackbirds. Be sure to bring along a pair of binoculars to search for eagles, which perch along rows of high trees that border the water.

Mammals are more difficult to see than birds because of their nocturnal habits and the dense habitats they choose. But if you are patient and interested enough to wait and watch, you might observe white-tailed deer, opossums, raccoons, and coyotes along the roads. You don't have to be a Boy Scout to detect the presence of mammals; just look for their tracks in the snow, dust, or mud.

Hunting and camping aren't allowed. Bring your own snacks, especially energy foods and a thermos of something warm to drink on a cold day. The refuge temperature is about 10 degrees colder than it is in Kansas City and there's a wind-chill factor, so wear a sweater, plus a parka, hat, gloves, and boots in winter.

The refuge headquarters is open daily, except for federal holidays. Free. (660) 442-3187; www.fws.gov/midwest/squawcreek.

where to eat

Camp Rulo River Club. P.O. Box 237, Rulo, NE 68431 (16 miles west of Squaw Creek on US 159). As you cross the bridge over the Missouri River into Rulo, you'll catch a sign to your left that says CAMP RULO RIVER CLUB. Situated on the banks of the Missouri, this place offers catfish and country music. Chicken and steak dinners are also offered at moderate prices. Weekends are the liveliest. Closed Monday. $$. (402) 245-4096.

Quackers Bar and Grill. 1012 State Street, Mound City. With a name like Quackers, the place has got to be low-key, casual, and filled with birding motifs. It's all of that, plus a great place for pizza, burgers, and tenderloin sandwiches any day of the week except Sunday. $. (660) 442-5502.

where to stay

Big Lake State Park Resort. Eleven miles northeast of Mound City, on Missouri Highway 111 and Highway 159, Bigelow, MO. Located on a natural oxbow lake, this lovely state park offers cabins with fireplaces, a meeting room, a dining room, and motel rooms and suites with kitchenettes. There's a swimming pool and fishing available as well. The resort is closed the end of October through the last weekend in March. A minimum of two nights' stay is required, but you'll want to spend at least that or more enjoying the tranquility of the area. $–$$. (660) 442-5432; www.mostateparks.com/biglake.htm.

regional information

northeast from kansas city

Excelsior Springs Chamber of Commerce, 101 East Broadway, Excelsior Springs, MO 64024; (816) 630-6161; www.exspgschamber.com.

Jamesport Community Association, Jamesport, MO 64648; (660) 684-6146; www.jamesport-mo.com.

Kearney Chamber of Commerce, P.O. Box 242, Kearney, MO 64060; (816) 628-4229; www.kearneymo.com.

Liberty Chamber of Commerce, 9 South Leonard Street, Liberty, MO 64068; (816) 781-5200; www.libertychamber.com.

Richmond Chamber of Commerce, 107 North Thorton, Richmond, MO 64085; (816) 776-6917; www.richmondmissouri.com.

Smithville Chamber of Commerce, Smithville, MO 64089; (816) 532-0946; www.smithvillemo.org.

east from kansas city

Arrow Rock Merchants Association, P.O. Box 147–B, Arrow Rock, MO 65320; (660) 837-3305; www.arrowrock.org.

Boonville Chamber of Commerce, Katy Depot, Spring and First Streets, Boonville, MO 65233; (660) 882-2721; www.boonvillemochamberofcommerce.com.

City of Independence Tourism Department, 111 East Maple Street, Independence, MO 64050; (816) 325-7111; www.visitindependence.com.

Columbia Convention and Visitors Bureau, 300 South Providence, Columbia, MO 65205; (800) 652-0987 or (573) 875-1231; www.visitcolumbiamo.com.

Concordia Chamber of Commerce, 802 South Gordon Street, Concordia, MO 64020; (660) 463-2454; www.concordiamo.com.

The Friends of Rocheport, 501 Third Street, Rocheport, MO 65279; (573) 698-3207 or (573) 698-3210; www.rocheport.com.

Hermann Tourism Group, 312 Schiller Street, P.O. Box 104, Hermann, MO 65041; (800) 932-8687; www.hermannmo.com.

Jefferson City Convention and Visitors Bureau, 213 Adams, P.O. Box 2227, Jefferson City, MO 65102; (800) 769-4183 or (573) 632-2820; www.visitjeffersoncity.com.

Kingdom of Callaway Chamber of Commerce, 409 Court Street, Fulton, MO 65251; (800) 257-3554; www.callawaychamber.com.

Lexington Tourism Bureau, P.O. Box 132, Lexington, MO 64067; (660) 259-4711; www .historiclexington.com.

New Franklin Chamber of Commerce, 130 East Broadway, New Franklin, MO 65274; (660) 848-2288; www.newfranklin.missouri.org.

Santa Fe Trail Growers Association, Route 1, Box 131–P, Waverly, MO 64096; (660) 252-0730.

Sedalia Chamber of Commerce, 600 East Third Street, Sedalia, MO 65301; (800) 827-5295; www.visitsedaliamo.com.

Warrensburg Chamber of Commerce, 100 South Holden Street, Warrensburg, MO 64093; (877) OLD-DRUM or (660) 747-3168; www.warrensburg.org.

southeast from kansas city

Lake of the Ozarks Convention and Visitor Bureau, P.O. Box 1498, Osage Beach, MO 65065; (800) 386-5253; www.funlake.com.

south from kansas city

Carthage Convention and Visitors Bureau, 402 South Garrison Street, Carthage, MO 64836; (417) 359-8181 or (866) 357-8687; www.visit-carthage.com.

southwest from kansas city

Chanute Chamber of Commerce, 21 North Lincoln Street, Chanute, KS 66720; (877) 431-3350 or (620) 431-3350; www.chanutechamber.com.

Crawford County Convention and Visitors Bureau, 117 West Fourth Street, P.O. Box 1115, Pittsburg, KS 66762; (800) 879-1112 or (620) 231-1212; www.visitcrawfordcounty.com.

Emporia County Convention and Visitors Bureau, 719 Commercial Street, P.O. Box 703, Emporia, KS 66801; (800) 279-3730 or (620) 342-1803; www.emporiakschamber.org.

Fort Scott Chamber of Commerce, P.O. Box 205, Fort Scott, KS 66701; (800) 245-FORT; www.fortscott.com.

Franklin County Convention and Tourism Bureau, 2011 East Logan Street, P.O. Box 203, Ottawa, KS 66067; (785) 242-1411; www.visitottawakansas.com.

The Garnett Area Chamber of Commerce, 419 South Oak Street, Garnett, KS 66032; (785) 448-6767; www.garnettchamber.org.

The Kansas Department of Wildlife and Parks, 14639 West Ninety-fifth Street, Lenexa, KS 66215; (913) 894-9113; www.kdwp.ks.state.us.

west from kansas city

Abilene Convention and Visitors Bureau, 201 Northwest Second Street, Abilene, KS 67410; (800) 569-5915; www.abilenekansas.org.

Bonner Springs/Edwardsville Chamber of Commerce, 205 East Second Street, P.O. Box 38, Bonner Springs, KS 66012; (913) 422-1020; www.wherelifeisgood.org.

Chase County Chamber of Commerce, 318 Broadway, Cottonwood Falls, KS 66845; (800) 431-6344; www.chasecountyks.org.

Council Grove/Morris County Visitors Bureau, 207 West Main Street, Council Grove, KS 66846; (800) 732-9211 or (620) 767-5882; www.councilgrove.com.

Lawrence Convention and Visitors Bureau, 785 Vermont Street, Suite 101, Box 586, Lawrence, KS 66044; (888) LAW-KANS or (785) 865-4499; www.visitlawrence.com.

Manhattan Convention and Visitors Bureau, 501 Poyntz Avenue, Manhattan, KS 66502; (785) 776-8829; www.manhattan.org.

Topeka Convention and Visitors Bureau, 1275 Southwest Topeka Boulevard, Topeka, KS 66612; (800) 235-1030 or (785) 234-1030; www.topekacvb.org.

Wamego Area Chamber of Commerce, P.O. Box 34, Wamego, KS 66547; (785) 456-7849; www.wamego.org.

northwest from kansas city

Atchison Chamber of Commerce, Santa Fe Depot Visitors Center, 200 South Tenth Street, P.O. Box 126, Atchison, KS 66002; (800) 234-1854 or (913) 367-2427; www.atchison kansas.net.

Leavenworth Area Convention and Visitors Bureau, 518 Shawnee Street, P.O. Box 44, Leavenworth, KS 66048; (800) 844-4114 or (913) 682-4113; www.lvarea.com.

Main Street Parkville Association, 207 Main Street, Suite B, Parkville, MO 64152; (816) 505-2227; www.parkvillemo.net.

St. Joseph Convention and Visitors Bureau, 109 South Fourth Street, P.O. Box 445, St. Joseph, MO 64502; (800) 785-0360 or (816) 233-6688; www.stjomo.com.

Weston Development Company, 502 Main Street, P.O. Box 53, Historic Weston, MO 64098; (816) 640-2909; www.westonmo.com.

festivals and celebrations

february

Step Back in Time Winter Festival, Jamesport, MO. First week of February. (816) 684-6682; www.jamesport-mo.com.

march

Wurstfest, Hermann, MO. Annual mid-March event. (800) 932-8687; www.hermannmo.com.

april

Big Muddy Folk Festival, Boonville, MO. Two-day event in early April. (660) 882-2721; www.boonvillemochamberofcommerce.com.

Dogwood Music Festival, Camdenton, MO. Annual mid-April event. (800) 769-1004; www.camdentonchamber.com.

Pony Express–Jesse James Days, St. Joseph, MO. First weekend in April. (800) 785-0360; www.stjomo.com.

Spring Homes Tour, Carthage, MO. Mid-April event. (417) 358-2373; www.visit-carthage .com/.

Tulip Festival, Wamego, KS. Third Saturday and Sunday of April. (785) 456-7849; www .wamego.org.

Tulip Time at the Binkley Gardens, Topeka, KS. Nine days in mid-April. (800) 235-1030; www.topeka.org.

may

AAUW Square Fair, Town Square, Garnett, KS. Saturday before Mother's Day. (785) 448-6767.

Apple Blossom Festival and Parade, St. Joseph, MO. First weekend in May. (800) 785-0360; www.stjomo.com.

Arrow Rock Annual Antique Show, Arrow Rock, MO. Third weekend in May. (816) 837-3470; www.arrowrock.org.

Civil War Reenactment, Carthage, MO. Mid-May event. (417) 358-2373; www.visit-carthage .com/.

Fort Leavenworth Homes Tour and Frontier Army Encampment, Fort Leavenworth, KS. First Saturday in May. (800) 444-4114; www.lvarea.com.

Gatsby Festival, Excelsior Springs, MO. Second weekend in May. (816) 630-6161; www .exmo.com.

Maifest, Hermann, MO. Mid-May event. (800) 932-8687; www.hermannmo.com.

May Day Festival, Jamesport, MO. Early May event. (816) 684-6682; www.jamesport-mo .com.

Memorial Day Weekend Salute to Veterans Parade and Air Show, Columbia, MO. (573) 443-2651; www.gocolumbiamo.com.

Mushroom Festival, Richmond, MO. First weekend in May. (816) 776-6916; www.richmond missouri.com.

Spring on the Square, Liberty, MO. Early May event. (816) 781-5200; www.libertymo.com.

Topeka Jazz Festival, Topeka, KS. Last weekend in May. (785) 234-2787; www.topeka cvb.org.

june

Art in the Park, Columbia, MO. First weekend in June. (573) 443-8838; www.gocolumbia mo.com.

Blind Boone Music Festival, Warrensburg, MO. Second weekend in June. (660) 747-3268; www.blindboonepark.org.

Country Stampede, Manhattan, KS. Held every June. (800) 795-8091.

Downtown Twilight Festival, Columbia, MO. Every Thursday evening of the month. (573) 442-6816; www.gocolumbiamo.com.

Flint Hills Rodeo, Strong City, KS. (620) 273-6480.

Fulton Street Fair, Fulton, MO. Three-day festival at the end of the month. (800) 257-3554; www.callawaychamber.com.

Good Ol' Days, Fort Scott, KS. First weekend in June. (800) 245-FORT; www.fortscott.com.

Heritage Days, Lexington, MO. Mid-June celebration. (660) 259-3082; www.historiclexington .com.

Parkville Jazz & Fine Arts River Jam, Parkville, MO. Third Friday and Saturday in June. (816) 505-2227; www.parkvillemo.com.

Scott Joplin Ragtime Festival, Sedalia, MO. First week in June. (660) 826-2271; www.visit sedaliamo.com.

Skunk Run Days, Ottawa, KS. Second weekend in June. (785) 242-1411; www.idir.net\~fetv.

Symphony on the Prairie, Flint Hills, KS. (620) 273-8955; www.symphonyintheflinthills.org.

Wah-Shun-Gah Days, Council Grove, KS. Third weekend in June. (800) 732-9211 or (620) 767-5882; www.councilgrove.com.

july

Amelia Earhart Festival, Atchison, KS. Annual festival in late July. (800) 234-1854; www .atchison.org.

Fiesta Mexicana Week, Topeka, KS. Weeklong mid-July festival. (800) 235-1030; www.topekacvb.org.

Fireworks Celebrations, Osage Beach, MO. Annual fireworks displays presented by Tan-Tar-A (800-826-8272) and the Lodge of Four Seasons (800-843-5253).

Fort Osage Independence Day, Sibley, MO. July 4. (816) 650-3278.

Fourth of July Celebration, Wamego, KS. (785) 456-7849; www.wamego.org.

Kansas River Valley Art Fair, Topeka, KS. Last weekend in July. (785) 368-3888; www.topeka.org.

Kaw Valley Rodeo and Riley County Fair, Manhattan, KS. Last week in July. (785) 537-6350; www.manhattan.org.

Missouri State Powwow, Sedalia, MO. Mid-July event. (800) 827-5295; www.visitsedalia mo.com.

Missouri Town 1855 Independence Day, Fleming Park, Blue Springs, MO. July 4. (816) 795-8200, ext. 1260; www.co.jackson.mo.us.

Platte County Fair, Tracy, MO. Third weekend in July. (816) 431-3247; www.plattecofair.com.

Sunflower State Games, Lawrence, KS. Two weekends in late July. (785) 842-7774; www.sunflowergames.org.

Wild Bill Hickok Rodeo and Western Heritage Festival, Abilene, KS. Last weekend of July. (800) 569-5915; www.ckff.net/schedule.html.

august

Great Stone Hill Grape Stomp, Hermann, MO. Second Saturday in August. (800) 932-8687; www.hermannmo.com.

Gus Macker 3-on-3 Basketball Tournament, Jefferson City, MO. Third weekend in August. (573) 634-3616; www.jeffersoncity.org.

Missouri River Festival of the Arts, Boonville, MO. Second week of August. (660) 882-2721; www.boonvillemochamberofcommerce.com.

Missouri State Fair, Sedalia, MO. (800) 422-FAIR; www.mostatefair.com.

Trails West, St. Joseph, MO. Third weekend in August. (800) 785-0360; www.stjoearts.org.

september

American Indian Heritage Weekend, Fort Scott, KS. Last weekend of September. (800) 245-FORT; www.fortscott.com.

Annual Ciderfest, Louisburg Cider Mill, Louisburg, KS. Last week in September and first week in October. (913) 837-5202; www.louisburgcidermill.com.

Annual Fall Festival and Crafts Fair, Jefferson City, MO. (573) 634-2824; www.jefferson city.org.

Annual Lawrence Indian Arts Show, Lawrence, KS. September and October. (785) 864-4245; www.visitlawrence.com.

Apple Jubilee, Waverly, MO. Mid-September event. (660) 493-2616.

Boone County Heritage Festival, Columbia, MO. Third weekend of September. (573) 874-7460; www.gocolumbiamo.com.

Boonslick Traditional Folk Music Festival, Arrow Rock, MO. Second Saturday in September. (660) 837-3335; www.arrowrock.org.

Capital Jazzfest/Balloon Race, Jefferson City, MO. (800)-CHILDREN; www.jefferson city.org.

Cider Days, Topeka, KS. Last weekend of September. (785) 272-9290; www.topekacvb.org.

Columbia Festival of the Arts, Columbia, MO. Last weekend of September. (573) 874-6386; www.gocolumbiamo.com.

Concordia Fall Festival, Concordia, MO. Early September. (816) 463-7056; www.concordia mo.com.

Downtown Twilight Festival, Columbia, MO. Every Thursday evening of the month. (573) 442-6816; www.visitcolumbiamo.com.

Fall Festival, Liberty, MO. (816) 781-5200; www.libertymo.com.

Fort Osage Rendezvous and Trade Fair, Sibley, MO. Second weekend in September. (816) 650-3278.

Heritage Day "Step Back in Time" Festival, Jamesport, MO. (660) 684-6682; www.james port-mo.com.

Jesse James Festival, Kearney, MO. Mid-September event. (816) 628-4229; www.jesse jamesfestival.com.

Lake Garnett Cruisers Annual Auto Show, Garnett, KS. Last weekend in September. (785) 448-5496.

Leavenworth River Fest, Leavenworth, KS. Second weekend in September. (800) 844-4114; www.lvarea.com.

Little Apple Festival, Manhattan, KS. Last weekend in September. (785) 587-2757; www .manhattan.org.

Little Balkans Days, Pittsburg, KS. Annual September event. (800) 879-1112 or (620) 231-1212; www.morningsun.net/cvb.

Old Marais River Run Car Show, Ottawa, KS. Third weekend in September. (785) 242-5799.

Ozark Ham and Turkey Festival, California, MO. Third Saturday in September. (573) 796-3040.

Power of the Past Antique Engine and Tractor Show, Ottawa, KS. Second weekend of September. (785) 242-1411.

Renaissance Festival, Bonner Springs, KS. Weekends in September and October. (800) 373-0357 or (816) 561-8005; www.kcrenfest.com.

Santa-Cali-Gon Festival, Independence, MO. Labor Day weekend. (816) 325-7111; www.santacaligon.com.

The Vintage Homes Tour, Lexington, MO. September of odd-numbered years. (660) 259-4711; www.historiclexington.com.

Wake Up to Missouri U.S.A. National Powerboat Championship Boat Races, Marina Bay Resort, Osage Beach, MO. (800) 386-5253; www.funlake.com.

Waterfest, Excelsior Springs, MO. Second Saturday in September. (816) 630-6161; www .exmo.com.

october

Apple Fest, Weston, MO. Early October event. (816) 640-2909; www.westonmo.com.

Apple Festival, Topeka, KS. Early October celebration. (785) 368-3888; www.topeka.org.

Arrow Rock Craft Festival, Arrow Rock, MO. Second weekend in October. (660) 837-3335; www.arrowrock.org.

Chisholm Trail Day Festival, Abilene, KS. First Saturday of October. (785) 263-2681; www.kansascattletowns.com/calendar/calendar.html.

Haunted Homes Tours, Atchison, KS. Halloween week. (800) 234-1854; www.atchison.org.

Maple Leaf Festival, Carthage, MO. Third weekend of the month. (417) 358-2373; www.visit-carthage.com/.

Missouri Town 1855 Fall Festival, Fleming Park, Blue Springs, MO. First weekend in October. (816) 795-8200, ext. 1260; www.jacksongov.org.

Octoberfest, Hermann, MO. Throughout the month. (800) 932-8687; www.hermannmo.com.

Oktoberfest, Atchison, KS. First weekend of the month. (800) 234-1854; www.atchison.org.

Oz Festival, Wamego, KS. October. (866) 458-TOTO.

Pioneer Harvest Fiesta, Fort Scott, KS. First weekend in October. (800) 245-FORT; www.fortscott.com.

Pony Express Pumpkin Fest, St. Joseph, MO. (800) 785-0360; www.stjomo.com.

Renaissance Festival, Bonner Springs, KS. Weekends in September and October. (800) 373-0357 or (816) 561-8005; www.kcrenfest.com.

River Rendezvous, Jefferson City, MO. Second weekend in October. (573) 761-5355; www .jeffersoncity.org.

Wamego Fall Festival, Wamego, KS. First Saturday of October. (785) 456-7849; www .wamego.org.

november

Annual Christmas Lighting Ceremony, Carthage, MO. Mid-November event. (800) 543-7975; www.visit-carthage.com/.

Annual Lake Lights Festival and Enchanted Holiday Park, Osage Beach, MO. Mid-November through January 1. (800) 386-5253; www.funlake.com.

Festival of Poinsettias, Lawrence, KS. Weekend before Thanksgiving through Christmas. (888) LAW-KANS or (785) 865-4499; www.visitlawrence.com.

Step Back in Time Christmas Festival, Jamesport, MO. Last week in November. (816) 684-6682; www.jamesport-mo.com.

Veterans Day Tribute, Emporia, KS. Early November. (800) 279-3730.

december

Christmas in Weston Candlelight Homes Tour, Weston, MO. First weekend in December. (816) 640-2909; www.westonmo.com.

Christmas on the River, Parkville, MO. First Thursday through Sunday in December. (816) 505-2227; www.parkvillemo.com.

Downtown Holiday Festival, Columbia, MO. First Friday in December. (573) 442-6816; www.gocolumbiamo.com.

First Night Columbia, Columbia, MO. December 31. (573) 817-2781; www.gocolumbia mo.com.

Frontier Candlelight Tour, Fort Scott, KS. First weekend in December. (620) 223-0310.

Homes for the Holidays, Fort Scott, KS. First weekend in December. (800) 245-FORT; www.fortscott.com.

Old-Time Holiday Happenings, Topeka, KS. Early December celebration. (785) 368- 3888; www.topeka.org.

Sparkling Arts Holiday Show, Columbia, MO. December 1 to January 8. (573) 443-8838; www.gocolumbiamo.com.

Squaw Creek National Wildlife Refuge Eagle Days, Mound City, MO. First full weekend in December. (660) 442-3187; www.fws.gov/midwest.

state parks, historic sites, conservation areas, u.s. army corps of engineers parks and lakes

kansas

Kansas Department of Wildlife and Parks, 14639 West Ninety-fifth Street, Lenexa, KS 66215; (913) 894-9113; www.kdwp.ks.state.us. The agency offers a guidebook to the state parks, provides maps, and assists with information on park services, including boating, fishing, hunting, camping, and wheelchair accessibility.

The Kansas Historical Society, 6425 Southwest Sixth Avenue, Topeka, KS 66615; (785) 272-8681; www.kshs.org. The society has information on state historic sites.

Kansas City District Corps of Engineers, 700 Federal Building, Kansas City, MO 64106; (816) 983-3632. Campers sixty-two or older can purchase Golden Age Passports for a modest cost and get half off on all camping fees in U.S. Army Corps of Engineers parks.

Kansas Travel and Tourism Web site: www.travelks.com.

missouri

Kansas City District Corps of Engineers, 700 Federal Building, Kansas City, MO 64106; (816) 983-3632. Campers sixty-two or older can purchase Golden Age Passports for a modest cost and get half off on all camping fees in U.S. Army Corps of Engineers parks.

Missouri Department of Conservation, P.O. Box 180, Jefferson City, MO 65102-0180; (573) 751-4115. Kansas City Office, 8616 East Sixty-third Street, Kansas City, MO 64133; (816) 356-2280; www.conservation.state.mo.us. Complete information on regulations for hunting and fishing permits can be found here, along with brochures on wheelchair-accessible conservation areas.

Missouri Department of Natural Resources, Division of State Parks, P.O. Box 176, Jefferson City, MO 65102; (800) 334-6946; www.mostateparks.com. The department has information on Missouri state parks and historic sites, parks, and campgrounds.

Missouri Department of Tourism Web site: www.visitmo.com.

about the authors

shifra stein

Author, artist, and workshop presenter, Shifra Stein has written more than thirty books and hundreds of articles for magazines and newspapers.

Her many guidebooks include the popular *Day Trips*® series for The Globe Pequot Press, as well as cookbooks such as *Wild About Kansas City Barbecue* and *Vegetables on the Grill* for Pig Out Publishing. She has also written several personal-power workbooks, including *Unlocking the Power Within: Journaling for Personal and Professional Growth.*

Equally at home with computer, pen, or brush, Ms. Stein is also an accomplished artist. Her "Art for the Health of It" workshops are offered through hospital and health-care facilities, cancer organizations, older adult education centers, and art centers.

Ms. Stein is available for speaking engagements. For more information, see her Web site at www.artforhealth.us or contact her at shifra@artforhealth.us.

diana lambdin meyer

Diana Lambdin Meyer of Parkville has contributed to dozens of travel guidebooks and written thousands of articles for newspapers and magazines during her freelance writing career that spans three decades. She is an award-winning member of the Midwest Travel Writers Association and the Society of American Travel Writers. She and her husband, Bruce, a professional photographer, travel the world in search of stories, education, and adventure, but the Midwest remains their home and their heart in all professional pursuits.

Diana has partnered with Shifra Stein to re-create *A Kid's Guide to Kansas City,* which is available at area bookstores.